TRUTH AND SUFFERING

FIGURES OF THE UNCONSCIOUS 20

TRUTH AND SUFFERING

Psychoanalysis, Science and the Production of Symptoms

Paulo Beer

Translation by Renata Takatu

LEUVEN UNIVERSITY PRESS

This book was produced with support of the São Paulo Research Foundation (FAPESP), processes 2016/03096-7, 2018/09753-5 and 2022/08353-9.

This book will be made open access within three years of publication thanks to Path to Open, a program developed in partnership between JSTOR, the American Council of Learned Societies (ACLS), University of Michigan Press, and The University of North Carolina Press to bring about equitable access and impact for the entire scholarly community, including authors, researchers, libraries, and university presses around the world.
Learn more at https://about.jstor.org/path-to-open/

Original title: Verdade e Sofrimento: psicanálise, ciência e a produção de sintomas
Authorized translation from the Portuguese language edition published by Editora Perspectiva.

ISBN 978 94 6270 406 0
eISBN 978 94 6166 553 9
https://doi.org/10.11116/9789461665539
D/2024/1869/10
NUR: 770

Cover design: Daniel Benneworth-Gray
Cover illustration: inspired by Karl Nordström, *Twilight in Spring II*, public domain.
Typesetting: Friedemann Vervoort

GPRC
Guaranteed
Peer Reviewed
Content
www.gprc.be

To Philippe Van Haute (†),
who taught me a lot about
assembling work and friendship.

To Luiza, Tereza, and Antônio,
my earth, my wind, and my fire.

Contents

Foreword

Psychoanalysis and its role in re-founding a politics of truth

Nelson da Silva Junior

This book comes out at a time that confirms its thesis and purpose: that science is a way of questioning the established, which requires a consistent critique of its excessively normative use, orientated towards establishing certainties. However, this is not the effect of a happy coincidence or the work of chance, but instead of an opportunity to respond to the issues that the dispute over truth have recently conquered in the social and political arena in the form of Fake News and denialism, powerful instruments mainly in the hands of conservative movements.[i] Moreover, there is nothing accidental about the precise timing of this edition, which began more than ten years ago when, in his master's degree,[ii] Paulo Beer's discomfort with the lack of rigour in tackling questions about the scientificity of psychoanalysis was already a clear motivation for his research.[iii]

The result of a doctoral thesis, this book broadens the scope of his master's degree. In this first research, he focused on the extra-clinical demonstration of the effects of psychoanalysis and, therefore, on the debate on the scientificity of psychoanalysis in empirical sciences orientated towards measurability. However, as is expected in any serious and consistent academic work, this successful demonstration opened a new question: How the theory and clinic of psychoanalysis, which does not fit easily with the quantitative methods of the empirical sciences, could be articulated with the demonstration of its effects by these exact sciences. This question required an unusual deepening of a debate that until then had been restricted to the field of epistemology, moving into the fields of philosophy of science, ontology, the politics of science, and ethics. It is essential to anticipate one of its most significant gains: this research recognises and solidly argues that psychoanalysis can lead in this debate. In this sense, Beer traces a path that takes an unprecedented and decisive step for the Lacanian project, explained in Seminar XI, which starts from the question of whether psychoanalysis *is a science* and transforms it into that of *what a science that includes psychoanalysis would be.*

This presentation will start with the general lines of force of the argumentative strategy used by the author to make this turn, trying to isolate how psychoanalysis assumes this privileged place in this debate. Next, it will delve into some significant and exciting themes without emphasising their function in our author's argument.

Lines of force

Firstly, the discussion has included two other objects that belong to both fields: *truth* and *psychic suffering*. Criticisms of psychoanalysis often seek their model of science in the field of biological psychiatry, which seeks to reduce psychic suffering to the effects of physiological processes in the central nervous system. Chemical efficacy, i.e. the production of psychic effects through medication, would retroactively indicate that biological processes are the primary causes of psychic suffering. This privilege would be exclusive to organicity, reducing to nothing any causality belonging to the field of representations, the symbolic and language, and therefore truth.

To combat this attempt at an explanatory monopoly on the causes of psychic suffering, Beer retrieves the discussion on truth in producing knowledge based on the works of philosopher of science Ian Hacking and psychoanalyst Jacques Lacan. He aims to "*reintroduce truth as a question that tensions the knowledge produced*". This idea is central to the work of both authors, albeit with different conceptual economies. Both Ian Hacking and Lacan mobilise, each in their own way, "*truth as a limit concept that brings together* [...] *epistemological, ontological, ethical and political problems*".

A major intellectual challenge is articulating two different theories and demonstrating elective affinities between them based on how they approach the relationship between truth and psychic suffering. Let us start by identifying two points in common between the investigated authors, as well as their differences.

Firstly, both conceive language as a doubly incomplete system: on the one hand, incomplete concerning reality, which implies an uncontrollable relationship with truth, and on the other hand, incomplete concerning itself. As a result, both reject metalanguage, as one of the Lacanian maxims summarises: *there is no truth about truth.* However, the two authors have a marked difference regarding the nature of incompleteness in language's relationship to reality. In Hacking, incompleteness is asymptotic, in the sense of graphs where a curve infinitely approaches a point without ever touching it. A mature reflection on the history of science nourishes Hacking's work on the philosophy of science, which allows him to approach science outside the evolutionist premise of knowledge, where science is seen as a totalising triumph over truth, overcoming myths, religions and ideologies. Hacking's reflection on science does not aim at the eventual untruths of other discourses. On the contrary, Hacking opposes science to itself, bringing to light the plurality of its forms of truth production.

In Lacan's view, the incompleteness of language comes from an equation of radical mutual exclusion between language and the thing, an exclusion that is the foundation of both. In this case, it is not a question of incompleteness in a continuous asymptotic approximation but of an impossibility of the encounter between language and the real.

Secondly, both regard subjects as performative effects of language; in other words, they conceive the essence, the ontological dimension of subjects as pure effects of language. Again, this book will explore fundamental differences between the two authors. In the lineage opened by Michel Foucault, Ian Hacking focuses on the open character of subjectivity in the face of knowledge, in other words, the ontological effects of the knowledge of the sciences in general on subjects. The mark here is, above all, one of variability. In his turn, Lacan radicalises the effects of the incompleteness of language and expands his equation of mutual exclusion to subjectivity, whose structure will be marked by non-being. The mark here will be the impossibility of an absolute identification of the subject with each of its variants conditioned by epistemic mutations throughout history. In the Lacanian conception of the performative dimension of the subject, it is crucial to differentiate the level of the production of subjectivities in each era from the level of the subject's structure. Subjectivities are mutable because the discourses of each era condition them, inevitably changing throughout history. However, the subject, according to Lacan, is never entirely conditioned by discourse, his faithful determination being instead the impossibility of representing everything through language. On this second level, the expression "production of subjectivities" would not be appropriate for Lacan since the impossibility of production marks it.

These differences in conceptions of the incompleteness of language and their respective ontological effects on subjects will also define differences in attitudes towards psychological suffering. According to Hacking, how subjects suffer depends on culture and scientific knowledge. As scientific knowledge changes, so does the nature of the subjects and their pains of the soul. This difference implies, according to Hacking, two types of pathologies: the indifferent types – which would have only a partial plasticity to knowledge, fundamentally restricted to differences in expression – and the interactive types, which would show an absolute plasticity, where pathologies would only be variants of particular and historically marked forms of knowledge. As an example, the indifferent type would be schizophrenia, and the interactive type would be hysteria. Still, according to Hacking, the indifferent types do not signal a possible form of truth about the immutable biological nature of the soul.

As Beer points out, based on the impossibility of mirroring language and reality, in Hacking's view, we should consider scientific truth as an effect, and even more precisely, as an indirect effect, of the effectiveness of scientific experimentation. For Hacking, the effects of its interventions on reality sustain the truth of a theory. This is what the philosopher called *entity realism,* which centres the discussion of scientific truth on the effects of experimentation. Its character is, therefore, transitory, incomplete, and fundamentally dependent on variations in what he called veracity; in other words, truth is an effect of the social conditions which enunciate it.

In Lacan's case, psychic suffering inherits its main lines from Freud: firstly, unavoidable suffering, which stems directly from the exclusionary relationship that language imposes on bodily experience; secondly, suffering which stems from defective relations to truth, and where truth acquires the function of the cause of suffering. For Lacan, these two origins of suffering structure the subjects' relationship with knowledge and truth in a dialectical relationship. Here, the truth is valid for its effect of rupturing knowledge by revealing it as mistaken, incomplete, or impossible, with the indication of another possible knowledge, which, if it stabilises, will, in turn, be the object of a new rupture through the emergence of another truth. Thus, from its function as a cause, truth is radicalised in Lacan's work as a "*vertical plunge into a conception of truth that gravitates around negative foundations, such as lack, impossibility...*"

The political re-founding of truth

Following this line of attack, the author mobilises both authors as a strategy for re-founding the politics of truth about psychic suffering against the main current canons. Indeed, a version of the truth as the adequacy of neurochemical processes in the brain monopolises its approaches and treatments. Based on Hacking, a broadly respected philosopher of science in empirical sciences, it is possible to find ways of legitimising truth according to psychoanalysis. Hacking's concept of *styles of reasoning* makes it possible to "*delineate the differences in the constitution of rationality and objects, as well as their strategies of support*". This concept can thus function as a platform for articulating the psychoanalytic clinic with other traditions of veracity, especially that of science, which works with the notion of truth as adequacy. At this point, psychoanalysis can tip the scales once the discussion about its scientificity is given due reflection.

The first step in Beer's strategy for re-founding a politics of truth is a critical re-reading of biological psychiatry's approach to psychological suffering, vigorously contesting the premise of the body as the sole cause and origin of what Hacking called indifferent entities.

In the case of schizophrenia, one of the most evident facts of this permeability of the biological to the symbolic was demonstrated around 50 years ago by research carried out by the World Health Organisation, namely the fact that patients diagnosed with schizophrenia in developing countries have higher rates of symptom remission than in developed countries.[iv] In addition to the apparent permeability of symptoms in a disease commonly seen as paradigmatic of the organic causality of all mental illness, here we have the exciting hint of a specific pathogenic factor of capitalism and its forms of life.

Another supposedly indifferent entity is depression. To approach it, Beer recounts the compelling case of the difficulties in introducing antidepressants in Japan, where the main barrier was the lack of cultural categories that would allow such a diagnosis. One of the problems with this introduction was that tests with antidepressants did not obtain significant results in local research, which prevented them from being approved by the government. However, indirect publicity campaigns with famous personalities and artists who talked about their depression changed people's view of this pathology. As a result of this cultural change, the results of clinical efficacy tests on antidepressants became so significant that they were "finally" approved for commercialisation. What is noteworthy is that the efficacy of antidepressants only became a scientific fact after the introduction of a new way of suffering in Japanese culture.

Another significant fact that indicates greater interactivity in objects that are theoretically indifferent when it comes to the human soul was the studies with active placebos, i.e. placebos without the active ingredient of antidepressants but containing elements that caused the side effects expected by such drugs. In this case, not so surprisingly, there was no significant difference between placebos and antidepressants.

In short, the difference between developed and developing countries in the remission of schizophrenia symptoms and the case of antidepressants in Japan, as well as active placebos, are arguments for questioning the idea of an absolute indifference given to the organic dimension in mental illnesses such as depression and schizophrenia. These studies show that the premise of an exclusively organic causality does not always hold for the psyche and also demonstrate the existence of types of causality that contradict this premise, namely social interaction, expectations, and beliefs, which are, in short, symbolic causes. Social interaction has effects that compete with the effects expected from the active ingredients of drugs in the field of biological psychiatry itself. These arguments stem from the field of organic psychiatry in particular and the field of the discourse of an organic causal determination of these mental disorders in general.

From the point of view of the relationship between language and biology, these facts are significant for the strategy of politically re-founding the truth about psychic suffering, as they demonstrate that the body is a more interactive entity than the psychoactive drug companies' version conveys. "*Interactivity,* he affirms, is *much broader than biological theories seem to realise so that taking the organic as a justification for indifference proves to be a fragile project.*" Beer thus points out that "*language is not limited to communication: language, the signifiers, intertwine with corporeal matter, constituting it irreversibly.*"

However, recognising these facts and their implications for what we mean by science is just one of the steps towards a political re-founding of truth. Some of the examples brought up by the author show that "good science" is often silenced as much as "bad science" is presented as accurate. These are cases in which the economic power of the big pharmaceutical industries is at stake and frames public dissemination and discussion. The power to shape political discussions has also increasingly been in the hands of large financial groups. Thus, it is worth asking about the chances of politicising science in this environment, given that the political arena is under solid threat.

In this sense, Beer wonders which language would be the most suitable for this critique because "*recognising the political dimension of knowledge production does not necessarily mean solving the problem.*" Therefore, this challenge outlines a second horizon: a conception of language capable of reconciling a science that does not monopolise truth with the political and institutional structures that define the priorities of science for each society at each historical moment.

Towards a fundamental agreement between science and politics: the absence of an ultimate truth.

The political arena has changed in a way that favours neither science nor the discussion of truth. Firstly, by obliterating the discussion of both. It is not news that the forms of communication that have taken place cannot be called debates, discussions or even dialogues. Instead, they are peremptory accusations with no room for reflection. A first step towards putting the question of science and truth back into the political arena is to recover the forms of communication that allow debate, the work of argument, and the openness that allows questions to advance as questions. Alternatively, to use the author's words, it is a matter of submitting science to the scrutiny of political criticism: "*science would present* [a] *potential for knowledge that is open to criticism, above all. This criticism must bear the mark of its political inscription since its constitution and effects are inseparable from power disputes.*"

In *Between Past and Future*, Hannah Arendt[v] proposes the present as this in-between, this gap without guarantees that allows an action to be a political act. It is interesting to note that the most typical stance of scientific research, doubt, is also the model for a political contextualisation of science. It is a sign that politics and science can not only coexist but share a homologous way with a refusal of totality: refusing it *a priori* as a beginning and an end. Indeed, as the author affirms:

> This lack refers to the fact that a new element can always emerge and make explicit that something is given as necessary and natural that can be understood and experienced differently. According to Mackenzie, this unnecessary character of established ways of thinking and experiencing will be localised as the foundation of the political: *it is a field of dispute and negotiation that is constituted from the impossibility of a single form of normative determination.* The political would, therefore, be the field inaugurated by negativity in its most robust sense since it would be *the recognition that the only trait that could be generalised as characteristic of being would be multiplicity: that which can be affirmed and which is always possible to be different from what one thinks it is.* We, therefore, return to the idea of difference or radical heterogeneity. In other words, power disputes exist and are justified because it is impossible to guarantee that one form of existence is more valuable than another.

It is under the condition of this openness, of this gap taken as a premise, that a more refined and consistent debate on the politics of truth can occur. The absence of guarantees does not equate to a "jack-of-all-trades", where the strongest has the most epistemic authority, which usually happens. The idea of a premise for the non-totality of knowledge indicates that there is a criterion for entry into this debate, namely that all participants have a consistent argument structurally open to revision, making their conceptions of truth explicit. This exigence already rules out Fake News and denialism, which emulate scientific discourse but leave out the incomplete, temporary, and fragmentary nature of its achievements. Nevertheless, the members admitted to the arena are subject to rules. Only in this way can the politics of truth be exercised consistently. *"It is therefore a question,"* he writes, "of *a truth that, at the same time as it presents possibilities for construction, also bears the mark of its negation, always in potency."* In other words, re-founding a politics of truth implies a re-founding of politics itself as an activity capable of welcoming a non-totalizing science in which the incompleteness of knowledge has a privileged place, explicitly protected. This proposition allows us to address the role of psychoanalysis in this possible debate on incomplete knowledge.

The new place of psychoanalysis in the philosophy of science

Let us return to what was labelled above as "one of the most important gains of this research", namely the privileged place that psychoanalysis would have in the philosophy of science.

Hacking's asymptotic relationship between truth and things allows truth to appear in various styles of reasoning. This relationship is part of one of the two great arcs of truth in the history of philosophy. Starting with Aristotle, the first arc conceives truth as the adequacy of things to the intellect. Kant takes it up in a relationship without ultimate adequacy, thus marking an insurmountable negativity between these two elements. One would not be wrong in saying that Paul Beer calls this negativity of this arc of truth a weak negativity. The adjective may come as a surprise, at least until we meet another negativity, this one with the adjective *strong.*

Indeed, truth traces another historical arc in which it assumes different types of rupture: Hegel thinks of it as contradiction, Heidegger as unveiling, and Lacan, truth as the negation of knowledge. What unifies this second arc of truth is that a negation of a negation is not equivalent to a position. In other words, the negation established by unveiling does not simply unveil what was veiled but rather the fact that something was concealed by apparently neutral forms until then considered to be fundamental to reality.

In order to present psychoanalysis as a theory and clinic necessary to the debate on psychological suffering, the challenge faced by Beer is to position *strong negativity* as a guarantee of *weak negativity,* which, in Hacking's thinking, is responsible for the open structure of science. Let us see how our author proceeds.

Lacan operates a diffraction in the psychoanalytic clinic, founded on the incompleteness of language, a step which distances him from the way Ian Hacking conceives it. For the latter, if the object is Kantianly unknowable – even though knowledge engages in an asymptotic negotiation with it – it cannot guarantee its truth through language alone. However, through negotiation with language, the truth of objects can reach some stability, and this is how the stability of styles of reasoning and theories arises in his work. For Lacan, it is the strong negativity that guarantees necessary stability. Strong negativity in the sense that it feeds on impossibility as a premise or as a principle, even if this principle, which organises the psychoanalytic clinic, is confirmed by its effects:

> If veracity is an effect of the impossibility of enunciating the truth about things – something that can be seen in the radical separation between signifier and signified – it is necessary to recognise the effects that the ways of dealing with this impossibility cause. According to Lacan, this is what psychoanalysis cannot give up; something that implies an intensification of this impossibility, which can be recognised by the active character of its opposition to knowledge.

Thus, language imposes a first "no" on an ontological level, whose incompleteness allows and, why not, *summons* a multiplicity of ontic affirmations, each of which equals a specific knowledge, scientific or not, but fleeting, paradoxically mistaken and, at the same time, necessary in its opposition to the fundamental incompleteness of language. The juxtaposition of Hacking's and Lacan's readings of psychic suffering constitutes a precise way of illustrating this difference between the two forms of negativity at play:

> There would be an effect caused by the fact that the subject inhabits language, which implies a division: on the one hand, there is possible knowledge (including about oneself); on the other, there is something that is not reduced to this knowledge, and which manifests itself as a

> truth that affirms the absence of original meaning. How the relationship between knowledge and truth is established is historical, producing different modes of subjectivity.

Up to this level, we are moving in the logic of weak negativity. In fact, according to Hacking's conception of historical ontology, the ways of suffering and healing are implicated in specific knowledge produced by established sciences. Nevertheless, he continues:

> The curious thing is that, in psychoanalysis, the most stable thing about the knowledge produced is the fact that this knowledge will always be rejectable in some way. No matter what can be said about them. It is not a stability based on indifference but on recognising something that structures interactivity. In other *words, if there is any indifference – something that does not change with the discourse produced – it would be concerning the impossibility, taken precisely as the central element of causality.* (emphasis added)

In this case, we are dealing with strong negativity, which crystallises more clearly in some Lacanian concepts such as *object a* and from the principle that *there is no sexual relationship.* Such are ultimately ontological equivalents of what Hacking considers to be the indifferent entities of the natural sciences that have an ontic status, even if not intelligible. *Radical indifference* in psychoanalysis has a foundational status from which the discussion of truth simultaneously engages an epistemological, ontological and ethical dimension.

How does this ontological positioning relate to scientific knowledge and science in general? The fact that in this clinic, truth is presented exclusively as a negation of knowledge, something that is more clearly present in the neurotic structure, is a correlate, for Lacan, of his reading of an irreversible rupture in the subject's relationship with knowledge, starting with Descartes' *cogito.* The hypothesis in question, namely that there is a refusal, in the modern scientific project, to deal with categories such as truth and subject, also configures the possibility for the emergence of psychoanalysis and its subject of the unconscious.

The Kantian subject of knowledge is a subject without an identity card. In other words, it is a subject deprived of all its historical determinations, every contingent cause, and everything that can or cannot be. The subject of knowledge is left only with what is necessary and what cannot fail to be. This subject is the only one explicitly accepted by science.[vi] In this Kantian moment par excellence, the language of science excludes the historicity of the subject and its truths. There is simply no place in scientific rationality for this "remainder", just as no names describe it. From then on, mutual negation organises the relations between knowledge and truth within discourse. Consequently, the splitting of the subject also corresponds to the birth of the subject of the unconscious, whose existence inferred by psychoanalytic theory is demonstrated by the effect of interpretations on the compromise solutions described by Freud: failed acts, forgetfulness, and symptoms.

Notably, the elements that scientific rationality necessarily excludes are also necessary. The subject with an identity card is as necessary to scientific endeavour as ordinary language's natural, imprecise, and equivocal logic is necessary to an article or an exposition of non-parametric logic. Thus, truth is one of the conditions of the very language that excludes it.

Let us return here to the difference between the two levels of this act of epistemic reoccupation that define how Hacking articulates Lacan in this book, namely the weak and the strong negativity. Firstly, Hacking, in his conception of scientific knowledge, assumes that reality is always in negotiation with the ways of approaching it. This epistemic stance allows for an articulation with psychoanalysis, as well as with other human sciences. Such an articulation is allowed by Hacking's weak negativity and explored by Beer in his master's programme.

However, at the level of Lacan's articulation of *strong negativity*, the relationship is a structural conflict between truth and knowledge. The conflict is not, however, thought of as the foundation of a mere psychoanalytic regional epistemology. Lacan considers conflict an ontological determinant when, for example, the subject of the unconscious is paradoxically *born from a lack of being*. There is an ontological negativity in the constitution of the Lacanian subject, which is why Beer presents the *strong negativity* as an element that is part of the same scientific epistemology that excludes it. This strong negativity, therefore, guarantees not an epistemic compatibility that allows for the articulation of natural and human sciences but a paradoxical Siamese constitution structured by the mutual exclusion between the subject of knowledge and the subject of the unconscious.

In his text, *Science and Truth,* Lacan presents two types of ontological effects on subjectivity. First, the structure of subjectivity is implicated in the very institution of scientific language by the foreclosure of the subject. Thus, negativity structures the relation between the subject of science and the subject of the unconscious. However, for Lacan, this structural exclusion operated by the subject of science is also what bases it. Thus, what is a problem for an ideal of science based on the indifference of objects is a logical necessity in Lacan's reading. This reading can integrate two hitherto incompatible *styles of reasoning*, an essential notion if we are to understand the extent of this integration.

Hacking proposes that we think of scientific theories through *reasoning* styles, which sustain the idea of the absence of an epistemological or ontological guarantee of scientific endeavour. Thus, he opens the possibility of considering science as composed of an open multiplicity of forms of consistent knowledge or, to use another of the philosopher's notions, correlated to the first, *stable* knowledge.

A style of reasoning is "*defined by delimiting the possibilities of constructing its objects, as well as establishing the basis for defining parameters of truth and falsity*." Based on this definition, he continues, "*it is possible to consider psychoanalysis as a style of reasoning in terms of Ian Hacking.* [...] *This style is structured* [...] *around strong negativity, in which truth can be located as a term that while giving a certain temporary substance to forms of enunciation, also presents the impossibility of total positivisation*." It is interesting to note that psychoanalysis not only constitutes a style of reasoning with its objects and parameters of truth and falsity but also does so in an intense and constant dialogue with other ways of thinking and producing knowledge. In fact, a style of reasoning can only exist among other styles. As demonstrated in this book, it is no coincidence that the psychoanalytic way of dealing with truth – as a question – never ceases to cause concern and discomfort. Uncomfortable both for itself whenever psychoanalytic theory proves to be non-identical to itself and its clinic and for others when it makes people speak about what they often prefer to keep quiet. Upholding truth as a question is an unavoidable urgency in times of negationism and other absolute certainties.

I want to end this preface on a more personal note: traits of this book are also the hallmarks of its author, and these have caught my attention since I had the privilege of meeting him and working with him: openness to reflective and argumentative dialogue, respect for opposing points of view without the seductions of a totalising synthesis, subtle, clear exposition and the ability to bring complex subjects to life with simplicity. A privilege that his readers will also be able to share with the book they have in their hands.

Notes

i Its author was recently called upon to take part in a debate that regularly resurfaces in the media: the attacks on psychoanalysis because of its non-scientific nature. On this occasion, it was the bestseller in Brazil: *Que bobagem!: pseudociências e outros absurdos que não merecem ser levados a sério [What a bullshit!: pseudosciences and other absurdities that do not deserve to be taken seriously,*] by Natália Pasternak and Carlos Orsi. Editora Contexto, 2023. His interventions, alongside those of Mário Eduardo Pereira, Christian Dunker and Vladimir Safatle, were fundamental in identifying the exclusively media function of these new attacks, demonstrating that the consistency of the arguments and honesty in analysing the references would not allow the book in question to be considered an example of a scientific work.

ii Published in the book: Beer, P. *Psicanálise e Ciência: Um Debate Necessário [Psychoanalysis and Science: A Necessary Debate*]. São Paulo: Blucher, 2017.

iii The latest case had been provoked by *The Black Book of Psychoanalysis: Living and Thinking Better without Freud*, organised by Catherine Meyer and published in France in 2005.

iv World Health Organisation. The International Pilot Study of Schizophrenia. Geneva: World Health Organization. 1973; Jablensky A et al. Schizophrenia: Manifestations, incidence and course in different cultures. A World Health Organisation 10-country study. Psychological Medicine, Monograph Supplement. 1992; 20: 1-97.

v Arendt, Hannah. Entre o passado e o Futuro. São Paulo: Perspectiva Publishing House, 1997.

vi In its latest version, this subject without a body and a soul, with only calculative reasoning, is reincarnated in the definition of the decision-making unit between excluding possibilities by the cost-benefit calculation, according to Gary Becker's formula. We see in this exclusion of the contingent one of the continuities between the emergence of the subject of knowledge and the corporate subject, the newborn of neoliberal discourse.

Introduction

Truth is one of the main subjects of contention in our world. Proving that something is true, being the one who tells the truth, denouncing the lack of truth in others: the list of possible forms of power linked to truth is long, and they are all influenced by intense affections. At present, the disputes over truth explicitly show the conflicting nature of the possibility of establishing consensus: Fake News, alternative facts, historical and scientific denial—these are all signs of some conflictual relationship with the truth, which simultaneously indicate that this is a realm of dispute. It also shows that what is in dispute does not necessarily concern the immediate object of the debate.

Take, for example, some of the denialist statements issued by Jair Bolsonaro during the COVID-19 pandemic. Beyond the occasional (and dramatic) issues regarding public health and the validity of scientific studies, what was at stake was a dispute over who has the right to say what is true (Beer, 2021). This could be a way of understanding why a president would create harmful conditions for the population he was supposed to govern: there was something else at stake, which has to do with the power of truth. However, when we step into this arena, we are already a long way from more traditional definitions of what truth is, especially when it comes to scientific thinking.

If we go back to how truth is traditionally understood, we can think of two main elements: on the one hand, it concerns the decisiveness of how pertinent knowledge and propositions are (and the eventual discernment regarding disagreements and the assessment of competing propositions); on the other hand, it operates within a spectrum that is both normative and disruptive.

In other words, the definition of what is true embodies the agreed ways in which something can be regarded as being true: we regard a theory as being true *because* we can observe it or else *because* we can produce the expected results from it. It is then about the parameters used to justify why something is true or false. In conjunction with this, the truth also yields definitions and norms (we know that a certain idea *is* true), just as it embraces the possibility of critique (although we believed that a certain idea *was* true, we found that another one *is* more adequate and, therefore, the previous idea *becomes false*).

Thus, the possibility of affirming and denying certainties is combined with the definition of how an idea can be affirmed or denied.

But this does not end the matter. After all, how we can claim that *x* is true or false depends on how we define *x*. This does not mean that first we define the modes of justification of the truth and then the objects, but rather that they are interdependent processes. In this sense, the issue of truth encompasses the relationship between knowledge and its objects, bearing a potential for justification and normativity (and disruption). If these few paragraphs are capable of pointing out the kind of broader issue that we will address in this book, we have yet to delimit an aspect to be considered: we will address the question of truth within the construction of knowledge on suffering.

Suffering is undoubtedly a broad category. We will start with debates connected to what is usually called psychic suffering, the kind of suffering that is often the target of interventions by clinical practices such as psychiatry or psychology. This kind of knowledge construction is particularly important because they show significant potential for controlling and directing ways of living through their clinical practices. If knowledge is constructed based on modes of understanding truth—both in terms of justification and in the definition of its very objects—a type of knowledge that shows such intense normative potential is worthy of having its assumptions called into question. Let us look at an example.

In 2009, the director of the centre for placebo studies at Harvard University, Irving Kirsch, published *The Emperor's New Drugs: Exploding the Antidepressant Myth*. A book that is the result of years of research (which is still being carried on to the present day), in which the author and various colleagues tackled a subject that is usually considered uncontroversial, both among lay people and specialists: the effectiveness of antidepressant medication. As the title of the book suggests, it is not a matter of merely reinforcing ideas that both common sense and a large part of the scientific community seem to accept and replicate but rather of calling into question how such drugs work.

In general terms, the surprising results of Kirsch's research can be summarised as follows: antidepressants are no more effective than placebos. This means that the therapeutic effects of several drugs considered to be antidepressants are no different from those of drugs which do not contain the active ingredient that should be responsible for the expected therapeutic effects. In everyday language, one could say that they work as well as sugar pills, provided, needless to say, that the sugar pills are administered as if they were the drugs with the expected active ingredient. Kirsch's research, as well as research by other authors who study placebo, lends a bit more sophistication to this idea: it is not just a matter of whether the drug (or the placebo) is given, but how this is done and the effects caused by the such drug. For example, it makes a difference whether the drug is given by a doctor or even whether it is given by a doctor who wears a lab coat or not; moreover, side effects, apparently irrelevant to the expected results, also matter. At this point, Kirsch explores a fact long known to those investigating the effects of antidepressants, precisely the high rate of the placebo effect.

Although it was known that such drugs showed an unusual percentage of placebo effect, the comparison with the drug effect still indicated significant effectiveness of the active ingredients. However, intrigued by this particular feature, Kirsch focuses on a specific type of study, which deals with so-called active placebos. This type of placebo, apart from not carrying the substance regarded as key to the performance of the drug, has others that provoke side effects like those expected. In other words, even though they did not include the antidepressant agent itself, they contained other agents that could lead the subjects taking the placebo to also experience symptoms such as headache, dry mouth, loss of libido, etc., in a way similar to what is expected as a side effect of the tested drug. According to Kirsch, when tested in this type of study, it was virtually impossible to differentiate between the effectiveness of 'real' antidepressants and the placebo.

This discovery has far-reaching consequences. Firstly, it points to a plausible explanation for the high incidence of the placebo effect in these drugs. However, by moving beyond this and rendering the differentiation impractical, we could reverse our thinking: it is not a drug with a high placebo rate, but a medication without an effective active ingredient that only works via placebo, whose performance might be increased by the significant presence of side effects.

We will return to this argument at different moments throughout the book and delve more deeply into it in chapter 5. However, we present it at this initial moment because it will help us to delimit the issue of truth. This is because depression can be taken as a paradigmatic case of the notion that there are different means for establishing true and false criteria and for building research objects. In this case, we must bear in mind that the 'discovery' of drugs capable of treating depression was responsible for establishing two core narratives. First, the etiological explanation that views depression as the effect of disturbances in serotonin reuptake responds to the supposed effectiveness of drugs that inhibit serotonin reuptake (the main target of Kirsch's studies). In other words, Kirsch challenges not only the effectiveness of a treatment but also the basis of a theory that would explain depression. Second, we must bear in mind that this drug-explanation combination reinforces a tendency to biologise what is traditionally called psychopathology.

This tendency, which is an effort to seek and determine markers as well as biochemical and physiological agents capable of explaining and treating disorders that cause suffering, has proved to be the focus of various research centres and governments. However, it did not achieve the expected results (Rose, 2018). We will go deeper into this discussion later, but for now, it is worth pointing out that this tendency establishes in advance a hierarchy between modes of creating knowledge and treatments that would be more or less appropriate (Rose, 2018); besides, it also operates within a way of thinking about truth and falsehood based on a very restricted type of object (biological objects, neurochemical objects, etc.). As Rose (2018) points out, this has translated into radical acts such as cuts to sociology research funding in favour of allocating these to brain mapping projects, for example. So far, these acts seem to reinforce a wager that shows no signs of delivering what is expected and harms by undermining lines of research that could bring more benefits.

Does this mean that biochemical, biophysiological, neurological research, etc., ought to be disregarded? Should the prescription of antidepressants be prohibited? This is precisely the kind of answer this book will not give the reader. It is not a matter of ignoring the value of specific fields such as neurosciences or biology but of making the debate more complex and sophisticated, which is rarely consistent with the adoption of rigid stances. The following pages aim to provide critical material so that these and other debates can move forward in a more interesting way. This means calling into question the fixed ideas that define scientific work as something that must lead to some totalising unity. It is not a matter of replacing one univocal understanding with another but rather of trying to create a critical space in which projects and assumptions can be challenged at their roots.

In times when denialist ideas are gaining in strength and popularity, it cannot be stressed enough that we must be careful when taking critical stances. Even at the risk of being tiresome to the reader, we will prioritise being cautious over avoiding repetition: a book written within the context of an authoritarian and denialist government cannot shy away from this. To be careful means, first and foremost, that critique is not aimed at ultimately overcoming an issue in any way. In fact, therein lies a difference between science and denialism: the former is marked by the constant search for openness and critical thinking, while the latter is based on the establishment of unquestionable truths (Beer, 2021). Openness and critical thinking should not lead to extreme relativism that prevents reaching consensus; it is, therefore, a matter of creating ways of evaluating and ranking knowledge that put themselves into question whenever possible and which are explicit about their assumptions and effects. Something that we will be doing here, beginning with the issue of truth.

In defending the importance of debate on the issue of truth within the context of knowledge production, we are asking how a shift in the definition of truth might affect the issue of psychological suffering. It is a question that comes from the understanding that truth, like scientific knowledge, has a contingent and variable nature. This situates the very issue of truth as something populating not only the fields of epistemology and ontology (traditionally associated with discussions in the philosophy of science) but also the fields of ethics and politics.

Truth between knowledge and politics

The relationship between truth and politics can be retrieved quickly. Suffice it to say, the slogan of Jair Bolsonaro's campaign had been uttered by Martin Luther King Jr. 50 years before, using the biblical quote "then you will know the truth, and the truth will set you free", John 8:32. Truth is mobilised by opposing sides, fairly naturally, as an object of power.

But this is not what we are focusing on. Here, it is a matter of thinking about the connection between truth and politics in the production of scientific knowledge. As Isabelle Stengers (1993) points out, politics is present at several moments when decisions must be made—whether when choosing between competing propositions or when delimiting the scientific field against what should not be considered science. However, this should not lead to the delegitimisation of epistemological and ontological work that is part and parcel of the practice of science.

Politics is present, first and foremost, because science is a public activity: the mobilised issues are part of a common ground, where the debate should revolve around how to establish parameters to produce knowledge of the best possible quality. This would be, according to Stengers, a political inscription of the making of science; however, as we insist and will continue to insist throughout the text, the results of epistemological and ontological work—of methodology, experimentation, demonstration, etc.—should not be diminished or disregarded on this account.

Such concern, which will permeate the whole book, is justified by the frequent denialist attacks experienced by many social groups. These attacks often make ill-intentioned use of debates on the variable nature of scientific doing and its intersections with the external world to delegitimise some forms of knowledge. We witness an inconsistent form of denial of rigorous studies as if the mere presence of intersections with the 'external' world would strip knowledge of its value.

While emphasising the imperative need to discuss the parameters in which the issue of truth is placed within the production of knowledge about suffering, we must remain alert to the effects produced by this discussion, especially since one of the areas that is inevitably impacted by the discussion proposed here is the one known as 'mental health', a term that is usually mobilised in public policy discussions—where the debate on how knowledge is produced shows its direct consequences on people's lives. And, in this sense, beyond denialist stances, we should also critically revisit hegemonic positions that end up normalising certain conceptions.

The issue of how legitimate clinical knowledge and practices are and their consequences for public mental health policies has been under discussion for some time. In my previous book, *Psicanálise e ciência: um debate necessário* [Psychoanalysis and Science: A Necessary Debate] (2017), the discussion was triggered by the closing of Centro de Referência da Infância e Adolescência [Centre of Reference for Childhood and Adolescence] (CRIA), a psychoanalysis service for children and teenagers offered by the Federal University of São Paulo, on the grounds that there was no scientific basis for the use of psychoanalysis in this type of service (Kupfer, 2013). This centre was reopened—temporarily at least—but the situation has only worsened in the last few years: on the one hand, there has been a growing belief in a psychiatric model based on biology for the treatment of suffering; on the other, practices without any substantiation or public debate have gained popularity, such as the use of religious treatments in therapeutic communities[1].

Silencing the truth

If we are initially oriented towards what might be called biological psychiatry (Rose, 2018), it is because we understand it to be a virtually mainstream clinical and research practice in most parts of the world (Watters, 2010). However, this predominance is not necessarily based on the inherent merits of its ideas and therapies but on an extremely combative mode of presentation whose distinguishing feature is not only the colonisation of new places but also the delegitimisation of competitors. Here is something that can easily resemble Stengers' analysis of the general history of modern science, which would require this kind of hegemony—since the distinction between science and non-science would be an unquestionable mark of its legitimacy (Stengers, 1993). According to the author, this kind of positioning is connected to the very issue of truth since the main frontier—to be fought tooth and nail—would be that between true knowledge and fictions.

However, this interpretation that delegitimisation and a kind of normative demarcation are related to a dispute over truth is already a consequence of reclaiming a debate about something that has often been silenced. This is an analysis common to several authors—Lacan and Hacking among them—which claims that modern science is somehow uninterested in (or even rejects) the issue of truth.

However, this rejection would not mean that it disregards knowledge as being true. Quite the contrary: it is as if nothing was to be discussed about the truth of knowledge produced according to the norms postulated by the scientific community. A way of normalising the truth, of reifying the assumptions underlying knowledge production. It is, thus, a rejection of the issue of truth as an enquiry into its variability, into the contingent character of knowledge—a rejection of questioning the truth rather than the quality of being true.

According to Rose (2018), what is surprising about contemporary biological psychiatry is that, even in the face of a widespread crisis regarding its research methods and therapies, the response has consistently been to avoid questioning what would be in play when it comes to its references to true knowledge. Instead, we see a stronger emphasis on biologism, an indisputable claim to the organic as the right path—an emphasis where the word evidence seems critical.

In her *How doctors think* (2005), Kathryn Montgomery gives a brief explanation of how the idea of evidence has evolved in recent decades regarding clinical practice. If, at first, pieces of evidence were occasionally used as a decision-making tool between specific techniques that raised doubts about their clinical use, the notion of evidence seems to have gained autonomy and is now independent of the well-defined context in which they were previously situated. Curiously, what we see is that even the term 'evidence'—which certainly has a much wider range than its application in this new epidemiological strand—seems to have become autonomous in relation to the group responsible for putting it in evidence, gaining different meanings, although always charged with an assumption of superiority in relation to other types of inference.

In the case of psychiatry, observational evidence (especially organic evidence) is raised to a position of a point of reference, as if it were able to indicate neutrally, only through observation, procedures to be adopted or therapeutic horizons to be defined. It is clear that there is a certain amplitude in the way the term 'evidence' is used; however, it is notable how the syntagma *evidence-based* seems to have become a synonym for legitimacy. It is as if there were some correspondence between evidence and truth, which, in contrast, would deviate from all the philosophical discussions that the term 'truth' seems to entail. In the field of psychiatry, this use is so widespread that it has led to direct responses, such as the project—led by Bill Fulford and John Sadler—called 'values-based psychiatry' (Fulford, 2008).

It must be noted that this kind of evidential rationality seems to be spreading uncritically, because of some demand for the suitability of no matter which disciplines to the same kind of support. This leads to attacks on the scientificity of psychoanalysis, usually centred on the accusation that the psychoanalytic practice and theory cannot produce legitimate validations. As argued previously (Beer, 2017; 2018), with minimal distancing we find that there is a generalisation of specific validation parameters, which must be challenged. Challenging that can be done by reintroducing the issue of truth into the production of knowledge.

Ways to ask about the truth

This brings us to how we will conduct our argument. Although truth occupies a central position in philosophy and the philosophy of science, there is much debate about its effective role in scientific practices. In fact, the term 'truth' proves to be rather tricky, revealing great complexity behind a signifier of common and trivial use. In his book *Theories of Truth* (1992), Richard Kirkham claims that the issue of truth is one of the key points in the work of numerous, if not all, great philosophers. Something close to what the philosopher Alain Badiou (2015) stated, for whom the enquiry about truth would be the very definition of the field of philosophy.

However, as Kirkham rightly asserts, the way the issue of truth arises for each author has specificities in relation to the goals that a given theory of truth may seek to achieve, the presuppositions on which it is built, the problems that it may or may not face, etc. This suggests that, although it is a term that often has universalist aspirations, the variety of ways to think about it indicates how difficult it is to find an absolute definition accepted by all.

Furthermore, we must bear in mind that not only because an author is concerned with the issue of truth will they necessarily be proposing a theory of truth. It is possible to simply adopt another author's theory of truth; or, as Kirkham points out, philosophers such as Hartry Field, Donald Davidson and Michael Dummett would not propose new theories of truth but rather delve into the question of whether any established theory of truth would be appropriate for a particular philosophical programme (Kirkham, 1992, p. 62). In this way, we need to distinguish between philosophical programmes and projects of a theory of truth, not with the intention of giving a final form to the infinite possibilities of subdivision and categorisation of layers of a philosophical project, but to demarcate that a theory of truth can either be the central object of an endeavour or something mobilised within a programme that has another object as its core.

More than that, a programme can combine different theories of truth. This is what Luís Claudio Figueiredo and Inês Loureiro (2018) indicate, for example, when commenting on Charles Hanly's proposition featured in the book *The Problem of Truth in Applied Psychoanalysis* (1991): even if it is possible to find moments in which psychoanalytic thought would work with an idea of truth by adequacy or correspondence (especially in Freud), this does not mean that it does not work with other meanings that define certain theories of truth, such as, for example, truth as coherence.

However, the way we will proceed does not suit any of the presented options: we will neither make an effort to define a theory of truth nor exhaustive attempts to recognise and present theories of truth in relation to the points at hand. They will be revisited in due course; however, they will not be at the centre of the argument we will present. This is because, as indicated, our main concern is to reintroduce truth as an issue that brings tension to the knowledge produced. And the selection of the two main authors we will use to accomplish this, the philosopher of science Ian Hacking and the psychoanalyst Jacques Lacan, is influenced by a certain refraction to discussions such as those proposed by Kirkham.

Hacking claims to have no significant interest in discussions about "the nature of truth" (2002a). Lacan, in turn, resorts to several different conceptions of truth throughout his teaching without making any effort to systematise them. He even presents modifications in relation to his references without establishing a direct dialogue with them in such a way that the issue of truth gains autonomy in his teaching.

Indeed, the selection of Lacan and Hacking circumscribes two authors about whom we cannot claim either that they propose a theory of truth or that they carry out a systematic study of different *theories* of truth. Here, we highlight the use of the term 'theory' as mobilised by Kirkham: systematic models established with the aim of defining elements and relations that guarantee the truth. For instance, we can point to another level of approach when Rose (2018) addresses the issue from the Foucauldian formula of *games of truth*. This construction is less concerned with the internal conditions and types of problems they aim to solve and more concerned with how different theories of truth can be mobilised within power relations. In this sense, Tarski's semantic theory (one of the cases studied by Kirkham and presented as a 'theory of truth') serves a different function from Foucault's since the former proposes a specific way of thinking about problems linked to the issue of truth in a local sense, with a focus on logic. In contrast, the latter proposes a structural understanding of how truth, as an issue, is mobilised within power relations.

As we have pointed out before, we intend to approach truth as a boundary concept that encompasses several issues: epistemological, ontological, ethical, and political problems. Within this framework, we might ask what would be the most appropriate way to address the issue of truth in the treatment of suffering, in the words of Rose. We believe that Ian Hacking and Jacques Lacan provide elements to answer this question. The interaction between them offers valuable parameters not only to think about truth as an issue that encompasses epistemology, ontology, ethics, and politics but also to think about the specificities of the field(s) of knowledge that deal with psychological suffering.

Ian Hacking and the critical advocacy of knowledge

Choosing Ian Hacking's work as one of the main references in our thesis was due to a series of factors, which could be summarised in the following statement: Hacking is a philosopher of science who is explicitly critical of normative conceptions on the making of science, but his critical position always responds, at the same time, to a defence of the value of knowledge produced scientifically.

Firstly, his approach to the natural sciences is sophisticated: the author criticises both representationalist and nominalist lines, which are guided by a critique of radical scientific rationalism based on his defence of the importance of experimentation. This is what we see, broadly speaking, when he postulates his *entity realism* in his book *Representing and Intervening* (1983). Nevertheless, whilst dedicating himself to these issues, he never failed to give voice to the influence of Foucauldian thought, which instituted the field of history as something inescapable in his thinking.

The Foucauldian influence makes him sensitive to the issue of truth and knowledge in their relations to power and becomes an integral part of his concerns. However, he takes this to a different destination than that of Foucault: he focuses on the contingency of knowledge implied by this mode of understanding and emphasises the stability of knowledge as something that should also be considered in terms of the relevance of its epistemological and ontological foundations. This is what he addresses in his project on *styles of reasoning*.

At this point, specifically, the issue of truth becomes relevant. Although Hacking never systematically engages in discussions about the nature of truth, he is constantly talking about *truth and (or) falsehood*, something that would be a foundational part of a style of reasoning. The author's idea is that a style of reasoning consists of a specific mode of considering the question of *truth and falsehood*, something inseparable from the possibilities of defining objects. In this way, Hacking introduces a way of approaching scientific thought that signals that epistemology and ontology are indissociable from one another. In addition, he states that there would be no external criterion that could serve as a guarantee for defining a style of reasoning; that is, the acceptance and stability of a style would have a self-referential nature.

This idea can be systematised in relation to the issue of truth, which he considers as something historical and timeless, but also of the order of the impossible. The styles of reasoning would then be modalities of truthfulness, understood as possibilities of enunciation of the truth (Hacking, 2006a). There would be a proposition of the issue of truth that unfolds in the relationship between truth and truthfulness, to the extent that truthfulness would be a historical—therefore circumstantial and incomplete—form of enunciation of the truth. However, there would be no external criterion for guaranteeing truthfulness. Hence the very relationship between truth and truthfulness would not be a relationship of adequacy.

This is a complex relationship which demands thorough work. However, it is already possible to identify two fundamental features that, since the beginning of the work, we have indicated as non-negotiable: that the issue of truth is reaffirmed as something inescapable, but that this should be done by being careful with the value of scientifically produced knowledge.

Hacking's contribution to our discussion does not end here. This is because the author has also put effort into thinking about the ontological effects of knowledge production, mobilised from categories such as *dialectical realism*, *dynamic nominalism* and *making up people* (Hacking, 2002a). This work, which departs from the conception that the established institutions and discourses define what individuals can experience, brings the philosopher's work directly into the field where we place our main interest on the issue of truth: in the production of knowledge about suffering.

From a very early introduction, we can see the justifications for choosing Hacking for this discussion. He is a philosopher of science who addresses the issue of the variability of knowledge without losing sight of the value of scientific production.

Truth in psychoanalysis as the denial of the established order

Dealing with the question of truth in psychoanalysis, even if centred on Lacan's studies, is a task that demands making choices that are not always evident. The so-called 'truth' and the issues related to this term are variable, so we need to be accurate about our choices to avoid getting lost in this universe. Broadly speaking, we will work on the issue of truth based on two guidelines: firstly, to establish what would be its relationship with knowledge; secondly, we argue that the consequences of the way the issue of truth is dealt with in psychoanalysis are enough to recognise, in the words of Hacking, a specific style of thinking, which would show an interesting way of insertion in the fields related to psychic suffering. In this sense, the issue of truth in psychoanalysis would be a key element of how its objects are delineated and how the parameters of truth and falsehood can be constituted.

As we know, truth emerges as an issue for Freud at a very early stage. In his "Studies on Hysteria", written in collaboration with Josef Breuer (Breuer & Freud, 1895), the issue of hysterical lying is already questioned in terms of an operation in which the truth seems to hide behind defensive structures. The treatment, based on speech, then starts to rely on a type of process of production of truth once it starts to be understood as a pathogenic cause. This problem is raised by Nelson da Silva Jr. (2017) based on the idea that there would be two pathogenic centres in Freudian theory, constituting an ellipse. The first would be the drive renunciation required for the transition to civilisation, which, according to the author, could also be linked to how language fails to deal with the reality of the body. This interpretation already bears the Lacanian mark of an approximation between the civilising process and the entry into language. In this first aspect, it is a matter not only of renunciation but also of suffering caused by an original impossibility. The second aspect would be connected to truth, understood as historical truth: this would also bear the mark of an inevitable loss in attempts to reconstruct and communicate this truth.

It is worth remembering that Freud will not restrict the question of truth to historical truth and also that, in Lacan, this term will acquire an even broader scope through the assimilation of linguistics into psychoanalysis. Lacan does not refrain from bringing fiction closer to truth, either in the early phases of his teaching (1953b/1979) or in more advanced phases (1969-70/2007). However, and this is evident in the writing of both psychoanalysts, truth will be constituted not only as a causal centre but also as a clinical operator. The very finding of a truth deficit as a cause for suffering (Silva Junior, 2017) places its retrieval reciprocally as a sign of treatment progress. On the other hand, this deficit must also be understood at the individual level, meaning that both repression and its lifting—as well as operations connected to these processes, such as interpretation or constructions—would orbit around the issue of truth. Not without reason, Lacan, in "Intervention on Transference", affirms that analysis consists of a dialectical movement that gravitates around truth (Lacan, [1951]1966/2006).

Such a consideration condenses a central movement that will be present in Lacan's various analyses of the issue of truth: it is a process, a dialectical process. This is indicative of a reading of Freud already infused with the influence of Hegelian dialectics, accessed by the psychoanalyst through Alexandre Kojève's teachings. As Silveira Sales (2007) points out, the way Kojève presents truth places it as a manifestation of an error since its effect is in opposition to what was established. As the author puts it, "truth is the very imbalance between reality and discourse. It is, therefore, taken from another angle, the truth of the impossibility of truth because nothing from 'reality' will find a place in language" (Silveira Sales, 2007, p.212). Thus, we see how truth simultaneously responds as the naming of an impossibility and the effect of a process. Truth is an effect insofar as it presents the mismatch between reality and discourse while also naming the impossibility of this mismatch.

This placing of truth within dialectics, usually presented as a movement that includes knowledge as a target of denial, indicates, therefore, that truth is constituted as something that is present in a given moment, and that inaugurates a new development. Or also, as what would be inscribed as an absence beyond the enunciation of knowledge: in the body, in the archives, in the traditions, and in the vestiges (Lacan, [1953a]1966/2006). And this also includes the so-called formations of the unconscious: jokes, dreams, and slips of the tongue, all as precursors of truth.

On the other hand, truth was also already linked to the success of an analyst's interpretation. This means that an interpretation would produce an effect of inversion, of the inauguration of a novelty from the denial of a crystallised narrative (knowledge). This is how he refers, in "Intervention on Transference", to the progress in the Dora case: dialectical inversions that produce new developments of truth, owing nothing to Hegelian analysis (Lacan, [1951]1966/2006). Truth as something that introduces a novelty: this seems to be a characteristic maintained in various propositions on the subject. It is, undoubtedly, a conception with a strong clinical emphasis: truth as something that presents itself as disruption, a critique of previously constituted knowledge—thus producing therapeutic effects.

However, this effect would be temporary, and what would have appeared as a novelty in relation to constituted knowledge would stabilise itself as another form of knowledge, thus displacing truth elsewhere. This is a construction largely compatible with various forms of the presentation of desire; indeed, Lacan links the issue of truth to unconscious desire [*Wunsch*]. In this sense, we can see that the specificity the term 'truth' assumes in psychoanalysis concerns its clinical localisation. Truth bears a close relationship with negativity, which is made explicit in the two impossibilities it posits: the fulfilment of desire and the completeness and appropriateness of language. We can see that if, on the one hand, it responds to strictly clinical questions, on the other, it could pose more general questions in relation to other forms of knowledge.

It is only worth pointing out that, later on, Lacan (1966a/2006) will reclaim the causal nature of truth, placing great emphasis on this issue, presented not only as the cause of psychic suffering but as a causal element relevant to all knowledge production. More specifically, he will demonstrate how truth, understood as this impossibility of convergence between discourse and reality, would be an element at once essential due to its causal character and rejected or silenced in the production and communication of knowledge.

We can therefore gather some insights from this first glimpse into the issue of truth in psychoanalysis. Firstly, as Silva Junior (2017) pointed out, it is a causal centre in Freudian psychopathology. Moreover, it is also understood as a clinical operator linked to the manifestations of the unconscious, repression, and lifting. In Lacan, it definitively takes on a broader scope in relation to the notion of historical truth, being located as a mismatch between discourse and reality (Silveira Sales, 2017). This interpretation is part of a dialectical mode of understanding in which truth takes the form of the denial of knowledge. It is, as indicated, a matter of truth as the temporary effect of denial, as well as the naming of a dialectical process that would reveal the impossibility of coincidence between discourse and reality, or else between object and desire. This initial presentation is enough, at least for now, to justify the importance of considering truth within Lacanian thought for our research.

At the very start, we can point out some of the developments of this issue. The first, already present in the aforementioned "Studies on Hysteria" (Breuer & Freud, 1895), concerns the possibilities of adapting clinical phenomena—and which, therefore, operate in a particular way in relation to truth, both as rationality and as an object—to what was regarded as the dominant scientific language:

> it still strikes me myself as strange that the case I write should read like short stories and that, as one might say, they lack the serious stamp of science. I must console myself with the reflection that the nature of the subject is evidently responsible for this, rather than any preference of my own. (Breuer & Freud, 1895, p. 160)

More emphatically, the attempts to explain and communicate about the unconscious have always been a great—and often thankless—effort, since there would always be a boundary between experience and communication. This boundary could perhaps be bypassed by the presentation of cases, since these could provide more appropriate working parameters than the scientific communication typical of physics and chemistry of the late 19th century (Forrester, 1996). Ultimately, this is something related to that which we have identified as elements that make it possible to consider a particular style of reasoning, which would, therefore, also raise the question of modes of theorisation and communication of the produced knowledge. If there is a tension between knowledge and truth, we must question the production of knowledge about the place of truth in its processes and about the effects of the possible ways of dealing with the fact.

Lacan and Hacking

If we resume what we have said about truthfulness—albeit briefly—we notice that in Hacking, as a way of enunciating the truth, there is an impossibility of the complete enunciation of truth contained in this idea. Inevitably, something would be left over, something that would be a key element when we consider the variability of knowledge. Still, in Hacking, the separation between truth and knowledge can be seen as a more radical feature since there would be no external guarantee for the truth of the different possibilities of enunciation of the truth. Something which, in turn, gets even more complex when considering the effects of knowledge on the possibilities of experience of individuals.

Psychoanalysis would put another spin on that question. This is because it is not only a matter of tension between truth and knowledge, understood in general terms, but also tension regarding a kind of object that already bears within it a character that is resistant to the possibility of being known. We attempt to present this as the particularity of truth in psychoanalysis, based on its double inscription as an impossibility.

The unconscious cannot be summarised as something that would escape consciousness, so it is not merely an ontological or epistemological question. The impossibilities that can be connected to it establish a dimension of constitutive absence—as we saw at the beginning of our presentation, based on the remarks by Silva Junior (2017). In general terms, what we intend to present as a possibility for considering that psychoanalysis dwells in a particular style of reasoning concerns the centrality of this absence and negativity as a fundament. A fundament in relation to which truth is a central term. If Hacking points out the ethical nature of the discussion about the retroactive effects of scientific discourse on individuals, psychoanalysis seems to take this discussion to its ultimate consequences by situating figures of absence as the epistemological and ontological foundation (or the lack of foundation), thus placing the question of ethics at the centre as a privileged problem.

In this way, we can more clearly locate the relevance of psychoanalysis in the discussion on the production of knowledge about suffering. This is a deep dive into a conception of truth that gravitates around negative fundaments, such as absence, impossible, etc. It is thus a dialogue that happens out of a specific kind of clinical experience; hence Hacking's approach to styles of reasoning will be of great help when it comes to delineating the boundaries of this conversation since it requires an exchange with other traditions. This way of bringing psychoanalysis into the debate will not only contribute to the discussion about suffering but will also help to sort out some old questions about psychoanalysis and science by demarcating the differences in the constitution of rationality and objects, as well as of their supporting strategies.

In this way, we will chart a course that, based on the issue of truth, will explore different aspects of knowledge production. We will start from a more general debate on the variability and value of scientific production, moving on to its ontological effects, in the work of Ian Hacking. Also, we will make a particular digression about truth in Lacanian psychoanalysis, from which the dialogue with Hacking will be resumed. Finally, we will address some problems about the production of knowledge about suffering, with the aim of thinking of other possible paths. We will constantly reiterate that this is a path committed to the defence of scientific knowledge, as well as the need to acknowledge the effects of producing such knowledge. A path that will seek to open up new doors, so that knowledge about suffering may serve as an instrument for the making up of new forms and not for adaptation to imposed norms.

Chapter 1

Science between truth and truthfulness

One way to think about the relationship between truth and knowledge is to take the relationship between these terms not in terms of adaptation or compatibility but in terms of tension. This means that, apart from the moments in which knowledge and truth display some kind of unity that makes it seem as if they are a perfect fit, a careful look at the historical processes and the lines of force at work in the production of knowledge indicates the need for a broader view. This kind of thinking gained momentum in the latter half of the 19th century, and on which we will base ourselves using Ian Hacking's work as a reference.

The tension between truth and knowledge can be attributed to the diagnosis that there might be a gap between theory and the world so that issues such as necessity and variability are treated as possibilities of enunciation of the truth, never in a direct relationship with it. This is a line of thought built around a critical position on a theory of truth that advocates adequacy or correspondence between knowledge and the world.

However, this does not result in a capitulation to the value of knowledge: on the contrary, there is an undeniable effort to defend science beyond a theory of adequacy. The choice for Hacking as a reference lies precisely in the fact that it enables dialogues with different positions in the philosophy of science, from a realist extreme to a constructivist one, sustaining a hybrid way to think about the value of knowledge. In this sense, we will begin with an introductory discussion on the issue of truth, and then delve into three themes that are central to this philosopher: first, his realism of entities, followed by his considerations on styles of reasoning, and finally, a critical approach to the idea of social construction of knowledge. The discussion on truth will bring into the picture the critique of the applications of theories of truth to scientific practice, introducing the separation between truth and truthfulness.

1.1. The question of truth in the philosophy of science

There are numerous ways of asking about the issue of truth, which consequently yields various ways of trying to answer it. Something skilfully inventoried by Richard Kirkham (1992) but which radically deviates from the path taken in this book. In fact, taking Hacking as a reference is nonetheless a curious choice: on several occasions, the philosopher asserts his lack of interest in discussions about the nature of truth, limiting it to more specific questions: in *Representing and Intervening* (1983), for instance, he asserts that he would not be interested in questions about truth, but in modes of truth and falsehood. In *The Social Construction of What?* (1999), he restates his eschewal of 'elevator words': words that would take the philosophical debate to 'a different level'—which was not particularly interesting to him because it stood apart from a more concrete discussion of scientific practices and their effects. Apart from being too brief, these detours were characterised by a remarkably low effort to explain their motives.

When Hacking publishes some texts between 2002 and 2012, and also through his courses offered at *Collège de France* between 2002 and 2006, he begins to appear more concerned with presenting his motivations for avoiding discussions of this kind. He was not refraining from talking about metaphysical issues, given that he himself affirms, in 1983, that his main interest in the postulation of his entity realism is *metaphysical*. Nor would it be accurate to say that he shies away from epistemological discussions, an implication more than evident in his books on statistical and probabilistic thinking, which have marked much of his career (Hacking, 1965; 1975a; 1990) and nearly all his books. What is curious, however, is that there is something that the author always seems to be addressing, despite his claims that he is not; something that does not explicitly appear in much of his writing but still seems to be there. Perhaps the fact that the author himself claims that he will not address this issue directly implies that, at the same time, he cannot dismiss it. And that which is part of this movement of presence and absence is tied up specifically with the issue of truth.

It is possible to argue that, although he does not deal with this issue directly, Hacking might be talking about it all along. After all, whether in the rigorous study of the emergence of a new style of reasoning, or in reflections on making up people, or in the sober criticism of the idea of the social construction of scientific knowledge, the question of truth would always be looming. It is an absolutely relevant remark, which does not diminish the novelty of how this question has been addressed from the 2000s onwards:

taken earnestly afterwards, his elaborations produce a clarifying effect in relation to his previous writings, helping to organise much of the author's project. Or perhaps, if we allow ourselves to be speculative, this more assertive approach might have been possible after the work done earlier. Regardless of the reason, we are interested in beginning our reflection at this point, as it already includes some assumptions present in the work that will follow.

Truth and truthfulness

We may think that some traditional ways of addressing the issue of truth have been consolidated in the Western philosophical tradition. Among them, the most famous notion in its connection with scientific thought is 'truth by adequacy' (or correspondence), which includes thinkers such as Aristotle, Descartes, and Kant. It is a branch that states, in general terms, that what is true is that which corresponds to what really is. It may feature certain modifications in relation to its objects, as Hacking (2002b, p.14-15) points out: in Descartes, what can be true are *ideas*; in Kant, *judgements*; in more recent philosophy, enunciations, sentences, and propositions. What remains, however, is that the character of truth concerns the adequacy or correspondence between these categories and the world.

However, the truth would not be limited to this conception in the history of Western thought. There is another category that is particularly interesting for thinking about science, and which, curiously enough, can be found in the Bible, mobilised by the words *emeth* or *emunah*, which would pertain to ideas of stability: "This truth is not about statements, judgments, or proposals. It speaks of constancy, safety, reliability." (Hacking, 2002b, p.15). This conjunction between truth as adequacy and constancy is revisited later, when the issue of truth is frankly addressed. Perhaps the main reason behind this more direct consideration of the issue of truth, even noted by the author, is the publication of a book called *Truth and Truthfulness: An Essay in Genealogy* by Bernard Williams (2002). Although the question of stability is central in Hacking's earlier works, it seems that Williams offers words that have been missing. Along these lines, he takes up an idea of atemporality often referenced to the idea of truth, indicating that there would be an ahistorical character to be considered when Aristotle taught that "to say of Being that it is, and of Non-Being that it is not, is true." [...] This definition is out of time, out of history. It runs through all informational discourse. If the concept of truth had a start, it was in the emergence of language itself—without doubt, a milestone in the history of humanity, perhaps even the dawn of our species. (Hacking, 2006a, p. 3)

He says the same thing about Tarski's famous statement about the whiteness of snow: snow is white if, and only if, snow is white. According to Hacking, these are purely formal enunciations. It is important to note that he acknowledges that this idea of truth without history and content would be a convention proposed by well-defined philosophical traditions and contradicted by other thinkers, such as Hegel or Foucault. And there, he makes clear that he chooses not to engage in a debate about the nature of truth: that would increase the complexity of certain discussions that could be simpler. At which point, he picks up on the suggestion he had heard from none other than John Langshaw Austin about avoiding words with an air of importance since the vast majority of problems would do without them and the problems they are loaded with (Hacking will call them, as previously mentioned, 'elevator words').

However, the author also raises another issue related to his choice not to discuss the nature of truth (2002b). The aim is not to dodge an overly dense discussion—which, as a matter of fact, is not consistent with the author's work, which has always delved into highly complex topics—nor to avoid problems that would only be relevant in very sophisticated discussions. As he states at this moment—and, curiously, this seems to be the only moment in which he clearly establishes this—his avoidance of the term 'truth' as something timeless has to do with a problem involved in the application of theories of truth to the sciences, pointing to an idea of circularity:

> Today's Aristotelians say what we say is true when it is in agreement or in correspondence with what is the case. It has often been objected to them that it was impossible to determine "what is the case" or "the facts" without resorting precisely to the proposal which is supposed to be consistent with the state of affairs. So there is a circularity in such a theory of truth. (Hacking, 2002b, p. 17)

Hacking also states, albeit briefly, that Austin's theory would not work for the sciences either, as the pragmatic character would not be enough to sustain the processes of scientific knowledge production. And, regarding the semantic theory of truth proposed by Tarski, often conjured up in evidentialist positions, it would be necessary to bear in mind that even Tarski suggests that each particular science determines the criterion of truth. That is, it is not correct to simply take the Tarskian conception of truth and apply it directly to the claim of observation as evidence—as Edward Erwin (2015) does, for example, when commenting on the standard for empirical evidence that should be pursued for the validation of psychoanalysis. At the very best, what is established is a circularity that asserts that what we unequivocally claim to be evident is evident; however, the transition from the logical proposition of 'if and only if' to empirical evidence remains unsubstantiated.

This becomes clearer by considering that the problems encountered in applying theories of truth by adequacy or Tarski's semantic theory to scientific knowledge would be examples of a bigger problem, which concerns the relationship between knowledge and its applications on objects[2]. After all, nothing prevents a theory from being coherent and establishing consistent logical relations without this meaning that it applies to the targeted objects. An impasse in the field of mathematics, presented by Paul Benacerraf (1973), would signal the disjunction between the theories that explain mathematical knowledge and those that explain the existence of mathematical objects, also understood as the theory of mathematical truth. The issue would then be that while mathematical thinking could produce proofs about the coherence of its thought, it would not be able to connect this demonstration with the truth of its objects. On the other hand, those capable of proving the existence of their objects would fail to demonstrate coherence in their thinking.

Hacking suggests this is similar to what goes on inside a laboratory: the transition from theory to facts does not respond to a general and timeless theory but to local and historical criteria. Criteria that would be linked to the possibilities of defining parameters for the true and the false, for objectivity, and that are related to the stability of the sciences. An idea condensed, three years later, into the term *truthfulness.* A term, according to him, less familiar to philosophers—who would be more accustomed to the *truth*—but which instrumentalises the discussion about truth in ways that think about specific events. In doing so, at this point, he even declares the specificity of its position within the philosophy of science:

> Because our philosophical research is linked to a history of science. It is a long duration history, and therefore very different from the histories of science we find today, but it is a history nonetheless. And I endorse the convention accepted by all great logicians, from Aristotle to Alfred Tarski: truth has no history, neither short nor long. (Hacking, 2006a, p. 3)

The author thus resumes the idea of truth as something purely formal and claims that there is something non-formal in all this, which lies in the fact that truth is linked to what is 'said'. The issue of formalisation of the truth—

referred to by Aristotle and Tarski—would be limited by the fact that every truth needs to be enunciated. The purity of truth, its atemporal and neutral character, would be lost at the moment of its enunciation. For if truth has no history, telling does. Truth, when told, requires someone to say it, and it is in this act of enunciation that the transition to truthfulness occurs. Truthfulness is linked to the act of telling the truth, which includes two aspects: the person telling the truth must provide accurate information (in conformity with reality), and they must be sincere. It is, therefore, about one issue related to the content and another to the intention of the enunciation.

However, limiting oneself to a definition that insists on the accuracy of the contents and the sincerity of the enunciation also brings back a circularity similar to the one pointed out previously. This requires truthfulness, as a concept, to be historicised. In other words, it should not be understood as a timeless and ahistorical event but as the result of several factors that come together and are tensioned throughout history. In addition, there would not be a single mode of enunciation. There are, therefore, different possibilities for saying the truth: "Truth has no history, but what we say, what we can say, that has a history." (Hacking, 2006a, p. 4). Thus, in very general terms, we see that Hacking's answer to the impossibility of ensuring the relationship between things and theories—because they are always, in some measure, circular—is based on historicisation. It is like a suture that would be contextually produced from local procedures that would serve as a one-off agreement on what should or should not be considered true. The big issue is, in this sense, to maintain that this agreement does not eliminate the value of knowledge. Such an answer must include a postulation of the robustness of knowledge that eschews a naive conception of representation.

Entity realism and critique of representation

Although only published in 1983, *Representing and Intervening* is a compilation of introductory courses Hacking had been offering at Stanford University over a number of years. This implies two considerations: first, the generalist nature of part of its content, where the author, by commenting on various traditions of the philosophy of science, locates his thinking; and second, the embryonic nature of the idea of styles of reasoning, which is mentioned only a few times throughout the book. Hacking says (2002b) that it was during a lecture by Alistair Cameron Crombie in 1978 that he first encountered the idea of 'style' associated with scientific thought, even though his earlier works already included compatible ideas. This can be seen, for example, in the influence of Foucault's work, which can be recognised as early as in *The emergence of probability* (1975a/2006).

If the idea of historicity of thought was already present in his recognition that, before the 19th century, there was nothing quite close to probabilistic thinking, the instrumentalisation of this idea through the term 'style' becomes more concrete at the end of the 1970s. In *Representing and Intervening* (1983), what we see are only a few isolated moments in which the author employs this term, even though one of his most important articles on the subject, entitled "Language, truth and reason", was published in 1982, that is, before the publication of the book. It is notable, however, how little influence this article, later republished in *Historical Ontology* (2002a), has on his line of argument. What we see are absolutely compatible texts, but they take rather different paths.

Representing and Intervening revolves around the critique of representation based on the advocacy of experimentation. He avoids discussions on the determination of truth-and-falsehood parameters by providing a more general description of the sciences, mobilising the thinking of great authors along more general lines. Even though the book is more carefully didactical, it still makes explicit Hacking's positioning on a very particular debate in the field of philosophy of science, even though it has far-reaching consequences. It concerns the discussion about whether or not invisible entities exist; and whether, as a result, they would or would not be purely theoretical entities.

This debate falls within the contention that began with the publication of *The Structure of Scientific Revolutions* by Thomas Kuhn (1962), known commonly as *Science Wars*. This contention, polarised between realists and nominalists, was supposedly initiated by Kuhn's publication because it was the first publication—from someone who was not far removed from scientific practice and rather prominent in the Anglo-Saxon world—that claimed a place for contingency in scientific activity. It would thus signal that science was influenced by issues other than mere epistemological problems. It is, then, in this book that Hacking points out that considerations such as these had already been made by authors such as Gaston Bachelard and Ludwik Fleck, although they did not gain the popularity that Kuhn did. This contention, which, interestingly enough, seems to be far from resolved, is discussed by the Canadian philosopher from the perspective of the issue of the reality of invisible entities; he later returns to this broad discussion (with regret, according to him), in *The Social Construction of What?* (1999), "How Inevitable Are the Results of Successful Science?" (2000) and the article we presented earlier, "'Vrai', les valeurs et les sciences" (2002b).

The great merit of this book is in defending the historicity of scientific knowledge without considering this historicity as an element that would delegitimise or eliminate the value of sciences. Resuming what we presented earlier, it is possible to recognise a discussion about truth, which would not depend, according to Hacking's positioning, on a capacity for total representation or on relations of absolute correspondence between theories and objects.

In dealing with the issue of the existence of invisible entities, Hacking argues for an apparently intermediate position: on the one hand, he rejects any idea of total correspondence between language and world; on the other, he also rejects radical idealism, according to which theories would have absolute independence from reality. However, this seemingly conciliatory stance turns out to be radical on some points. This is, after all, a critical account of the notion of representation, indicated as something always problematic. This connects to the problem presented earlier since representation could be understood precisely as the 'transition' between theory and things. In addition, he also criticises theoretical realism, which would argue for the correspondence between theoretical statements and things themselves (since they also require correspondence that is dependent on representation). Thus, the question of truth is central, being dealt with, at first, based on the proposition that representation and intervention are indissociable.

Intervention

The main line of argument postulates that notions of truth and reality should not be so closely linked to the issue of representation as is the case in immediate correlations between evidence and fact; instead, they should be examined from the point of view of the effects of intervention. In fact, any representation would include a dimension of intervention since it is not simply a matter of observing and noting how things really are but instead of producing them. In this way, *entity realism* is distinguished by the proposition that it is possible to infer the existence of theoretical entities from the effects produced in interventions: if it is possible to make use of an entity to produce something new, then it is possible to assert the existence of that entity. Experimental work, therefore, becomes central to postulating the existence of unobservable entities, leading to a subversion in which intervention says more about the truth of something than the theory itself:

> Science is said to have two aims: theory and experiment. Theories try to say how the world is. Experiment and subsequent technology change the world. We represent and we intervene. We represent in order to intervene, and we intervene in the light of representations. Most of today's debate about scientific realism is couched in terms of theory, representation, and truth. The discussions are illuminating but not decisive. This is partly because they are so infected with intractable metaphysics. I suspect there can be no final argument for or against realism at the level of representation. When we turn from representation to intervention, to spraying niobium balls with positrons, anti-realism has less of a grip. [...] The final arbitrator in philosophy is not how we think but what we do. (Hacking, 1983, p. 31)

Regarding this, Hacking declares that he is more interested in the issue of the existence of entities than in questioning strategies for establishing truth-and-falsehood. Much of the introduction to the Brazilian edition of the book (Hacking, 2012a) is devoted to arguments on this issue. Something different from what he did in much of his work, making clear at this point that he is interested in metaphysical questions rather than epistemological discussions. This is a sensitive issue since part of his critics perceive his work as a proposition of epistemological differentiation. On the one hand, there are those who make a nominalist interpretation, claiming that there would be an underlying advocacy of ideas of inference to the best explanation (Resnik, 1994; Reiner & Pierson, 1995). On the other hand, the author also steers away from some of its defenders, such as Mauricio Suárez (2006), who perceives Hacking's claims about the manipulation of entities as if just a simple manipulation (which does not necessarily cause any effects) were enough to affirm the existence of the entity, while also attributing to the (simple) manipulation some sort of causal value. Hacking reminds us that he is not only talking about manipulation in a general sense but specifically about constant and methodical manipulations that create new phenomena. Besides, he steers away from causal inference, especially if taken as a type of guarantee.

In doing so, the philosopher circumscribes a separation between two distinct dimensions related to the truth in a way that is compatible with the problem posed in his 2002 article. Truth here is understood as something connected to the existence of the entities, not to the correctness of the theories. Bearing in mind that the alleged problem would lie precisely in the link between these two elements. Considering the case of depression, briefly introduced at the beginning of this chapter, we can assume that depression exists even if the theories that try to explain it are wrong. This may even change what we understand as depression, but it does not put its existence in check.

It is also necessary to consider that his entity realism poses a second problem of great interest for the philosophy of science: based on the argument that one can infer the existence of entities but not necessarily the appropriateness of the knowledge produced about them, Hacking suggests that the main engine of science would be experimentation. Not only because of its applicability in terms of validation but especially due to the experiments' potential to produce and establish new facts.

In this sense, the permanent insufficiency of established knowledge that undermines a position linked to theoretical realism is combined with the idea of the autonomous existence of the real, in which things exist beyond what is said or known about them. We would recognise this when this reality came into conflict with established theories. Besides, in a distinctly Kuhnian heritage, experiments would be privileged moments for recognising crises and producing new facts that were not foreseen in theory, thus presenting a disruptive power capable of demanding epistemological reorganisations.

There is, therefore, contained in the critique of representation the recognition of a double operation of the real: while the author still acknowledges a degree of stability in the prevailing theories, he also points to the disruptive character, that is, to the world as something that is presented as different from what is expected. This kind of positioning allows us to resume, once again, some considerations about the truth: on the one hand, the opposition between truth and truthfulness (Hacking, 2006a) indicates that the possible modes of enunciation of the truth always leave something out and that this can be a destabilising element in theories. Experiments would act as a tensioning mechanism between truth and truthfulness: they would put into play the enunciations about the truth to confirm their relevance and recognise their flaws or incompleteness. This does not mean that truth would be fully captured or stabilised; on the contrary, it could destabilise both one-off enunciations and models of truthfulness (as general possibilities constituted of the enunciation of the truth).

Realism

It is possible that, in scientific thought, theories can always be questioned and proved wrong or even that an original incompatibility between theory and truth in its timeless and absolute character is presupposed. However, this does not necessarily lead to an anti-realist position. If the discussion can be presented as the opposition between the argument that scientific theories correspond to things themselves, on the realists' side, and the claim that there is no relationship at all between statements and things, on the anti-realists' side, Hacking's analysis indicates that there are several intermediate positions that must be considered.

Realism, taken broadly, advocates for a relationship of correspondence between theories and entities, states and processes. Truth appears, then, as a qualifier that concerns adequacy, placing itself in opposition to falsehood. But the main point is that this adequacy concerns not only the formal statements that must be logically coherent but also the literal transition from what is proposed to the state of things. It is precisely at this point that it opposes anti-realism in that the latter would claim that the truth of everything that is described and operated upon in enunciations as theoretical entities cannot be proved:

> Some anti-realists hold back because they believe theories are intellectual tools which cannot be understood as literal statements of how the world is. Others say that theories must be taken literally – there is no other way to understand them. But, such anti-realists contend, however much we may use the theories we do not have compelling reasons to believe they are right. Likewise anti-realists of either stripe will not include theoretical entities among the kinds of things that really exist in the world: turbines yes, but photons no. (Hacking, 1983, p. 21)

We should draw attention to the end of this quotation, as it indicates the specificity of the discussion presented. It is, first and foremost, a contention over theoretical entities, that is, entities that are not observable but play an effective role in scientific practice. When the book was written, the discussion about the existence of electrons fitted perfectly into this quarrel since it was still just a 'theoretical entity' without the possibility of direct observation. This is perhaps one of the questions that, surprisingly, continues to be highly relevant today since one of the most prevalent strands of anti-realism argues that one should only consider that which can be directly observed. For Hacking, the issue of observation—or, more specifically, of what can be observed—is quite important since it is directly connected to how causal relations are understood by anti-realist currents, since causes would never be observable, indicating a clear distance from their entity realism.

If, on the one hand, it may seem somewhat naive to postulate that theories can arrive at the truth of things as they really are, on the other hand, an absolutely anti-realist stance that advocates that only what can be observed should be taken into account seems to share a problem quite close to the former, namely that observation is presented as an effective way of accessing things themselves, and that it could dispense with causal hypotheses.

Hacking, as stated earlier, describes himself as an entity realist or as an advocate of experimental realism. Such a statement implies the division of realism into the realism of theories, in which "The question about theories is whether they are true, or are true-or-false, or are candidates for truth, or aim at the truth", and the realism of entities, in which "The question [...] is whether they exist." (Hacking, 1983/2012, p. 27). According to the author, it is possible to be a realist of theories without being a realist of entities, that is, to argue that theories are true without affirming the existence of the theoretical entities. On the other hand, the realism of entities can work without a belief in the literality of theories, affirming that one can postulate the existence of something without necessarily being able to describe it correctly or completely[3].

The realism of entities is not based on the explanation one can or cannot give about a phenomenon or entity; it is based on the capacity to produce effects from the intervention in an entity. In this way, a theoretical entity will only be satisfactory if it is an existing entity, which implies that there is something that is satisfactorily used in a theory and, to that end, it is necessary that one can produce effects from that theory. Such a path hinges on the inseparability between representation and intervention, which will culminate in Hacking's interest in what can be called 'reality': something which is neither stable nor transcendent but a product of constant *renegotiation*. This consideration is important given that, as the author himself stated, anti-realist theories have been gaining importance in recent decades. The most famous among them is known as *positivism*.

According to Hacking, positivism can be understood from the premise that "Nothing can be known to be real except what might be observed." (Hacking, 1983/2012, p. 41). Again, this is an affirmation that is extremely close to that which has been mobilised by biological psychiatry in its foundation (Rose, 2018). In doing so, it is worth saying that the author combines under the name 'positivism' traditions that did not necessarily call themselves that way, such as Hume's empiricism or the constructive empiricism of Bas van Fraassen. His justification is that all these disciplines would share six presuppositions that define this mode of thought[4]: emphasis on verification, the privilege of observation, rejection of causality, contempt for explanations, rejection of theoretical entities, and rejection of metaphysics (*ibidem*, p. 108).

Our interest focuses, at this point, on a positivist trait that, besides being notorious in today's scientific production, is at the core of our main concern: the overestimation of empirical observation in relation to other modes of explanation, experimentation, and validation. In this regard, Hacking comments on the work of Bas van Fraassen, who presents a more current and balanced version of the points just made. However, the problem he raised concerning the transition from theory to facts (or things) would continue to be a problem:

> The positivist enthusiasm for verifiability was only temporarily connected with meaning, in the days of logical positivism. More generally it represents a desire for positive science, for knowledge that can be settled as true, and whose facts are determined with precision. Van Fraassen's constructive empiricism shares this enthusiasm. (Hacking, 1983/2012, p. 52)

The author points out that if we return to the terms employed in "'Vrai': La Science, Les Valeurs", an attempt at an epistemological resolution for the transition from theories to truth would persist, albeit in a more sophisticated way. He answers based on two points: the first concerns language; the second intervention.

The question of language

Language is a perennial question in studies about science. The very possibility of making sense of the world demands a conceptual approach if we are to think about the relationship between theory and thing. In this field, it is possible to assume various positions, from denying the importance of these questions, based on the overemphasis on observation, to arguments that flirt with a vertiginous relativism. Hacking signals his sympathy for nominalist projects, but with many reservations. Curiously, his comments on the subject are much more detailed than his positions, as it can be seen in *Why Does Language Matter to Philosophy?* (1975b/1999). In this book, the author takes stock of great thinkers who have taken language as a philosophical object; it is a thorough book, in which, however, Hacking hardly positions himself.

The most interesting point to our discussion about incommensurability: a term made popular by Kuhn in the philosophy of science (1962) in its employment related to the impossibility of connecting elements of different theories, but which consists of a broader philosophical question about the possibility of understanding or translating an idea. If a term only takes on its meaning within an established network of meanings, attempts at understanding would always be flawed, as they would take the terms out of their context. Hacking briefly mobilises (in *Representing and Intervening*) some philosophers who have addressed this question, such as Donald Davidson and Dudley Shapere. Still, his main concern is actually with the question of the incommensurability of meaning, starting with the work of Hilary Putnam.

In an essay entitled "The Meaning of 'Meaning'" (1979), Putnam directly addresses the question of meaning, based on whether elements with the same name correspond to the same entities in different theories. Putnam's answer, broadly speaking, is that meaning is the gathering of different elements: from syntactic and semantic functions, their original or natural references (if there are any), and their extensions and stereotypes, which encompass the contextual meanings that are related to words. This results, therefore, in an understanding of language that is not based on an idea of correspondence between thing and meaning but on a socially-defined relationship—which is, however, not without some kind of connection to the reference.

That, at least, is the explanation that Hacking finds most useful to his entity realism. He makes this position clear by commenting on other texts by Putnam (1982), written at a later moment when the philosopher would have experienced a more radical nominalist turn, arguing for *internal realism*. For Hacking, however, the main problem with the development that radicalises Putnam's nominalism is that it would end up constituting itself as a system of thought that external events could not interpellate: "Putnam has become conservative. For Kant there was no way out of our conceptual scheme. Putnam gives no reason to suppose there is any way either." (Hacking, 1983, p. 111).

Therefore, we see that the way Hacking mobilises language in its discussions defines something that responds to social relations but is nonetheless interpellated by elements external to established systems. Something not far from how he refers to the question of reality: also inspired by Putnam's work, he refers to reality as something constantly being renegotiated. He thus makes explicit what some commentators call a 'modest realism' (Mendonça, 2012): something that eschews idealism and anti-realism since it always insists on interpellations that are not reducible to language while refusing proposals of total adequacy between theories and truth.

Intervention and causality

The second point presented earlier deals with the inclusion of the question of intervention into the way scientific procedure is understood. As stated, positivist currents advocate the idea of observation as something independent of the theories at stake. This argument has been subject to much criticism, usually on the grounds that neutral observation is impossible. Rather, observations would be loaded with theory, and this would call into question the privilege of observation. Hacking, however, does not agree with this criticism.

It does not mean that he disagrees with the idea that observation is influenced by theories. From the outset, this is where he distances himself from positivism, and he does not refrain from demonstrating that he disagrees with this separation in most cases. According to him, for the most part, science would work in such a way that observations are not pre- or atheoretical. However, even in cases where this happens, that does not mean that observation is reduced to theory. It is possible to distinguish between observation and theory, as much as the two are intertwined. And this would not change the value of the observation since this relationship would not prevent observations from producing points of instability in theories. Something similar to his critique of Putnam's internal nominalism: Hacking always emphasises the disruptive value of that which can destabilise an established system of thought.

Therefore, his issue does not have to do with one of the ideas found in the critique of observation, which would argue that theoretical contamination would render observation virtually sterile. This does not hold, according to the philosopher. However, observation must be understood not as a privileged activity but as a procedure, a necessary skill for any experimentation. And experimentation—indeed, a privileged process within scientific production—cannot be understood as a modality of knowledge production based on reproductions of real phenomena.

The distinction between experimentation and the reproduction of reality takes place on several levels, ranging from the production of instruments that enable a particular kind of observation to the creation of events that would never have existed:

> To update the example, 20 years ago there were no masers or lasers in the universe. Perhaps that is wrong, perhaps there were one or two. (Some cosmological phenomena have recently been suggested as maser phenomena.) Yet now the universe has tens of thousands of lasers, many

> of them within three or four miles of me as I write. (Hacking, 1983/, p. 226-27)

This is an illustrative example when it comes to the creation of phenomena. Experiments, even if they try to reproduce phenomena found in everyday life, do so in a specific way. Even when experiments are replicated, this is done with some methodological modification, whether in the method of measurement, or observation, or control, etc. All these cases are examples of how there is an active intervention in the production of scientific knowledge. Even in the non-experimental sciences, intervention could not be ruled out since even language modifies (albeit not completely) the idea we have about objects. This is, therefore, the heart of Hacking's critique of the extremes of realist or anti-realist positions, which passes through a critique of the idea of representation which necessarily includes a consideration of intervention. This leads the author, when revisiting his articles from the 2000s, to argue that truthfulness is linked to causality. For it is based on the produced effects that it would be possible to infer the existence of entities, as well as to produce some kind of productive knowledge: "We are completely convinced of the reality of electrons when we regularly set out to build — and often enough succeed in building — new kinds of device that use various well-understood causal properties of electrons to interfere in other more hypothetical parts of nature" (Hacking, 1983/2012, p. 265).

It is, in this sense, a wager on intervention as a way of producing causal explanations. The affirmation of existence is thereby a by-product since it is only possible to produce a cause from that which exists. The main interest would then be the causal potentiality, the possibility of producing transformations. In this sense, the relevance of truthfulness models would be provided by their transformative capacity. Therefore, it is possible to consider that the central axis of entity realism is *the possibility of enunciating the truth from the recognition of the effects that can be caused.*

This is a critical stance towards the idea that the value of knowledge is linked to the possibility of direct observation of its entities or of representation. On the contrary, his emphasis is directed at scientific doing as a process from which the causal potential of entities can be gathered, which must have their existence affirmed precisely because they are located as the cause of something. This interpretation poses problems to a naive defence of biologistic views as if, because they can be located or observed in the body, they provide an ultimate truth—as it is repeatedly claimed in relation to depression. Hacking avoids the word 'evidence', not without reason, since this term would tend to be understood under a fixed mindset, where the direct observation of entities would be valued more than their effects. What Hacking therefore asserts, in his version of realism, is the reality of effects. This is a possible interpretation of one of the author's latest remarks on the subject: "My attack on scientific anti-realism is analogous to Marx's onslaught on the idealism of his day. Both say that the point is not to understand the world but to change it." (Hacking, 1983/2012, p. 274).

As we know, however, this statement is part of a broader project, defined not only by a case for experimentation but by a proposal for understanding the value of knowledge based on recognising its necessary features and contingencies. Thus, we proceed with his styles of reasoning.

1.2 Styles of reasoning

As presented so far, we see there is a great effort by Ian Hacking to resolve a poignant question at the end of the 20th century: the existence, or not, of unobservable theoretical entities. Although some of the examples mobilised by the author are no longer relevant to this discussion—technological advances have made the observation of electrons possible, for example—this does not mean that it has lost its vitality. Rather, perhaps even more complex cases might benefit from the philosopher's remarks on his entity realism, such as discussions about whether or not the localisation of brain markers is required for the acceptance of theories of mental disorders. This discussion can be found in the brief presentation on the debate about depression at the beginning of this chapter. However, it is not restricted to this case since there is a trend of massive investment in research aimed at brain localisation as a primary goal, as aptly described by Nikolas Rose (2018). We will not delve deeply into this debate yet, for to do so satisfactorily there are still other conceptual tools that we need to establish.

For now, it is worth noting that we have gathered two paths traced by Hacking: on the one hand, the refusal of a general theory of truth based on the understanding that truth is only accessible in its historicised and partial forms, named as truthfulness; on the other hand, the advocacy of the value of scientific knowledge grounded in the possibility of producing effects from the intervention in entities—which, consequently, would prove the existence of these same entities. It is, therefore, a general positioning on the historicity of knowledge, and a specific proposal that addresses both the truth of the existence of entities and the value of experimentation, focusing on the effects of interventions rather than a naive idea of observation. The following pages will elaborate on the first point, linked to the historical character of the forms of truth.

Published in 1982, "Language, Truth and Reason"—republished in *Historical Ontology* (2002a/2009)—falls within a line of philosophy of science that viewed with some concern the growth of relativist tendencies. It is worth remembering, for example, that one of the most hard-hitting books within this debate, *Laboratory Life: The Construction of Scientific Facts,* written by Bruno Latour and Steve Woolgar, had been published in 1979. Even though Hacking does not fail to acknowledge the merits of Latour and Woolgar, as he does in *The Social Construction of What?* (1999), he also points out that if the quarrel termed *Science Wars* had been initiated by the publication of *The Structure of Scientific Revolutions* by Thomas Kuhn (1962/2013), then *Laboratory Life* would be the book responsible for throwing gasoline on a debate hitherto restrained. Moreover, the prominent Edinburgh school, captained by Barry Barnes and David Bloor, established the sociology of science as a relevant field populated by authors of varying degrees of radicalism. In the collection where the text in question was originally published, articles by various authors with different stances towards scientific relativism were brought together. The one by Hacking was reportedly considered the second most relativistic, only behind the chapter written by Barnes and Bloor.

As the title indicates, it is a moment when the author dwells on the question of truth (as does the whole book it is part of), although, as previously noted, he does so to shift the discussion to the truth-and-falsehood syntagma. It is also the first moment when Hacking, based on a lecture by Alistair Crombie he attended in 1978, employs the term *style* to talk about modes of reasoning. Crombie would come to publish his mammoth work more than a decade later, entitled *Styles of Scientific Thinking in the European Tradition* (1994). In addition to Crombie, we can also recognise a heavy influence of Foucault—already found in his 1975 book on the emergence of probabilistic thinking—as well as of Paul Feyerabend's impactful *Against Method* (1975/1993). There is, however, a marked distance from Crombie right from the outset, and that concerns the fact that the term *style* was originally articulated to *thinking*, and not *reasoning*: "I prefer to speak of styles of (scientific) 'reasoning' rather than Crombie's 'thinking'. This is partly because thinking is too much in the head for my liking. [...] Crombie's last word in the title of his book is 'Arts'; mine would be 'Artisan.'" (Hacking, 2002a, p. 180-81).

This change serves more as a mark specifically directed towards Crombie but one of great importance to Hacking's thinking. More than that, it works as a distinct mark in relation to Koyré, Crombie's teacher, to whom Hacking imputes an overly rationalist conception of science, even if he does not fail to acknowledge his importance and influence on his own thinking. This already indicates his view of scientific practice as something that significantly exceeds the sum of the scientists' minds. According to him, the thought itself is constituted from various socially established possibilities, which should be considered when addressing the question of the truthfulness of an idea. It is not for nothing that in an article revisiting this publication 30 years later, he states that he remains implicated with his project of *styles*, although he no longer finds it relevant to call them styles of reasoning: "'Styles of scientific thinking & doing' is a better label; the styles can also be called genres, or, ways of finding out" (Hacking, 2012b, p. 599). We can even see how production continues to be a key issue for the author: it is not just about thinking but about doing things.

The very possibility of a proposition being "a candidate for being true-or-false, depends on whether we have ways to reason about it." (Hacking, 2002a, p. 160). This means that a style of reasoning is not a way of defining possibilities for assessing the truth or falsehood of a question but that the very possibilities of enunciating a question, as well as the parameters of truth and falsehood, are produced within a specific style. This does not mean there is no truth or falsehood, nor does it lead to complete relativism. Only that the modes of assessing truth and falsehood are supportive of the possibilities of constructing their own propositions:

> My worry is about truth-or-falsehood. Consider Hamlet's maxim, that nothing's either good or bad but thinking makes it so. If we transfer this to truth and falsehood, it is ambiguous between (a) nothing which is true is true, and nothing which is false is false, but thinking makes it so, and (b) nothing's either true-or-false but thinking makes it so. It is (b) that preoccupies me. My relativist worry is, to repeat, that the sense of a proposition *p*, the way in which it points to truth or falsehood, hinges on the style of reasoning appropriate to *p*. Hence we cannot criticize that style of reasoning as a way of getting to p or to not-*p*, because *p* simply is that proposition whose truth value is determined in this way. (Hacking, 2002a, p. 160)

With this, Hacking suggests there is a difference between relativism and subjectivism: thinking that we can make something true or false out of our own thinking would be a form of subjectivism, whereas relativism would be the recognition that there are candidates for truth and falsehood inherent to the way of thinking. This can also serve as a reorganiser for perennial issues such as incommensurability or conceptual schemes. Rather than being seen as problems concerning truth, they should be taken as issues concerning truth and falsehood. The main point is that there would be no possibility of considering the truth of something independently of the style of reasoning in which it is presented: propositions only exist within styles and, therefore, within parameters of truth and falsehood. Two decades later, the author will name this movement after the tension between truth and truthfulness so that the latter would respond to the particular possibilities of enunciation of the truth, being, therefore, a circumscription of a timeless truth into historical forms of truth and falsehood.

The styles and the sciences

In this sense, the word *style* proves useful as it indicates something that is not limited to the field of epistemology, being borrowed from aesthetics. It is also quite wide-ranging and can be used to varying degrees. In addition to postulating six 'main'[5] styles, Crombie himself indicated there were intermediate styles.

Interestingly, Hacking refers to these six main styles in a strict manner, at least in large part of his work. Something that happens, for example, when he denies John Forrester's (1996) proposition about the existence of a case thinking style into which psychoanalysis could be included. What seems most surprising about this positioning is that the way Hacking himself develops the idea of styles of reasoning does not seem to accommodate such a rigid approach.

Indeed, when he revisited the subject in 2012, he claimed he would have made a mistake trying to circumscribe the styles to this list and some derivatives. In commenting on some appropriations of authors who have used his ideas to define 'other' styles, including Arnold Davidson's advocacy of psychiatry as a style of reasoning, he says: "He [Arnold Davidson] and many others were right and I was wrong. Of course the phrase can be applied to a host of, well, styles of reasoning, and it was stupid to try to patent it, and restrict it to members of a list" (Hacking, 2012b, p. 601).

According to Hacking, there is something similar between the notion of a style of reasoning and, for example, translation issues or the very notion of a Kuhnian paradigm. These notions work quite well when problems of continuity and understanding arise: "Translation is hard when one gets to whole new ranges of possibility that make no sense for the favored styles of reasoning of an-other culture." (Hacking, 2002a/2009, p. 161). The expression "whole new" in this passage is key, for it indicates the nature of a notion difficult to circumscribe: it seems obvious in borderline cases, but it is difficult to establish the threshold. Let us recall, for instance, the various criticisms of Kuhn's lack of definition of his notion of paradigm and of a certain lack of interest on the author's part in producing a more precise notion (Kuhn, 1977/2011). Hacking takes up a similar stance on the notion of style, abstaining from an exegesis of the term and merely assessing how other contemporary authors employ it.

On the other hand, it is worth noting that there are important differences between the notion of styles of reasoning and that of paradigm. The former is far more encompassing, comprising transversality between different specific sciences, whereas the idea of paradigm is restricted to one part of a particular science. In addition, Kuhn insists on the idea of rupture between different paradigms, or at least on the extent to which they indicate that scientific knowledge is not cumulative. Hacking agrees with this idea, although he points out that this would not be correct in relation to styles:

> *Knowledge* is less cumulative than we thought. As argued Pierre Duhem, a century ago, the *explanations* of phenomena are always subject to radical revisions. But there are other things that accumulate. According to Duhem, scientific classifications are more stable than explanations. [...] There is an *accumulation* of styles, but the paradigms, for Kuhn, replace each other; they do not accumulate. (Hacking, 2006b, p.7)

Thus, we see that a trait of the styles of reasoning is their cumulative character. They do not need to be a rupture from what preceded them in order to introduce novelties. On the other hand, specific theories or sciences are not synonymous with styles of reasoning: they establish themselves in one style or in more than one. Just as indicated by the difference concerning the notion of paradigm, the issue of amplitude becomes necessary in locating across specific styles and disciplines. In fact, the relationship between a style and a particular science is not only one of amplitude, but of function: style structures the possibilities of thinking, and this structure can include different expressions.

In the same way, a specific science is a smaller structure that holds different paradigms. It is also worth noting that styles can be combined in research projects, just as the combination of styles can lead to a new one.

A problem produced within a discipline may trigger the beginning of a process that would lead to a style of reasoning, but this does not mean that the style would remain restricted to the discipline in question. The possibilities contained in a discipline thus depend on the existence of the style of reasoning within which the discipline exists, establishing the historical character of modes of thought. And as stated previously, one of the traits of this establishment is defining the possibilities of propositions and the parameters of truth and falsehood:

> They would not be possibilities, candidates for truth or falsehood, unless that style were in existence. The existence of the style arises from historical events. Hence, although whichever propositions are true may depend on the data, the fact that they are candidates for being true is a consequence of a historical event. Conversely, the rationality of a style of reasoning as a way of bearing on the truth of a class of propositions does not seem open for independent criticism, because the very sense of what can be established by that style depends upon the style itself. (Hacking, 2002a, p. 167)

In the context of determining the possibilities of truth and falsehood, another question dear to scientific thought is defined: objectivity. According to the author, the idea of objectivity is directly linked to the idea of truth since it would indicate nothing less than established ways for getting to the truth of things. With the emergence of a new style of thinking, fields of possibilities open up. Hacking makes several references to Althusser's use of the word *continent* to refer to this. The best example, perhaps one of the few consensuses in the field of philosophy of science, is Galileo's crystallisation of a style of reasoning: it is not about the application of previous ideas to other objects or of new ideas on old objects; it is about the establishment of another mode of reasoning, defining new possibilities for objects and for truths and falsehoods. This is what is termed *systematic experimentation* (Hacking, 2012b, p. 602).

Furthermore, the term 'crystallisation' should not be ignored: it points to the understanding that, although Galileo used various instruments in innovative ways, the invention is not entirely his but something due to the crystallisation of innovations that had been underway for some time. This term was a subject of debate in the publishing of his *The Emergence of Probability*

(1975a), in which Hacking argues that before the 17th century, there was no probabilistic thinking in Europe. This is not to say that its foundations had not yet been invented but that several elements required for probabilistic thinking had not yet been combined in the way that we have come to know it. Once they were, that way of thinking crystallised.

A style emerges as something restricted from local and small interactions. Over time, they gain amplitude and become established as a norm. They become the right way to reason within a field. There would be, for Hacking, a frequent inversion on the question of objectivity: it would not be an *a priori* but rather something constituted within the style of reasoning itself. More than that, a style would be responsible for introducing various elements, such as: "objects; evidence; sentences, new ways of being a candidate for truth or falsehood; laws, or at any rate modalities; possibilities" (Hacking, 2002a, p. 189).

Methods of reasoning and objects

In this way, we come close to defining a style of reasoning. Something that does not precede the novelties it introduces but is constituted as the novelties appear and become self-sustaining. A style of reasoning is therefore recognised by the introduction of novelties: styles of reasoning define new objects and methods of reasoning (Hacking, 2002b; 2006b; 2006c). The other elements may be seen as branches of these two more general categories: one more directly related to ontological issues; the other to epistemological issues. The way we think restricts the possibilities of approaching objects, just as the possible ways of approaching define how one can think about objects. This, in turn, goes back to the issue of possibilities for enunciating the truth or truthfulness: "Objects need methods of reasoning so that we can tell the truth about them. Conversely, a method of reasoning without a new type of object is sterile and will never distinguish a style of thinking." (Hacking, 2006c, p. 14).

We see, therefore, that the issue of truth and falsehood gains prominence as a contingent mode of knowledge production. The author is categorical in stating that new objects, new clauses, new laws are everyday inventions that occur all the time. However, what defines a style would be a novelty concerning truth and falsehood. To this end, he uses the term *positive* in a rather broad sense, referring to the possibility that certain elements may acquire a positive value in relation to the truth. This value is historically determined and has no element outside the style to be sustained. Broadly speaking, this indicates that while it is possible to distinguish truths and falsehoods within a specific style, no general theory unifies the different ways of doing this. Furthermore, the very idea of correspondence would always be subordinated to a particular style, from which it would be possible to prove that a theory corresponds to a fact. For example, it is not possible to prove the truthfulness of an idea such as "30% of depressed patients get better when they take medicine" outside of a probabilistic or statistical style. Just as thinking statistically cannot demonstrate the correspondence of an idea to a particular case.

If a sentence can only be regarded as true within a style of reasoning, this means that styles are standards of objectivity since they define the parameters that delimit the possibilities for differentiating between true and false. On the other hand, it means that the truth thus produced is restricted by the possibilities contained in such a style. The way of thinking truth is made possible by the way of thinking, and the way of thinking is not unique. From this point onwards, Hacking will claim that styles are self-authenticating so that the paths constructed and enabled by each style to reach truth or falsehood are what we call objectivity. Something which, according to the philosopher, never fails to produce a strange feeling of circularity.

Self-reference

His concern is with constructionism. He devotes an entire book to this topic, and we will address some points in detail later. For now, we should delineate the proposed differentiation: according to the author, constructionists would believe that it is possible to produce facts according to what one wants to prove; not the style of reasoning, because it is not about constructing facts, but assessing candidates for truth and falsehood that were already established, although the definition of truth and falsehood is historical. However, this is radically distant from the idea that it is possible to construct facts from what is intended to be demonstrated.

At this point, we come back to the issue of truth as constancy. Stability is a central quality in scientific thinking since it demonstrates that theories are sound and relevant both in relation to the practical problems concerning them and to the thinking of other scientists who might prove them wrong. Kuhn devoted much of *The Structure of Scientific Revolutions* (1962/2013), not coincidentally, to the issue of crises and the characterisation of normal science as something that develops at almost full stability, while revolutionary science would be that which responds to the instability of its constructs. More often than not, instability is caused by problems that existing theories or paradigms cannot solve. A style of reasoning should, by definition, be more stable than a paradigm or specific theories. Furthermore, the stability of a style of reasoning comes both from its usability (whether practical or theoretical) and from the fact that the parameters of truth and falsehood must be criticised to be disproved. At this point, self-reference shows an interesting facet:

> The apparent circularity in the self-authenticating styles is to be welcomed. It helps explain why, although styles may evolve or be abandoned, they are curiously immune to anything akin to refutation. There is no higher standard to which they directly answer. The remarkable thing about styles is that they are stable, enduring, accumulating over the long haul. Moreover, in a shorter time frame, the knowledge that we acquire using them is moderately stable. It is our knowledges that are subject to revolution, to mutation, and to several kinds of oblivion; it is the content of what we find out, not how we find out, that is refuted. Here lies the source of a certain kind of stability (Hacking, 2002a, p. 192)

We see, thus, that Hacking places his proposition about styles of reasoning as, on the one hand, a constant feature in the history of science (science is always made out of styles of reasoning), and on the other, as a contingent, historical, and self-authenticating stabilisation of modes of enunciation of the truth. Contingent and historical because they respond to historical events, i.e. they could be (and are) different depending on how they emerge, and there is no general rule defining that emergence. Self-authenticating because there is no external element to validate its truthfulness. We have, in this sense, a fairly precise description of what he calls truthfulness.

In 2012, he revisited this issue to dwell a little on the debates raised. According to the author, self-authentication would function as an antidote to projects that seek the unique foundations of knowledge, as epistemology used to do (and sometimes still does), or that the logician would seek in relation to the foundations of reason. Styles have no foundation; they are the very mode of reasoning in the sciences:

> To say that these styles of thinking & doing are self-authenticating is to say that they are autonomous: they do not answer to some other, higher, or deeper, standard of truth and reason than their own. To repeat: No foundation. The style does not answer to some external canon of truth independent of itself (Hacking, 2012b, p. 605)

In addition, there would be stabilising techniques: ways of accommodating and adapting a style of reasoning to the problems posed. Hacking addresses this issue in a few papers, notably one on statistics (1992b) and another on laboratory (1992a)[5]. But stabilising techniques are potentially infinite, sharing only the fact that they are necessary for the survival of a style. They are, in fact, what allows a style to be adapted to answer the problems it encounters. But again, there is no way of generalising what makes a style succeed or fail to adapt. Broadly speaking, we may conclude that since no external criterion guarantees the relevance of a style, the only possible answer to explain the existence of a style is pragmatic: a style exists and is used because it works. So, it remains. Why we think it works depends on a number of negotiated elements. Either because they increase how much we know about something or because they please us. But, in the last instance—because there is, in fact, no last instance—the only explanation is this: "There is no external canon, of the sort demanded by correspondence theories of truth. But there are still standards, pragmatic ones" (Hacking, 2012b, p. 605).

Styles and history

At this point, we can recognise why Hacking is considered one of the great exponents of *Science Studies,* which have allegedly supplanted a tradition of philosophy of science that had a solid epistemological and foundationalist tendency by including history as an inescapable field for the understanding of the scientific activity. After all, the pragmatic argument mentioned earlier is nevertheless a recourse to historical thinking: we only consider the styles that were and are relevant in history. There is no epistemological or methodological reason to explain it, as there is no external criterion to sustain it.

In *As políticas da razão* [The Politics of Reason] (1993), Isabelle Stengers criticises Popper's proposition of falsifiability as an element of normative epistemology (or methodology) through a line of argument highly compatible with Hacking's thought. According to the author, broadly speaking, since the very criteria of falsifiability (or of truth and falsehood) depend on the context, falsifiability would be unable to define what should or should not be considered scientific; rather, it would only be able to recognise what *has or has not* been considered scientific. She claims, in this sense, that this is an operator pertaining to the history of science, not philosophy. It is evident that such a remark on Popper's work is absolutely different from that on Hacking's work, especially for its acknowledgement of the place of history in science studies. In fact, one of the chapters in *Historical Ontology*, entitled "'Style' for Historians and Philosophers", originally published in 1992, deals directly with this issue, indicating the points where he engages with historical thought and the places where he uses the work of historians for another purpose: to do philosophy.

However, as we see, towards the end of his philosophical argumentation on styles of reasoning—published 20 years after the text "'Style' for Historians and Philosophers" and 30 years after his first article on styles of reasoning ("Language, Truth and Reason")—history returns. It returns with a certain disguise of pragmatic philosophy, which is necessary to mobilise notions of agreement and negotiation, which the author constantly revisits, but without concealing its historiographical weight. Which, we reiterate, is not a problem for the author, on the contrary. Hacking advocates the value of science not despite but because of the lack of an external criterion to guarantee its truth. The fact that what is produced are local modes of enunciation of the truth does not diminish its value.

This is what can be observed, for example, when he claims that "'self-justification', far from implying a kind of subjectivism, is the founder of scientific objectivity and reproducibility" (Hacking, 2002b, p. 19), meaning that in this game of pragmatic negotiation the objective would be *that* which is stabilised. It even indicates that stabilising techniques are entirely different from one another—which makes sense since what they stabilise is also notably different. These analyses show, however, that some techniques are more effective than others. More than that, the author proposes stability as one of the core characteristics of a style: "Each style persists, in its peculiar and individual way, because it has harnessed its own techniques of self-stabilization. That is what constitutes something as a style of reasoning" (Hacking, 2002a, p. 194).

We see, therefore, that along with the production of novelties in relation to the parameters of truth and falsehood and the possibilities of constructing objects, a style is also marked by the capability of science to produce techniques. These are not techniques for applying their knowledge to solve everyday problems but techniques for producing and maintaining the production of knowledge. This is what the author calls "philosophical technology: a study of the ways in which the styles of reasoning provide stable knowledge and become not the uncoverers of objective truth but rather the standards of objectivity" (Hacking, 2002a, p. 198). It is not by chance that this philosophical technology complements the remark the author makes about the word thought: it is not an abstract invention or the sum of ideas but a process that begins as something relatively ordinary and whose success is based not only on its capability of producing relevant knowledge but also on its reproductive and self-stabilising potential. It concerns the establishment of methods of discovery that transcend the minds and operate through their presence in a wide range of areas in people's lives.

Nevertheless, not recognising the existence of an external criterion and defending the stability and self-authentication of styles of reasoning as constitutive features of scientific practice can lead to various interpretations. The sum of these elements seems to have a direct influence on constructionist and subjectivist tendencies, which can both pose important and necessary questions to scientific practice and how society perceives it, and lead to certain types of denialism that see the absence of transcendental criteria for guaranteeing the value of knowledge as a reason for devaluing scientific practice, or to a naive and irresponsible relativisation. This is a key issue for this work, as we have been reiterating since we believe it is crucial to examine scientific practice without falling into ignorant denialism. So let us look at the way Hacking addresses this issue.

1.3 Social construction and radical relativism

According to Hacking, the publication of *The Social Construction of What?* (1999) was particularly motivated by certain comments that regarded his book on the sciences of memory (Hacking, 1995/2000) as a fine exemplar of constructionist thought. Nothing could be more wrong. In fact, at various moments in the book, the philosopher shows his distancing from the idea of social construction, but this tendency of interpretation still persists.

More generally, this feeling may come from a very hurried reading of the path the author had been following: let us remember that even though his first book on the logic of statistical inference (Hacking, 1965) can be framed as a study of a more rationalist approach in the field of philosophy of science, his 1970s publications on probabilistic thinking (1975a/2006) and language (1975b/1999) already demonstrate a strong influence of Foucauldian thought, bringing the philosopher's work closer to debates influenced by the field of history. This movement towards variability in scientific thinking became stronger in the 1980s, as we can observe both by the fact that *Representing and Intervening* (1983) is more concerned with criticising radical realisms than nominalisms and especially by the publication of "Language, Truth and Reason" (1982), a text we discussed in detail in the previous section, in which Hacking is explicitly concerned with arguing that *reason* has a history. The early 1990s, with the publication of *The Taming of Chance* (1990) and "'Style' for

Historians and Philosophers" (1992c), deepened the 'styles project' (Hacking, 2012b), positioning the author as a critic of normative and foundationalist projects. However, he also rejected radical relativisms such as subjectivism or social constructionism.

In this vein, it is not surprising that the publication of a book that discusses in detail how mental disorders can be considered retroactive effects of discourses on individuals has been assimilated as a piece of social constructionism. Some of his categories, such as *dynamic nominalism*, *making up people*, *moving targets*, among others, come close to the vocabulary employed by more radical relativists. We will deal with the issue of mental health disorders later; for now, we will make some observations on his critique of the idea of social construction.

What is constructed

Hacking's critique of the idea of social construction is quite thorough, including a detailed inventory of the ways that the idea of construction is presented. They are organised from six possible levels of constructionist positioning so that the passage from one to another would entail a gain in radicality: historical < ironic < reformist < unmasking < rebellious < revolutionary (Hacking, 1999, p. 19). If they all start from the recognition that there would be external, variable, and historical issues involved in the production of knowledge and forms of socialisation, both the scope of this variability and the effects it produces on the value of established forms of knowledge would be different in each case. In this sense, historical constructionism would point to the contextual character of knowledge production. In contrast, revolutionary constructionism, on the other hand, would take the contingency of knowledge as a reason for discrediting it and replacing it with other forms of knowledge.

There is no disagreement as to whether knowledge and various other activities linked to its production are historically determined. More than this, there is also the recognition of the role of discourses in determining the possibilities of the experience of individuals, as we shall see below. However, this does not mean that the term 'construction' is the most appropriate since it would be loaded with a spectrum of meanings that indicates a capacity to decide and rectify what will be produced. Broadly speaking, Hacking raises two concerns. The first relates to the difference between various cases: there are situations and objects (or types of objects) that are more susceptible to the influence of the discourses produced, which means that the issue of variance (or inevitability) must be modulated. Secondly, even in cases where we can consider that discursive influence plays an important role, the word 'construction' would still not be the most appropriate.

First, we must be clear about what is on the table. If we say something is socially constructed, what is this something? This something can be an object, an idea, a theory, a fact, etc. These elements present different levels of semantic degrees so that some connect to more immediate ideas, while others result from complex rationalisations. The degree of contingency tends to grow along with complexity, so it would make more sense to speak of construction in relation to theories than to objects. For example, in taking up Andrew Pickering's work on quarks (Pickering, 1984), claiming that while the idea of quarks can be constructed, quarks themselves are not. Pickering reportedly replied, in a letter in 1997, saying

> I would never say that Constructing Quarks is about 'the idea of quarks.' That may be your take on constructionism are the natural sciences, but it is not mine. My idea is that if one comes at the world in a certain way—your heterogeneous matrix—one can elicit certain phenomena that can be construed as evidence for quarks. (Pickering *apud* Hacking, 1999, p. 30)

This passage interests us because it clearly indicates Hacking's position on the issue. He does not disagree with Pickering, quite the contrary. He states that, in fact, "if you came at the world in another way, you could elicit other phenomena that could be construed as evidence for a different (not formally incompatible, but different) successful physics" (Hacking, 1999, p. 31). This is totally compatible with what we have seen up to now about his idea of *styles of reasoning*; something presented almost 20 years earlier. We should remember, after all, that the author states that truthfulness is the possibility of the enunciation of truth, so contingency is always involved in the enunciation. This does not mean—and Pickering would also agree—that anything can be true: objects resist classifications and ideas and, in this sense, constrain 'creative freedom'. The main point where Hacking distances himself, at least in relation to Pickering, is his use of the word construction. For the Canadian philosopher, using it is a bad way to advance the debate, as it ends up flattening out issues that always deserve to be considered in more detail.

The biggest risk when talking about constructionism would be to overextend the imaginable freedom in determining what is or is not considered a fact or in the influence that nominalism would have on the freedom to determine how we understand the world. For the philosopher, the issue would be that, in much of the discussion, moral issues would be overinflated and obscure the resistance faced by the discursive field. He nevertheless asserts that the moral issue is central in cases of interactive kinds. But beyond this, there would also be a tide of normalisation under the name of 'social construction', which would cause several discussions to be reduced to moral discussions. In this sense, as already stated, the author raises the need for a rigorous delineation of what would, or would not, be constructed. This is such a central issue that it even lends itself to the name of the book. It is a matter, first of all, of delimiting *what* we are talking about when we talk about social construction.

The clearest example he mobilises about the moralisation of the discussion on knowledge production is what he calls unmasking. This kind of constructionist approach would be based on the assumption that exposing the political and moral influences involved in the production of knowledge would directly affect the quality of the knowledge established. For example, unmasking the selfish interests of scientists would result in the loss of value of their research results. This idea makes no sense; first, because the results would not necessarily fit the original interests, but also because the value of the results lies beyond the interests of those who produce them. Unmasking is not about refuting truthfulness, for it does not show that the results are wrong, but simply that they are influenced by political and moral issues (Hacking, 1999, p. 58). Something which is, by the way, inherent in any process of knowledge production.

This specific case is interesting as it indicates a more general positioning of Hacking. He does not deny the idiosyncrasies of scientific activity but claims that this does not exhaust the issue. In this sense, there would be two ways of approaching the issue: one that is concerned with the scientific activity itself, and another, with the assembly of truths into the body of knowledge. Although neither respond to any superior external instance—nor are they internalist practices that do not respond to issues external to the scientific community—this would not justify the idea that the paths taken in knowledge production could be planned so successfully as to justify the use of the word 'construction'.

According to Hacking, the most interesting way of dealing with the issue of variability in the knowledge produced (or that could be produced) is based on account of three categories: contingency, nominalism, and explanations of stability.

Contingency, nominalism, and stability

The first of these, *contingency*, concerns the possibilities for developing scientific thought once its foundations are already established. It is a matter of considering the variability of possible paths within the styles of reasoning currently in use or even the possibility of a new style of reasoning emerging and becoming stabilised. The mere claim that knowledge could have developed in another way, through another path, and reached other results is considered absurd by a good number of scientists. But history does not fail to demonstrate moments when this has happened. An example mobilised by the author is the impossibility of deciding between three different laws of gravitation in the 17th century (Hacking, 1999, p. 78). In this case, the acceptance of Newton's law would not have occurred for epistemological or experimental reasons since the laws would be equivalent in these senses. But only one of them survived. This leads to another consideration: several procedures working towards equalising accepted theories and erasing incompatible features in other theories that may have been assimilated. This would give an impression of greater uniformity, albeit violently produced. Contingency would not only exist but also be erased by the process itself.

Hacking, however, argues that it is a possibility that should be considered, although he does not find it so relevant. This happens by considering two elements as being key to the functioning of science: the power of established tradition (knowledge, techniques, equipment, etc.) and the resistance of objects. Combining these elements would limit the possibilities for variation, but this does not mean there would be only one way.

The author elaborates the second point, nominalism, in a more supportive way. This point combines several developments that have already been presented above, in particular his critique of representation and his idea of styles of reasoning as a historical process that defines the possibilities for the creation of objects and of truths and falsehoods. In general, it is possible to say that Hacking's thought imputes, within the current debate, the tension between truth and truthfulness to the issue of nominalism: there are established modes that define the possibilities of thinking and acting. They change dynamically and accumulate, but these facts can only be recognised by looking at a long stretch of time.

The main difference between what Hacking calls contingency and what operates under the name of 'nominalism' concerns the dynamics of change. Styles of reasoning, or even minimally detectable changes in language, are only possible in historical processes. The change happens over a long stretch of time, and it is a complex process. However, such a change could take knowledge to entirely different places. Let us remember how he states that styles of reasoning start as trivial questions and gradually stabilise. The way he presents the issue of contingency concerns one-off decisions, simultaneous paths that can be followed, that is, issues that are subordinate to these more general structures, which leads, in turn, to *stability*.

How the issue of stability is relevant to the debate about social construction is specifically concerned with explanations of stability. The crucial point, in this sense, is whether the stability of scientific knowledge is explained in a way that is internal or external to the field of science. Stability is an essential feature of a style of reasoning, and its explanation is pragmatic: the style fits. However, this discussion is not about styles of reasoning but about specific sciences and their theories. But taking fitness into account is not without interest. This does not mean that its uses can be foreseen, nor does it define whether this use value will come from inside or outside the scientific community. Since *Representing and Intervening* (1983/2012), Hacking uses as an example the idea that success in science can be measured by its recognition within its own community, as Imre Lakatos (1970) would suggest with his idea of cumulative research programmes. According to the Canadian philosopher, this criterion would substitute truth as a reference for success.

Authors such as Bruno Latour and Isabelle Stengers present an externalist view: they believe that much of the instabilities—like stability—ultimately respond to issues external to the scientific community. In contrast, says Stengers (2000), authors such as Thomas Kuhn or even Gaston Bachelard were internalists in a way different from Lakatos: as much as they advocated a non-cumulative nature of knowledge, they understood disruption as an effect of the inner workings of the community. Hacking's stance here is similar to that adopted in relation to contingency: he does not deny that external factors influence the definition of stability; however, he does not believe this is so relevant. We see, in this way, that the author's critical stance in relation to social construction is based on a kind of respect for resistance: resistance from the world or from things or resistance from established ways of thinking and doing.

The possibility of disruption is always there, creating some sort of bridge between the notion of object resistance (which he borrows from Pickering, we must remember) and his advocacy of experimentation. Experimentation may be regarded, in this sense, as something so important because it is the best way to defeat the established order. The established order, in turn, would be the product of a certain inertia but also of a successful fitting between theory and the world (a robust fitting, to borrow another expression from Pickering). However, Hacking is adamant in stating that while this fitting may be perennial or even inexorable (as expected of scientific laws), this does not mean it is the only possible one. In this sense, these supposedly immutable theories are criticised not because they are false but because they are merely one of the options.

Variability

He develops this question more thoroughly in an article called "How Inevitable Are the Results of Successful Science?" (Hacking, 2000). As the title makes quite clear, the question is whether successful sciences would reach the same results on remotely similar objects or topics. To answer this, the three categories presented here so far are reduced to two: the issue of stability is assigned to the word success (resorting to Lakatos), while what is treated under the name of *nominalism* is included in the category *contingency*. Hacking frames the question in a rather interesting way, retrieving Evelyn Fox-Keller's argument—in her book *Reflections on Gender and Science* (1985)—about the reproduction of a military language in the sciences, based on the logic of enslaver and enslaved person. Building on this, Hacking asks himself: would we reach similar results if we used other words to talk about biology?

His argument revolves around a central notion, the notion of *question*. According to him, questions only make sense within their contexts, an idea that brings the philosopher closer to the concept of contingency. In that context, a question that makes sense is a *live* question. As we have seen, something compatible with his work on styles of reasoning. However, once a live question is asked, and there are possible ways to answer it. The contingency is dramatically reduced: "aspects of the world determine what the answer is, even though only people in a scientific society find out the answer" (Hacking, 2000, p. 69). This article's great value is its conciseness: the philosopher manages to clearly define what he imputes to contingency and what is necessary. In brief, one can say that questions are contingent, and answers are required.

But the required nature of answers exists within a system that interconnects, firstly, the contingency of questions that defines which are the possible answers; next to that, the contingency of that which leads to specific kinds of outcomes to be considered successful outcomes; and, finally, the restrictive nature of the real. That is, answers are required within a contingent and self-authenticating system, but they are required once the restrictions that come from both the (historical) thought and the (indifferent) real are put in place. This indicates, however, that they are not unique: "The results of successful science are not inevitable; we could have had equally successful science with different (but not incompatible) results" (Hacking, 2000, p. 71). This suggests that, even if they are not inevitable, it is not possible to sustain any answer or even construct facts at will. There is something that resists the possibility of complete relativisation of knowledge. Revisiting the play between truth and truthfulness, it would be possible to affirm that there is something in truthfulness that refers back to the truth and historicises the enunciations about the truth, but at the same time, holds some permanence.

Following this presentation of some central debates on the production of knowledge, it will be possible to address the question of truth in relation to suffering. To this end, the tension between the idea of timeless truth and the notion of truthfulness as possibilities for the enunciation of the truth is a good organiser, being able to situate the movements between, on the one hand, the recognition of the variability and contingency of knowledge and, on the other, the affirmation of the value of knowledge and the restrictions to its production.

The notion of styles of reasoning indicates the need for recognising the historical character of knowledge, which relates to the possibilities of structuring thought and the objects addressed. This fits into an understanding that makes no separation between intervention and representation, suggesting a way of apprehending language that regards signification as something that escapes an idea of adequacy, demanding an understanding of the social factors involved in the definition of shared meanings. On the other hand, the inseparability between representation and intervention locates experimentation as a privileged factor of scientific practice, for it can produce disruptive effects and introduce novelties. The emphasis on effects will be deepened in the next chapter, in which ontological effects will be considered in a specific way within the classification of objects that would respond to the classification itself, leading to a direct approach to phenomena linked to suffering.

Chapter 2

Historical ontology and transient mental illnesses

In the previous chapter, we covered some debates concerning how we can consider the relationship between truth and science. As we have seen, it is not a matter of seeking a relationship of complete adequacy between them but rather of reflecting on how science can produce valuable knowledge even when dealing with a great deal of variability. In this way, we can make some progress if we understand this relationship from the perspective of the historicisation of truth as the middle term of social negotiations and interactions with reality. However, it does not exhaust the question of the subject's presence. This question can be broken down into two problems: first, whether there would be some kind of consideration of subjectivity in the transition from formal propositions to their application possibilities, at which point the subject would become the 'enunciator of the truth'; second, what would be the effects of this particular kind of knowledge production on subjectivity.

The first question can be routed into the proposition of styles of reasoning. We must remember that taking 'objectivity' as a technique of stabilising and defining the possibilities for reaching the truth implies an ever-present dimension of negotiation, as well as an idea of effectiveness that does not meet an epistemological or methodological criterion with any guarantee. This means, broadly speaking, that the very techniques of objectivation would not wholly exclude subjectivity, but would at least have a stabilising effect, avoiding very large oscillations in the production of knowledge. This is thus located in his account of the contingency of knowledge, which, we reiterate, must always be considered within its interaction with the real as something restrictive in relation to theoretical plasticity.

The second problem raised, however, opens a new chapter. In fact, thinking about the effects of knowledge production on subjectivity is nevertheless part of an ancient discussion on the separation between natural sciences and social sciences.

One possible way to move forward with this discussion is by considering the question of truth from the perspective of the specificity of the object to which it is linked. This proposition is justified for a few reasons: firstly, as Foucault points out in his *The Order of Things* (1966/2016), it is by taking the (human) subject as the object of knowledge production that a field of problematics is inaugurated in science because there is some sort of mirroring. These problematics—which somehow introduce the discussion on the ethics and politics of knowledge—will play a key role in the confrontations in epistemology and philosophy of science that are still ongoing. In this sense, we see how certain particularities of an object would demand an epistemological reorganisation, directly affecting formulations and modifications in the structure of the way of thinking that intends to handle this type of object. This would include, at most, modifications in the choice and use of certain notions of truth. On the other hand, the very fact that there are differences among objects that establish the need for considering truth regimes with distinct functionalities implies a retroactive effect: the need to consider the specificities of the object retroacts on a general conception of truth since the applicability of its parameters responds to the characteristics of the object in question. This is contained in the reciprocity, indicated by Hacking, about forms of truth and falsehood and the possibilities for considering objects.

These are some initial questions in this debate, which has gained remarkable complexity in the history of epistemology and philosophy of science. We initially present the issue in such a comprehensive way to situate the debate that we will develop. The question of the object has proved to be a complex problem to solve, especially when the attempts to do it insist on some definitive categorisation that is simultaneously broad, rigorous, and precise, as is usually the case in propositions of radical division between the natural sciences and the human sciences. However, significant progress has been made, among which we will highlight how Hacking advanced the debate on problems related to psychopathology and to categorisations of the individuals' modes of experience within different contexts based on his studies on transient mental illnesses. On the other hand, we must not forget the problematization made by psychoanalysis in relation to this, especially concerning the reifying potential present in psychology, which Lacan revisits, in "Science and Truth" (1966/2006), when referring to Canguilhem[6].

Therefore, we can see that beyond epistemological and ontological questions at play in this discussion, they are also inescapably influenced by ethical issues since it directly affects the definition of what we believe could or should be the target of the intervention of others.

2.1 Truth, evidence, and biological objects

The discussion we are going through here anchors its interest in the affirmation that various positionings, which, at first, are recognised as purely epistemological choices, will inevitably have, whether intentionally or not, ontological, ethical, and political consequences. More than that, we see that the advocacy of certain ways of dealing with the truth seems to hinder rather than help us address some problems, something evident in biological psychiatry, which insists on a rationality that is highly problematic and ineffective in relation to the questions it tries to solve (Rose, 2018; Silva Junior, 2016). The case of psychiatry demonstrates a series of mistakes made within a contemporary trend that advocates 'evidence-based' clinical practices but takes the term 'evidence' in a naive or simplistic sense.

It is important to remember that if the idea of evidence is mobilised in such a way that might be criticised for its naivety, it is not because the importance of this term in the philosophy of science is being denied—quite the contrary. The problem lies in the emancipation of this idea, in the placement of 'evidence' as some kind of guarantee for the truth of an enunciation—whatever it may be—but which, by mobilising a term that would be carrying an imaginary baggage smaller than 'truth', would reinforce an idea of independence, of autonomy in relation to the one who enunciates it. Not a few discussions are held about what evidence would be, about different types of evidence, evidence *in itself* and secondary evidence etc. The question of evidence does not fail to raise metaphysical reflections, not least because evidence is produced within rationality, not found (Hacking, 1999; 2000), which makes them not so evident. The contemporary usage of the term, however, seems to yield this assumption: as if, beyond everything that can be discussed, there were that which can simply be ascertained. As we see clearly in Erwin (2015) and can infer from Insel (2013), there is a naive empiricism in placing empirical evidence indisputably as the best kind of evidence; for, even if the term is being seriously discussed and rigorously addressed, its employment disregards much of this work and merely reproduces a positivist ideology, whereby one must believe only in what can be seen[7].

In this sense, the employment of the term 'evidence' seems to offer two modalities of flexibilisation and emancipation in relation to these 'deviant' questions: (1) the evidence refer to something much more immediate, indisputable, something that can simply be seen, thus stripping the term 'truth' of some of its weight; (2) the insistence on the employment of the term 'evidence' in clinical practices may have the effect of obliterating an ethical perspective based on alterity, normalising and naturalising moral patterns from a presumably epistemic basis, as if there were, in fact, no relevant ethical discussions. Thus, grounding clinical practices on this perspective, as if evidence was something that is simply found, has a double effect of erasing the ethical and political dimensions, as well as disregarding the performative character of knowledge on the modes of experience.

Revisiting Insel's speech presented in the introduction, what we see is not only a reductionist monism that states that the cause of mental disorders should be attributed primarily to organic functions but also the placement of this monism within a mode of thought that eschews discussions that add complexity to the questions. Even the way he states this, arguing for laboratory tests as the ideal standard, shows how a complex discussion is trampled on in the resort to observation. Creating such standards of truthfulness directly affects the type of knowledge that will be produced and, hence, on the diagnoses and therapies informed by that knowledge. In fact, if these questions are emptied of their ethical and political nature, this will have effects that must be understood not only in relation to the theoretical corpus that will be built but also in relation to the effects that these ideas will have on the subjects' ways of experiencing.

At this point, we return to the question of the object, which lies at the heart of the discussion held so far. Beyond defining positivist reasoning as the standard model of rationality, the movement here illustrated by Insel's statement indicates yet another point that must be considered: the equalisation of questions concerning distinct objects. When he claims that patients deserve better and that psychiatry should work like other areas of medicine—such as cardiology—he is not only generalising the localisationist rationality but also proposing a non-differentiation of objects that are treated (and constructed) in different ways.

This, which is termed organicism, biologism, or which was earlier called 'reductionist monism', indicates the radical disregard for the effects of language on objects—effects which do not occur in the same way in all objects (or subjects). This presumption to purify that which is organic in psychic functioning perhaps explains a yearning to act effectively on more stable or less complex bases. It may indicate, on the other hand, a way of dealing with an old sense of uneasiness about something that Freud describes as the narcissistic wound resulting from the Self[8] no longer being the master of its own house (1917a/2010), whereby the establishment and the possibility of organic manipulation of the psyche would bring some comfort; or simply an alternative whose conclusions back up therapeutics with the greatest potential for commercialisation and profitability by large corporations. Regardless of the motivation (or combination of motivations), the fact is that this discussion is part of a long-standing problem in the philosophy of science, which deals with the differences among objects.

Some notes on the discussions about the differences in objects

A few paragraphs above, we mentioned that there are problems with attempts that aim to be broad, rigorous, and precise to make a definitive categorisation of the differences among objects. We must stress that we use the terms 'rigorous' and 'precise' inspired by Gilles-Gaston Granger's use of them in *Pensée formelle et sciences de l'homme* [Formal Thought and the Sciences of Man] (1960/1967), in which precision and rigour are mobilised in situations that are at first contradictory to each other. He states, for example, that rigour would be linked to mathematical formalisation, displaying the quality of generalisable stability; on the other hand, precision would be linked to the detailed consideration of particularities—found, for example, in a historical account. In this way, the proposition made by the author considers that the more rigorous a sentence is, the less precise it would be since the distancing from details would be due to the formalisation process.

On the other hand, it would be very difficult to formalise highly precise sentences; therefore, any generalisation based on them would be inaccurate. This is how Granger suggests, at the limit, that mathematics is the extreme point of formalisation and rigour, and history is an example of precision. He thus proposes the separation between formal and empirical sciences, which concerns their possibilities of formalisation. Formalisation is, in fact, located as a central feature of scientific thinking: on the one hand, because it enables the expansion of a theory's ability to develop and act from the rigorous generalisation of its key ideas. On the other, for being responsible for the public nature of science since the replicability of knowledge production processes—made possible by axiomatic reduction and the resulting application to other objects or situations—would liberate the produced knowledge from its original conditions of production. Thus, other researchers could not only reproduce but also deny knowledge (Granger, 1993).

However, we can see that even if formalisation is regarded as a central feature of scientific practice, this means neither that he presents a normative epistemological or methodological model for a general definition of what science is nor that he disregards the differences in objects (as evidenced even in the very title of his 1960 book). In relation to the difference between objects, Granger affirms the need to consider the existing complexification when dealing with some cases in which language would have an active role since it would hardly be possible to turn human facts into objects because they carry meanings that interact with the research being done.

Thus, these practices should work with an idea of representation, not of reduction to abstract schemes. Something that is compatible, for instance, in the communication of knowledge through clinical cases. In relation to a normative methodology, Granger states that he does not believe in the utility of such an endeavour, describing his effort as the definition of a vision and a language for science (1993). Language, as we see it, is related to formalisation and mathematical language. Vision is inseparable from language and is a project of knowledge production with the greatest possible indifference to external issues. While he is not suggesting that science should, in fact, be autonomous in relation to what transcends its field, neither does he fail to advocate that this autonomy should be a goal.

Although our comment on Granger's understanding of this issue is secondary, mobilised for the sake of contextualising the debate we will conduct, it is important to note that the direct affirmation of the non-establishment of a normative methodology[9] can be understood as positioning in relation to Karl Popper's work, an epistemologist who became known for his advocacy of a normative epistemology that would be able to set parameters for defining scientific practice without differentiating between types of sciences, in addition, of course, to his famous proposition of the principle of falsifiability (Popper, 1934/2002). The position in relation to Popper interests us not only because he is constantly being invoked because of his criticism of psychoanalysis but especially because he was one of the players in a heated argument about the differences among objects.

In very general terms, concerning the criticism aimed at psychoanalysis, it is only worth pointing out that, beyond a certain fragility stemming from a restricted interpretation of the field, his criticisms were answered, in his own terms, by Adolf Grünbaum (1984). Grünbaum has solidly demonstrated how untenable was the affirmation that psychoanalysis could not be proved wrong[10]. If such criticism is enjoying unexpected longevity, this seems more related to the persisting difficulties with psychoanalysis—which are often poorly defined—than to its epistemological value per se[11].

The elevation of falsifiability to an essential condition of scientific practice raised an intense debate, not because it questioned the importance of the possible contradictions among theories within scientific thought but because of the generalisation of falsifiability as a prescriptive feature. If several authors have positioned themselves critically in relation to the uniqueness of scientific practice proposed by Popper, including those mentioned above[12], there is a particular author with whom Popper engaged in an active exchange of ideas and who seems to have made a special impact on the Viennese philosopher. We are talking about Friedrich von Hayek, one of the founders of neoliberal thinking, who, in addition to his extensive work on economics, has also devoted himself to various other topics, such as psychology, law, and philosophy of science.

Hayek presented his differences by insisting on the difference between objects. Such insistence proved relevant since Popper advocated a scientific monism, that is, a series of understandings—which often brought him closer to positivism, although some differences remained unbridgeable[13]—that should be equally valid for both natural and social sciences. By criticising Popper's idea, Hayek introduces the proposition of distinguishing between what he termed as phenomena of simple regularities (also called essentially simple structures) and phenomena of complex regularities, or essentially complex structures (Fernandez, 2000). This distinction, presented in his text "Scientism and the Study of Society" (1942), stems from the realisation of how difficult it is to mathematise social facts and that it is impossible to observe all the variables involved. In this way, the instability created by complexity and the irreducibility of phenomena to mathematisation would make it impossible to produce explanations and predictions that are rigorous enough.

As Fernandez (2000) argues, the influence of Hayek's thought on Popper is notable, so in *Conjectures and Refutations* (1963/2002), we can recognise the acceptance of distinct criteria and expectations between the human and the natural sciences. This would be one of the reasons for upholding falsifiability as a key criterion in establishing a normative epistemology for science, which is not without its problems. Apart from those indicated above, falsifiability as a normative criterion becomes problematic within a historical comprehension of the parameters of truthfulness that underpin a mode of knowledge production, as seen in Hacking (1982).

In any case, these brief paragraphs were intended to present how the debate about the differences among objects has been and continues to be relevant within the fields of epistemology and philosophy of science. Together with the problem related to contemporary psychiatry, which also touches on issues relevant to psychoanalysis, we believe that this discussion proves its pertinence since there seems to be tension over the fact that the specificity of the object poses inevitable questions to the knowledge that will be produced.

The object and the subject between psychoanalysis and the philosophy of science

Although both the philosophy of science and epistemology have been inevitably occupied by the question of the object in their recent (and perhaps not so recent) histories, this does not mean that the question is settled. Despite some thinkers, who could be distinguished by their inflexibility on the matter, having changed their positions—such as Popper, as we have just pointed out—it is clear that merely considering that different objects demand different epistemological constructions is a statement which risks being forgotten due to its general nature. In fact, this statement—which could be considered an epistemological maxim—only gains relevance when it has some materiality. In other words, this recourse is only pertinent in situations that demand a different type of epistemological construction from the one locally in vogue.

If we take the debate between Popper and Hayek as an example, it is possible that the difference between physics and economics would be so striking that there would be no further complications when implementing this idea once it was accepted by both. However, if we delve a bit into Hayek's work to the point of finding certain psychological bases for his economic theories (Hayek, 1952), the crystal-clear differentiation between objects of simple and complex phenomena seems to get a bit hazy, with blurry boundaries. It is worth remembering that projects that aim to understand brain functioning as the first step on a long journey—or, rather, as the first brick in a high wall—are not new. On top of this first brick, many others would be added, underpinned by an understanding of knowledge which is absolutely suited to that which is known as Popper's scientific monism but with even more radical realistic overtones. This is the case, for instance, of Roy Bhaskar in his *A Realist Theory of Science* (1975/2008), a book in which he proposes the establishment of a realistic understanding of cognition as the basis of a solid scientific realism.

For Bhaskar, psychology would be an especially interesting field because it was the point of intersection between what was so far susceptible to realistic theorisation and what was not. According to him, from a sufficiently solid understanding of cognition, events hitherto refractory to realistic standards of objectivity could be adapted to them. It would thus be possible to establish the cognitive bases of representation and produce realistic knowledge from them. It was, therefore, a sort of Cape of Good Hope: something that, if transposed, would open up a vast field of possibilities. Hayek, by contrast, found in psychology, at first, a case for methodological differentiation, insisting on the impossibility of knowing a structure as or even more complex than the one involved in the act of knowing (Hayek, 1952). Whether from one side or the other, the fact is that the question of the object gains complexity not only because of the epistemology that can be derived from it but because the classification of objects per se does not afford such definitive positions. Let us recall, as indicated a few pages back, that brain mapping projects for a more 'adequate' treatment of mental disorders are the current big wager of psychiatry (Insel, 2013), even though its refreshing discourse also indicates that little progress has been made since Bhaskar's propositions (Rose, 2018)—to borrow a recent example, of course, since this ambition can be identified with frightening similarity in previous centuries.

The fact is that, regardless of the type of discussion that can be established when the objects are more decidedly social or natural, the one we propose here is built precisely upon a point of debate, estrangement, and dispute over the nature of the object. Lacan, in his seminar on *The Psychoses* (1955-56/1997), devotes some sessions to the causal nature of psychotic disorders, advocating that language should be considered as opposed to biological or psychogenic traditions. Something that is also found in his "Presentation on Psychic Causality" (Lacan, [1946]1966/2006). In the following years, his discussion became more complex as the negative character of the question of the object (or objects) intensified.

Hacking, on the other hand, takes debates related to psychopathology and the classification of individuals to discuss differences in the relationship between categorisation and objects, dealing with transient illnesses (neuroses, in his definition), but also commenting on non-transient illnesses (such as schizophrenia, according to him). From his work, we can also infer the tension between subject and object, although in a way that is radically different from Lacan's. Both authors make important advances in this field, especially by not sticking to the discussions hitherto established and by proposing new terms for the debate.

If Hacking became renowned for his works on 'hard' topics such as probability and statistics (Hacking, 1965; 1975/2006), devoting himself more avidly to discussions on psychopathology and differences in objects from the 1990s onwards, it is a known fact that his interest in these topics predates this—for his reading of Foucault was present in 'early' moments of his work, but also for having published sparse texts such as "Making Up People" (1983), which would later be compiled in *Historical Ontology* (2002a).

As we shall see below, Hacking proposes a displacement of the traditional debate on the nature of objects by assimilating, as a central feature, language as an operator: there are interactive and indifferent kinds, and the difference between them is the interaction between the specific object and the categorisation at stake. This route makes it possible for the separation between biological and cultural to be addressed in its own right, something that is often circumvented without taking the vitality out of the discussion. More than that, this proposition—which, in its latest form, bears the name of 'dynamic nominalism' (Hacking, 2002a)—indicates a distinctive regime of truth in which the definition of the modes of knowing is directly related to modes of ontological experience, of how individuals experience themselves. This is, thus, a powerful statement in relation to the question of truth.

On the other hand, as briefly indicated in relation to Lacan's treatment of the question of psychosis, we can see that the centrality of language is a point in common between the authors. However, it is developed in different ways. The subject's relationship with language—whether belonging, dwelling, or inseparability indubitably—will take up Lacan's entire teachings and is an inescapable point for rigorously treating how he and his successors have addressed the question of truth. In fact, the French psychoanalyst will be much more concerned than the Canadian philosopher with theorising the effects of language, the latter being more devoted to historical studies and their underlying philosophical discussions.

Influences

Before we begin the appreciation of the debate as such, there is one last question that seems noteworthy to us because it might contribute to finding the points where the two forms of thinking we are dealing with converge and move away from each other. These are Lacan's and Hacking's epistemological influences. It is well-known that Lacan resorted to numerous authors, often explicitly, other times in a more discreet manner. While it is possible to notice the influence of great names from philosophy and epistemology in his work, such as Hegel and Heidegger (Simanke, 2002; Iannini, 2012), it is to Alexandre Koyré, a Russian-born French philosopher and historian of science, that Lacan attributes much of his ideas on the more specifically epistemological debates. This reference is clear in "Science and Truth" (1966a/2006), among other works. It is possible to say that Koyré was of great importance for the Lacanian view on the emergence of modern science and its subject, something the author explored in several books (Koyré, 1939/1966; 1957/1968; 1961/2011).

However, Koyré's influence is obviously not limited to Lacan's thought. One of the marks of his work, described as a confrontation with historiographical positivism, allegedly opened up the possibility of thinking about the history and the philosophy of science in a way different from that which prevailed until then (Lacerda Abrahão, 2015, p. 203). Such importance is unequivocal in the work of Thomas Kuhn—even the author himself acknowledges the importance of Koyré in his formative years, pointing him out as the founder of a new historiography of science—and it can also be recognised, albeit with some restrictions, in the writings of Paul Feyerabend (Lacerda Abrahão, 2015, p. 210).

Following a rather generalistic genealogical line, it would be possible to include Ian Hacking in this succession since the author does not deny the influences of Kuhn and Feyerabend in his work. In this sense, a broad field named 'historical philosophy of science' would be an umbrella containing all three authors and could provide some clues to the points of convergence between Hacking and Lacan. In fact, both exhibit key differences with positivist thinking—something that could, without much difficulty, be attributed to the studies of Koyré, who is interested in the subtleties and 'external' influences found in the history of science as much as in questions with greater epistemological weight.

However, even if this kind of philosophy of science, which holds historiography in a privileged place, can be attributed to Koyré's thought, we must bear in mind that this tradition[14] includes several authors who offer different ways of working at this intersection. In this sense, the differences claimed by Hacking in relation to Kuhn and Feyerabend become more powerful, in particular, for demonstrating an interest in more ordinary questions, less central or with less impact than a 'scientific revolution', proposing a way of thinking which is more focused on subtleties than on generalisations (Hacking, 1999). Hacking, in this aspect, would be concerned less with scientific theories and more with science as something embedded in culture.

He then moves closer to Alistair Cameron Crombie, an author whose interest in the idea of 'styles of scientific reasoning' (Crombie, 1994) shows greater care for this kind of detail. Something which, however, brings Hacking closer once again to the thought of Koyré, who was Crombie's teacher. Although, we must remember that Crombie had a heated argument with Koyré about the emergence of modern science, arguing that there was no such radical break between it and medieval science. At the same time, Koyré considered that the precedence of theorisation over experimentation was a clear sign of separation (Koyré, 1961/2011).

Nevertheless, the influence of Michel Foucault's work on Hacking also seems to have deepened this kind of thinking, indicating yet another element that localises the differences between him and Lacan. Such influence can be found as early as 1975, both in *The Emergence of Probability* (Hacking, 1975a/2006) and in *Why Does Language Matter to Philosophy?* (1975b/1997), taking shape from the 1990s onwards, when the author delves into a field closer to Foucault's. The emphasis on how sciences are constituted and developed—not in general lines, but in their details—can be recognised in these two major influences. In this sense, even if it is possible to recognise his proximity to Koyré when it comes to the differences with positivist historiography and with a tradition of doing philosophy of science in a way that is indissociable from history, he presents important points of disagreement, although relevant only in a more specific framework.

It is undeniable that there are differences between Lacan and Hacking, which is expected since the kinds of theorisation that each proposes to carry out are radically different. It is not uncommon for Lacan to state the difference between psychoanalysis and philosophy, even contrasting the two fields at various times, particularly in his seminar on *The Other Side of Psychoanalysis* (Lacan, 1969-70/2007). It is not clear whether that which Lacan calls philosophy is precisely the same thing as that which Hacking is concerned with, and it is not our role to follow this discussion at this point, as it would be a clear digression. But we must emphasise that the two authors have different goals when constructing their thoughts.

It is worth remembering that while he has dealt with issues in the field of psychopathology, Hacking does not report any clinical experience. On the other hand, and here we reiterate the importance of this historical review, it is also worth stressing that the differences between the authors do not stem only from their objectives or practical commitments. They share a conceptual framework, each demonstrating greater proximity to different and conflicting traditions. This should be taken into account, along with the orientations related to what they aim for in their intellectual activities. These are certainly not independent series; however, it is always necessary to emphasise these aspects to avoid an interpretation that inflates intentions to the detriment of history since history indicates both the influences and the possibilities for constituting a thought.

2.2 Making up people

Even if he showed his interest quite earlier, in the late 1990s and early 2000s, Hacking does his most in-depth work on the so-called 'interactive kinds'.

This production shows a certain type of progression in that issues presented in previous books are revisited in those that come later, achieving greater consistency and conceptual depth. In this way, if the first two books devoted to this kind of consideration—*Rewriting the Soul: Multiple Personality and the Sciences of Memory* (1995/2000) and *Mad Travelers* (1998)—operate as two major 'case studies', their themes are revisited in a more analytical stance in *The Social Construction of What?* (1999) and *Historical Ontology* (2002a/2009).

Hacking begins the book that concludes this series of publications, *Historical Ontology* (2002a), by revisiting his statement about a distinction between social and natural sciences. This is supported by the argument that what distinguishes the social sciences is the fact that there is a retroactive effect of the knowledge produced on the object. In contrast, the objects of the natural sciences would be more stable. However, more than just a differentiation between types of phenomena, the author suggests the notion of *historical ontology* as the central organiser of the different concepts that are mobilised in this discussion so that it would work as a kind of general definition of his thesis on the relationship between knowledge and experience.

This relation between differentiation—between types of phenomena (social and natural) and the status ascribed to the ideas stemming from this very differentiation—circumscribes the initial tension to which the ensuing discussion never fails to respond. However, it is clear that the discussion transcends this initial tension since several points at the heart of this differentiation gain autonomy by showing an interest in unfolding that goes beyond the mere distinction between types. What started as a reflection embedded in the tradition of discussions about methodological and epistemological unity thus becomes a specific and rigorous study of the inseparability between epistemology and ontology: "But in social phenomena we may generate kinds of people and kinds of action as we devise new classifications and categories. My claim is that we "make up people" in a stronger sense than we "make up" the world. (Hacking, 2002a, p. 40)

This does not mean, as previously presented, that natural objects are not understood in terms of an epistemic framework—to retrieve a Foucauldian term widely used throughout Hacking's work. He recognises, for example, the relevance of Kuhn's propositions, even advocating that they be classified as a 'revolutionary nominalism'. What is at play here is opposition to an idea of strict nominalism, which would be linked to the pretence that naming objects would have object-creating effects far more comprehensive than those related to the mode of 'access', whereby naming interferes with how the phenomenon can be addressed. In relation to natural science objects, therefore, nominalism would be found in the fact that there is always a historical and contingent starting point for the production of knowledge; in other words, there is no epistemological 'ground zero', as stated in *The Social Construction of What?* (Hacking, 1999). In this way, a scientific revolution could even transform the categories used to classify and name the world—producing extremely far-reaching and profound effects—but this would not mean a change in the world per se. However, for Hacking, the world per se is never accessible. This is what he calls *revolutionary nominalism*, and which carries the idea that underlying the historicisation of these dimensions, "the possibilities for truth, and hence of what can be found out, and of methods of verification, are themselves molded in time" (Hacking, 2002a, p. 4).

This discussion, which is grounded in the natural sciences and runs through not only the *historical epistemology* programmes, such as the one directed by Lorraine Daston at the Max Planck Institute but also the idea of the creation of phenomena, developed by Hacking in *Representing and Intervening* (1983), has the function of circumscribing the specificity of the discussion about objects in the social sciences. It is, therefore, a preparation that first establishes the historicity and contingency of the bases of production for any kind of knowledge, to then delve into an opening of a second inflexion point, which concerns objects that interact with language. To this end, he starts from Foucault's three axes of knowledge, power, and ethics to argue for the historicisation of how we constitute ourselves as objects of knowledge, subjects of power, and moral agents.

It should be noted that this is not a new question. Apart from *Historical Ontology* (2002a) being a compilation of texts written between 1973 and 1999, this specific discussion on the 'making up people' is presented here as a kind of product from discussions held in other books and articles published between 1975 and 1998. Stabilising this discussion under the syntagma 'historical ontology' has to do with understanding that the conditions of possibility for distinct forms of experience are historically determined: "Historical ontology is not so much about the formation of character as about the space of possibilities for character formation that surround a person, and create the potentials for "individual experience." (Hacking, 2002a, p. 24).

We see, therefore, the comprehensive character of the proposition, which does not concern singular facts, but rather a 'space of possibilities' and the creation of 'potentials'[15]. This is about being careful with demands for precision or inevitability as if this type of proposition could produce accurate predictions or categories with a high degree of specificity. This is not the case since it is a matter of developing a broad structure that can manifest itself in different ways, whose multiplicity is not anticipated, and neither is detrimental to the proposed idea.

A good example of this is the notion of trauma. If at first, it was physical and physiological issues that were named under this signifier, at a certain moment, it became fixed in everyday language as a definer of 'psychic wounds'. As he points out in *Rewriting the Soul: Multiple Personality and the Sciences of Memory* (1995), the notion of trauma gained this status before Freud—contrary to popular belief—and its evolution over time shows how the importance it is gaining produces effects on subjectivity.

In *Historical Ontology*, Hacking revisits the guideline found in the Diagnostic and Statistical Manual (DSM) since the 1980s to abolish the term 'neurosis', which was then assimilated by other diagnostic frameworks, particularly post-traumatic stress disorder. By referring to the book *The Harmony of Illusions* by Allan Young (1995), he points out how this shift from neurosis to post-traumatic stress disorder produces the understanding that symptoms are triggered by external events, not by a structural issue. This would not be a problem since "no adult human life lacks events that can now be counted as "traumatic" — recounted, told, experienced as, traumatic." (Hacking, 2002a, p. 24)

Hacking thus points out that one can recognise the effects produced by the naming of trauma as a distinguishing feature of individuals in the three categories indicated: in recognising people as traumatised; in the instances of power that proceed to view trauma as an issue to be tackled (from training courses to courts and so on)[16]; and in moral assimilation in which trauma appears as an event that is not only explanatory for inappropriate actions, but also provides a kind of absolution: "Trauma offers not only a new sense of who others are, and why some may be that way, but it also produces a new sense of self, of who one is and why one is as one is" (Hacking, 2002a, p. 20).

He also mobilises a second example, which presents a clearer picture of the constitutive character of this naming. According to the philosopher, it is the notion of child development, which has become—at least in the last 150 years—one of the categories for understanding childhood. As soon as a baby is born, or even before this happens, there is already a discourse in place whereby certain characteristics will be, at all times, compared with a standard of normality, and the individual's relationship with this standard will be a distinctive feature of their constitution. As the author asserts, "Our idea of what a child is has been formed by a scientific theory of development. It forms our whole body of practices of child-rearing today, and, in turn, forms our concept of the child." (Hacking, 2002a, p. 21). This discourse shapes not only the children but also the parents and their whole environment, which then begins to be determined by the knowledge about the child's world. Besides, this environment should not be limited only to 'ideas'; trivial things—like toys, games, etc. —are also produced within this discourse. Suffice it to notice that any product aimed at children brings along some kind of consideration about the developmental stage to which it is appropriate.

Hacking claims that his interest in this topic is threefold: "would like to know if there could be a general theory of making up people, or whether each example is so peculiar that it demands its own nongeneralisable story; and I want to know how this idea of "making up people" affects our very idea of what it is to be an individual" (Hacking, 2002a, p. 100).

The way of answering these questions, albeit an incomplete one, according to the author himself, involves resuming the distinction between nominalism and realism, but at their extremes: it aims to delineate what it defines as *dynamic nominalism* so that, while it does not consider that much is gained by applying entity realism to social objects, it rejects static nominalism, which argues that categories created for classification do not interact with their objects.

The idea of dynamic nominalism proves to support the consideration that human actions cannot be dissociated from their descriptive character. However, it does not stop there: if, on the one hand, intentionality depends on description, on the other, we must bear in mind that the set of possibilities for action—constrained, therefore, by the possibilities for description—also concerns the possibilities for identification, so that there is a common ground between 'modes of acting' and 'modes of being'. In this way, Hacking answers the third question he asks about how dynamic nominalism affects the idea of what it means to be an individual: *to be an individual is to be something possible at a particular historical moment.* Which, in turn, underpins how he views this discussion as an ontological one. As he states,

> In fact, "ontology" turns out to be perfect, for we are concerned with two types of being: on the one hand, rather Aristotelian universals—trauma or child development—and on the other hand, the particulars that fall under them—this psychic pain or that developing child. The universal is not timeless but historical, and it and its instances, the children or the victims of trauma, are formed and changed as the universal emerges. I have called this process dynamic nominalism, because it so strongly connects what comes into existence with the historical dynamics of naming and the subsequent use of name (Hacking, 2002a, p. 26)

As for the first two questions, whether there is a general theory or the examples are so particular that they demand a particular history, his answer dismantles, at least partially, the opposition between them. On the one hand, there is something particular in each of the cases, which is why the author claims that there is no *general history*. However, this does not preclude the possibility of a *general theory*, which would be based precisely on dynamic nominalism. In this sense, a partial operation is included, which appears across cases, but not always in the same way. These are two vectors; one produces the labelling and the other puts tension on it. Thus, Hacking establishes his theory of 'making up people' by presenting a retroactive and dialectical linguistic operation, which causes naming to create and modify types of human beings and acts, which in turn modify the possibilities of naming.

Interactive kinds and retroaction

According to Hacking, it is necessary to give a precise definition of what is meant when talking about dynamic nominalism. It is not simply a matter of people changing their behaviour based on interaction with other people or significant events, nor is it about intentional choices that may or may not be made. This is not a psychological category intended to explain human behaviour but a discussion within the philosophy of science that aims to reflect on the effects of knowledge production on certain objects. More specifically, he is not referring only to certain objects but to the relationship established between certain kinds of objects and certain kinds of knowledge or of categorisations.

In fact, the term 'kind' is chosen based on the differentiation between indifferent and interactive kinds. A word borrowed from Goodman (1954) and his paradox about the colour of emeralds: some say emeralds are green, others that they are blue. They could be considered grue if this word were firmly established in culture. What follows is rather than considering the word green (or the greenness) to be something intrinsic to the object or experience, it responds to the habit of using the word green. Thus, Goodman suggests that the construction of an object is inseparable from its classification in the sense that it is realised based on pre-established agreements.

This statement should be understood within the scope of the question on the act of classification, which inextricably combines category and object. A kind can then be regarded as a kind of *classification*, understood as an action that combines language and object. There are kinds whose classification does not pose questions related to the performativity of language; this does not mean that there is a direct relation between enunciation and the world, something that has already been pointed out at various moments about the very idea of 'general' nominalism found in Hacking's thought. However, indifferent kinds demonstrate a passivity towards what is being categorised, i.e., the category itself does not change the possibilities for the existence of the object and, therefore, does not modify the categorisation process itself. We emphasise that this is not indicative of a stagnant idea or a theoretical realism regarding categories but rather an understanding of the effects caused by the action of defining categories on the very process of categorisation. The categories created to talk about a rock, for example, do not modify the possibilities of existence of what is categorised. Saying that the rock is made up of carbon does not change its molecular structure. This does not mean that there are no other possible categories or modes of categorisation. It simply means that affirming a certain category does not change the categorisation itself.

On the other hand, there are interactive kinds, in which the classification modifies the elements mobilised through its own process. We must be careful in understanding that we are not talking about general changes that discourse can produce in an object but specific changes linked to what is mobilised in that particular category. It is thus something more specific than differentiation between objects since some objects react to language and others do not. This differentiation is important because even objects that react to language do not react in the same way in all cases. A discourse about depression, for example, may have a retroactive effect on the categorisation of depression itself—by modifying whether depressive symptoms are legitimate forms of suffering or the very experience that individuals have with their suffering—whereas a discourse about a broken arm presents no such effect. This does not mean that what is said about a broken arm does not affect the individuals who hear it, but rather that it does not change the fact of whether the arm is broken or not. To put it simplistically: categorising an arm as broken may bring effects (it may even cause depressive symptoms in the subject whose arm is broken), but this is not an interactive kind since it does not modify the object of the categorisation itself (the broken arm).

Such a definition is important, especially because it is a way through which Hacking proposes his argument without entering a discussion about the objects themselves. He is not arguing over whether we are talking about the same object when we talk about depression or orthopaedics, nor about the general and necessary definitions of objects (or subjects) influenced by language. He is talking about specific cases in which the process of categorisation brings a discourse that modifies its own object so that the category itself, which brings discourse and object together, must be understood as an interactive kind. For instance:

> I want to focus not on the children but on the classification, those kinds of children, fidgety, hyperactive, attention-deficient. They are interactive kinds. I do not mean that hyperactive children, the individuals, are "interactive." Obviously hyperactive children, like any other children, interact with innumerable people and things in innumerable ways. "Interactive" is a new concept that applies not to people but to classifications, to kinds, to the kinds that can influence what is classified. And because kinds can interact with what is classified, the classification itself may be modified or replaced. (Hacking, 1999, p. 103)

Such a definition concerns the interaction with produced meanings and not simply with actions. It claims, for example, that quarks are indifferent because they do not respond to classification; this does not mean they are passive. In the same way, plutonium interacts with other elements but not with the classification. These elements are indifferent to meaning, not action (Hacking, 1999, p. 105). Interactive kinds are those that are modified by the meanings produced in the classification, particularly in relation to what is being categorised. And this interaction produces modalities of retroaction, which can work in confirming and establishing ways of experiencing that will be strongly present and socially recognised, but which can also produce the inadequacy of certain categories that become obsolete as an effect of categorisation itself.

In this way, interactive kinds make the categorisation process more complex, creating what the author describes as a looping effect, in which the classification modifies its object. As pointed out, this may occur to the point of rendering the category inadequate to the current state: "There can be strong interactions. What was known about people of a kind may become false because people of that kind have changed in virtue of how they have been classified, what they believe about themselves, or because of how they have been treated as so classified" (Hacking, 1999, p. 104).

The effects of invention and establishment of forms of experience are thus central in explaining the existence of transient mental illnesses, which exist only in a specific place and time. This idea, extended to a general functioning in *Historical Ontology* (2002a), is mobilised in *Rewriting the Soul* (1995) under the name of 'feedback effect' in an attempt to explain how events linked to scientific categorisation produce new ways of being.

Thus, we can see how Hacking's books maintain a dialogue with each other and produce a way of addressing these questions. What is presented in 1995 and 1998 as the *feedback effect* gets named in 1999 as the *looping effect* and gains greater conceptual weight in 2002 with the *dynamic nominalism*. Along with these categories, Hacking also briefly discusses the interplay between interactional kinds and biological effects, named *biofeedback*, to destine discursive modifications that produce effects on the body. Such an operation poses a complex question since it would modify what the author often considers indifferent kinds.

At this point, careful reading is necessary. In talking about interactive kinds, there is no discussion about the language effects on individuals in general, but specifically about the effects of classifications on the possibilities of existence and determination of subjectivities. And about the complexity that this retroaction introduces into the production of knowledge about these kinds, claiming that it would be the only explanation for how certain names and named things could fit together so well.

This way of approaching the question shifts the traditional debate on the differentiation between natural and social sciences from the distinction between objects to a consideration of kinds of classification. Social sciences (of social objects) do not necessarily deal with interactive kinds, or not only with interactive kinds; just as certain problems can be understood as being composed simultaneously of interactive and indifferent kinds—such as psychopathology, according to the author. He claims, for example, that depression is a case of biological illness—which he then considers as an indifferent kind—but that it is expressed out of cultural elements and is also an interactive[17] kind. Furthermore, it shows biolooping effects since behavioural treatments can modify serotonin levels: "by living in this way, adopting certain types of behaviour, a certain chemical condition of the brain, thought to be correlated with depression, is alleviated. We have a dynamics working at the level of classification and at the level of biolooping." (Hacking, 1999, p. 123)[18].

Something similar to what he says about autism, commenting on the tension that lies in the opposition between biological understandings and the consideration of other factors that should be taken into account:

> Here we want to say both that childhood autism is (is identical to) a certain biological pathology P, and so is a "natural" kind or an indifferent kind. At the same time, we want to say that childhood autism is an interactive kind, interacting with autistic children, evolving and changing as the children change (Hacking, 1999, p. 119)

This discussion is central to us since it condenses a great potentiality from Hacking's propositions but also shows a mistake in the analysis. This is particularly clear in relation to depression, where the author does not seem to recognise the retroactive effect that the very understanding of depression as a biological—and therefore indifferent—object can cause. That is, what are the effects of an interactive kind being presented as an indifferent kind? One can readily think of power effects resulting from regarding contingent characteristics as necessary. We will explore this in more detail later.

On the other hand, at this point, Hacking expresses his disagreement with both social constructionism and rigid designations for psychopathologies (Hacking, 1999, p. 122), pointing out that these issues would be better addressed from a dynamic, rather than semantic, mode of understanding. This means that, even if he claims a privilege in relation to biological causality, he still acknowledges the importance of that which also appears as interactive. In general terms, he argues for the necessity of regarding the problems indicated as processes in which classification and experience mutually modify each other and not as stagnant attempts at definition. This positioning can be understood as a dialectical relationship between truth and knowledge, especially if we take the ontological effects of the discourses on knowledge as truth effects on individuals. The classification dynamics should thus be seen as a key element that can be better understood from his considerations on transient mental illnesses.

2.3 The transient mental illnesses

The central importance we give to the question of transient mental illnesses in Hacking's work is justified by the organising value this debate has within the author's thought. Indeed, its theoretical path is decidedly marked by the consideration of pathologies that were once highly prevalent and important but which do not necessarily continue to exist. Thus, the exploration of transient illnesses is not a deviation or simply one case among others but rather a privileged way of approaching what had been indicated before as a point of interest. This point of interest will later be established as the centre of gravity of his considerations on knowledge production about social objects, demanding a return to his nominalist inspirations.

Broadly speaking, Hacking's assertion of a nominalist position responds to something that had already been within his sphere of interest for some years, which concerns how it is possible to *make up people* (Hacking, [1983]2002).

It is important to note that the term *make up* is not foreign to the author, nor to his writings on natural science—a field where its use may have been most alien, in fact. In *Representing and Intervening* (1983), Hacking argues that scientific practice invents phenomena rather than simply reproducing those found in the natural world. It even creates phenomena that never existed before, such as lasers and masers (Hacking, 1983). Regarding the making up of people, the author refers to the fact that the existence of human beings cannot be separated from the ways we think and understand this very existence; therefore, by modifying the way we deal with the question of existence, we also modify the possible ways of experiencing existence.

As we see, this proposition with a clear Foucauldian influence indicates an intertwining between epistemology and ontology since the establishment of conditions of possibility for thinking about existence produces specific modes of subjection. Thus, the ways to define truth, or the parameters of truthfulness and falsehood, constitute a first demarcation of the field of possibilities that establishes what will be possible and acceptable to think and will lack legitimacy. This is, therefore, the first point indicating that notions of truth need to be taken as more than a strictly epistemological statement.

Based on the idea of making up of people, Hacking proposes a conceptual framework to support his thought. It is into this framework that enters his *dynamic nominalism* (or dialectical realism), a concept used to indicate the retroactive effect of discourse on the individual. To do so, he also needs to establish other terms, such as *interactive kinds*, *looping and feedback effects*, as part of a conceptual constellation that shapes his historical ontology. As indicated, these concepts are shaped throughout his books in a writing movement that shows a clear concern that is not only conceptual but also aesthetic. Concerning this aspect, it is curious to note how in both *Rewriting the Soul* and *Mad Travelers*, the author takes on a writing that is far more narrative—including, in the latter, some formal experiments.

This facet of greater formal freedom seems to respond to a debate he has been establishing since 1975 when writing *Why Does Language Matter to Philosophy?* concerning incommensurability: he suggests that the relationship between incommensurability and translation (understood not only as the translation from one language to another but also as the adaptation of ideas to another context) would, in many cases, assume the form of an impossibility of understanding any phenomenon outside its world of origin. Almost 30 years later, in *Historical Ontology* (2002a), Hacking clearly states that incommensurability should be limited to the impossibility of direct comparison between phenomena from different conceptual frameworks but that this does not mean an impossibility of understanding. Comprehension, in turn, could be produced from the reconstitution of thought, something that would not, however, be so easy to put into practice. In this sense, it seems to us that historical and narrative caution, as well as differences in style that can be found in these two books, are part of an attempt to reconstruct the thought of a particular moment, something made necessary by the delimitation of the very object:

> By a "transient mental illness" I mean an illness that appears at a time, in a place, and later fades away. It may spread from place to place and reappear from time to time. It may be selective for social class or gender, preferring poor women or rich men. I do not mean that it comes and goes in this or that patient, but that this type of madness exists only at certain times and places. The most famous candidate for a transient mental illness is hysteria, or at any rate its florid French manifestations toward the end of the nineteenth century. (Hacking, 1998, p. 1)

If the author's conceptual proposition concerns the assertion of modes of existence that are made possible by established knowledges available at a given moment, then the reconstruction of not only these knowledges but, in particular, of the meaning they held at those given moments is not just an illustration but an indispensable point of argumentative demonstration. This justifies the peculiarity of these two books and the need for part of them to be retrieved in our work.

The centrality of knowledge and the niches

Published in 1995, *Rewriting the Soul: Multiple Personality and the Sciences of Memory* (1995) is the first book by Ian Hacking devoted to an in-depth and detailed examination of how social context influences—or even constitutes—the way individuals think of and experience themselves. In this specific case, the author is concerned with demonstrating how a specifically circumscribed mental disorder is constituted as an effect of previous events in such a way that the prevailing mode of thinking about what a human being is—their normality and their pathologies—not only circumscribes the limits within which these issues can be understood but also modifies how those who live under this discourse experience things.

Thus, the book's main goal is not only to describe and contextualise the multiple personality disorder or dissociative identity disorder—as it is currently termed—but the way the sciences of memory operate in the establishment of a new way of thinking about and experiencing the soul, in the author's words. This emphasis is found in the book's title, *Rewriting the Soul: Multiple Personality and the Sciences of Memory*, but it was lost in the Brazilian translation when the beginning, which refers to the idea of 'rewriting the soul', was removed. As argued by the author, the phenomenon of multiple personality is general, concerning memory, description, past, and soul. It is necessary to observe how 'obvious' it has become. This was only possible once 'memory became the way to have knowledge of the soul.' (Hacking, 1995, p. 109).

In this respect, multiple personality is presented as one case among other possible effects of establishing a specific way to think of the soul. Thus, this disorder—which emerged a few decades ago and seems to be geographically restricted to the United States—can be defined by splitting the psyche into different personalities, where there is a mnemic rupture between the experiences lived by each of them.

The central thesis concerns the localisation of the definition and conceptualisation of *memory* as a possible way of addressing questions that, up to a point in time (the mid-19th century), could not be assimilated by the prevailing scientific thought or by the more general discourse produced by it. Memory is described as a field in which numerous categories—cognitive, affective, mystical, and so on—converge. At the same time, Hacking ties his interest to the nearly definitive and inevitable nature of how statements about memory are presented. He turns to a particular case of what he calls memory-thinking (the multiple personality) to discuss this supposed inevitability. According to him, this disease had been overlooked for some years, and by the time the book was written, it was of great importance in North America.

More than that, there is a quite specific wager on the performative character of the discourse on memory and the establishment of multiple personality as a disorder: the fundamental feature of this relationship must be sought in the etiological explanations of the disorder, whose foundations would hold the definitions of that which is understood as an individual: "The soul that we are constantly constructing we construct according to an explanatory model of how we came to be the way we are" (Hacking, 1995, p. 95).

There is a confluence of theories of causation, that which is presented as inevitable, and modes of subjection. The author continues, "a seemingly innocent theory on causation (which might as a matter of empirical fact be true or false) becomes formative and regulatory" (Hacking, 1995, p. 95). In his investigation, he takes Foucauldian archaeology as a reference to demonstrate how 'new' ideas become unavoidable. In the latter half of the 20th century, multiple personality demonstrates how this unavoidability is constructed, both by its contextual specificity and by the possibility of tracing its 'origins', which can be identified in another specific time and place: in France, between 1874 and 1886. There is a special emphasis on how scientific knowledge interferes with the production of symptoms and diseases. Symptoms whose truthfulness the author does not challenge, which grants their construction a strong epistemological status: the knowledges being circulated have true ontological effects.

The choice for this 19th-century period is made for two reasons. Firstly, because there was a wave of multiple personality cases in France between 1874 and 1886. Before that, cases of double consciousness or other types of dissociation were reported, but they were not as important as they became after 1875. The second reason is how these cases came to be understood: based on the diagnosis of hysteria, but not only (something relevant for the cases of fugue as well, which will be addressed later). Hacking is looking for a trait that can give more consistency to the rise in the number of cases, even to the studies on hysteria. According to him, the cases of double consciousness found in England were not memory-related; this seems to be something new in France.

Although it was linked to hysteria, especially by Charcot, multiplicity led to some diagnostic disagreements. Janet considered it to be a special case of bipolar disorder, and there were also some associations with schizophrenia. However, Hacking states that the most accepted version was the connection with hysteria, which would also explain its demise in several places—related to the decline in the importance of hysteria in French psychiatric debates. The same is said about fugue, which, in turn, was at the centre of a debate between epilepsy and hysteria, the latter having won out. According to the author, diagnostic quarrels play an important role in establishing a transient illness since they allow traits related to the condition to circulate in society.

Just as in the case of double personality, there was an epidemic of this illness in the early 20th century characterised by three factors: an irresistible compulsion to travel, carried out in an intelligible and apparently normal way, followed by amnesia (Hacking, 1998, p. 47). And just like double personality, it quickly disappeared. If, to some researchers, these demises are questions to be answered, Hacking is more interested in the fact that double personality has survived (transformed into multiple personality) and can be found today in the United States.

The presence of multiple personality disorder is surprising not only for its specificity and strong occurrence in culture but also for its conceptual weakness. Its rise would be correlated to the revival of its presence in culture, driven by the publication of novels and the making of films based on the stories of multiples. It is worth saying that, unlike the cases described in the late 19th century, it is no longer a question of double personality but of a much larger number, roughly stable around 16 different personalities. The novels and films played an important part in intensifying the spread of the disorder. This was not by chance but by a confluence of the relevance of causes that are responsible for the condition's development, and their acceptance and mobilisation within social movements that bring together those affected and those responsible for therapies.

We can see, at this point, that, along with the centrality of the idea of cause in determining a pathology, there is also the account of cultural elements that would be ready to be mobilised. Hacking gives a thorough description of this in relation to multiple personality. Still, it is only in *Mad Travelers* that he will name this idea more assertively, appealing to the idea of *niche*: "the concatenation of an extraordinarily large number of diverse types of elements which for a moment provide a stable home for certain types of manifestation of illness." (Hacking, 1998, p. 13).

The idea of niche carries with it the multiplicity of factors required for considering the emergence of a pathology. This is of special importance as it also locates the centrality the author ascribes to scientific knowledge by asserting its prominent role in determining possibilities of experience. However, this does not entail a direct and inevitable cause-and-effect relationship but rather the establishment of a field of possibilities. In fact, the very choice of the word 'niche', which refers to the ecological niche, carries this idea since it responds to the understanding that a niche is that which determines evolutionary possibilities without implying predictability.

More specifically, Hacking (1998, p.2) claims that four vectors play a special role in establishing a transient illness: (1) a framework of diagnosis; (2) being placed in between two elements of contemporary culture in a polarised fashion: one virtuous and the other vicious; (3) visibility, meaning that the disorder should be visible as something to escape; (4) despite the pain that is produced, the disorder should also bring some relief.

Therefore, we can see a great effort to qualify the niche not only as a framework of potentialities that sustains different final expressions but also as something whose consistency is beyond merely a discourse, in a Foucauldian sense[19]. Hacking is thus interested in institutions, social movements, groupings, etc., that are part of that constitution, and from that, he draws, in *Mad Travelers*, a few general lines.

As previously indicated, the diagnostic framework is important for the illness not only to dwell in the scientific community but also to extend its reach beyond the walls of knowledge production. To this end, as already stated, diagnostic quarrels were of great help, which was the case for both double personality and fugue. The question of polarization between two cultural elements of opposing valences is an idea missing from his book on multiple personalities. However, the author does make some comments on this later on. In the case of fugue, Hacking points to this polarization because of its insertion between an imaginary of popularisation and valorisation of tourism, counterbalanced by the criminalisation of vagrancy. The *fugueurs* would be between these extremes: poor but not miserable, an urban citizen in a moment when tourism gained popularity with companies like Thomas Cook and Son (Hacking, 1998, p. 26-27).

Thus, we see how these vectors are intertwined. If the first two seem to establish more general lines of determination, the others concern more particular issues: the scientific discourse also depends on the social acknowledgement of suffering, while suffering itself and the nature of 'relief' brought about by pathology respond directly to the specificity of the group within which it is manifested. If tourism occupied a privileged position and its popularisation was presented as an alternative to the constraints of a worker's life—but not exactly of a low-paid worker—there is another constraint to this alternative, which is precisely vagrancy. For Hacking, suffering, recognition, knowledge, and cultural elements are part of the same web, where it is not possible to disentangle one thread from the other completely.

2.4 Multiple personality

This intertwining can be found in the case of multiple personalities. The cultural context that welcomed and boosted this disorder in such a unique way can be considered from three central points that have been mobilised: (1) the election of *child abuse* as an urgent and general problem, whose widespread and devastating presence in society should be tackled by everyone; (2) the tendency towards the medicalisation of therapeutic processes and the active stance, on the part of doctors, in establishing an etiology that preserves its functions; and, finally, (3) the acknowledgement of memory, but more specifically of lost memories, as the core etiological element of the disorder in question.

The centrality of child abuse is perhaps where it most differs from the picture of the previous century since, apart from occupying a much less important place in the etiology (if it ever occupied any place at all), child abuse would, according to Hacking, be a non-existent category between 1874 and 1886 (at least in today's terms). Of course, something similar to what we now understand as abuse was happening; however, the repulsiveness of it was not the same.

According to the author, it can be stated that cruelty towards children was a recognised fact, which, however, would undergo important changes within its spectrum. The first point of modification, and perhaps one of the most interesting for thinking about how political issues permeate this type of process, is that cruelty towards children in 1874 was understood as something related to social class, with greater prevalence in the lower classes. It was thus an effect of poverty, which is expressly erased from contemporary North American discourse. Part of the potency of the child abuse category comes from its universality, something that does not predominantly afflict the poorest; therefore, it should not be understood as a social issue. Such a position was of great interest to the American government since it consisted in establishing a problem of general interest that would not bring consequences for the workings of the economy nor criticism of income distribution and inequality. Added to this is the inclusion of the sexual issue in the category of abuse, which was not present in the idea of cruelty.

The sum of these things would have created a huge social impact, mobilising several sectors of American society: it is worth remembering that Nixon even made a televised statement and signed a presidential order to fight child abuse in 1974. It is not only about establishing a kind but about delineating a form of suffering that will be presented as adequate. We must emphasise that this does not remove the aspect of truth from suffering; however, it shows how the ways of suffering respond to their environment, being mobilised in the delineation of debates and showing political valence. The detachment of the connection to poverty shows how there is a steering towards a more interesting field to the ideas prevailing at the time.

If it was not linked to poverty and class difference, how did they think of abuse? Two lines of approach consolidated. The first consists of the approximation between child abuse and evil, in the sense that children would be abused because of the evilness of certain people. In conjunction with that, in second place the association with sexuality, in the sense that sexual perversions and disorders would also play a big part in that.

Lastly, a major difference is the destination given to the problem. If cruelty towards children, even if acknowledged, did not seem to be a reason for major interventions in the 19th century, child abuse is understood as something unacceptable, which implies fighting the abusers and treating the victims. This treatment is fully embraced by medical discourse—which, of course, is reproduced across mechanisms that do not necessarily need to be occupied by doctors, such as support groups and other kinds of organisations. However, it is the medical discourse, markedly from pediatricians and psychiatrists, that will sustain the seriousness of child abuse and also endorse the need for treatment as a preventive intervention by backing the idea that being abused in childhood would be a cause of abusive behaviour in adulthood (Hacking, 1995 p. 89). In this way, medical authority composes and subscribes to the centrality of child abuse as the great evil to be combated, endorsing the circumscription of a problem that belongs to everyone but which would not have social origins. This can even be seen as a movement to capture the enunciation of the truth: the medical discourse presents itself as the one capable of telling what is really happening, and the legitimacy granted to it produces effects.

The potency of this kind can be identified in the number of reported cases of abuse in the US. There is a rise from 7,000 (1967) to 1.1 million (1982). According to the author, this would have happened due to its presence in culture and to a widening definition of child abuse, which is now understood as the cause of any 'deviation' that results in a development that is not 'optimal'. (Hacking, 1999, p. 144). The scientific discourse was playing a central role in this, especially based on the false knowledge about repeated abuse (abused as a child, abuser as an adult), which had been present from the beginning. This whole process, according to Hacking, should be understood from his idea of interactive kind, taking into account the possibility of re-signifying past experiences from current elements made available:

> Consciousness is not raised but changed. Someone now sees herself as abused as a child, because she has a new concept in terms of which to understand herself. This is perhaps the strongest and most challenging application of Goodman's dictum, that worlds are constituted by kinds. Child abuse is a new kind that has changed the past of many people, and so changed their very sense of who they are and how they have come to be. (Hacking, 1999, p. 162)

Regarding multiple personality disorder (MPD), the role of medicalisation (understood as discourse, not only as practice) is quite clear, as it plays an active role in the attempts to substantiate the condition scientifically. As the disorder gains popularity, the urge to verify its scientific basis is so strong that different attempts are made, although none seem to achieve solid results.

Attempts at validation

According to Hacking, a disease can be known by two distinct routes: through a combination of etiology, semiology, and therapy or through measuring its presence and manifestation in the population.

The combination of etiology, semiology, and therapy, in the case of multiplicity, made use of causal theories as a focal point for the argument, relating both the classifications of symptoms and therapy to what was presented as the great etiological event: a trauma resulting from child abuse. The philosopher points to a certain naivety in how the patients' accounts were handled, often taken literally as objective descriptions. Although, as the author points out, this has been a highly complex topic of discussion since Freud, it was actively ignored by multiplicity theorists. As he asserts, "A therapist can hardly resist such evidence, and yet there is reason to worry that the process of therapy and healing concretises a story into a fact." (Hacking, 1995, p. 90) so that the absence of a strict methodological and conceptual work to deal with what was part of the therapy contributed to making the etiological hypotheses very fragile. For Hacking, the value of these accounts would lie in their being an explanation by the patients themselves about what happened to them. Still, they would have little value as a generalisation or causal explanation. This is why the author is emphatic when stating, "Psychiatry did not discover that early and repeated child abuse causes multiple personality. It forged that connection, in the way that a blacksmith turns formless molten metal into tempered steel" (Hacking, 1995, p. 94).

In relation to measurement propositions, they focused on the hypothesis presented by Frank Putnam (1989) whereby dissociation would work in a kind of *continuum*, which could be gauged from creating a measurement system. Many questionnaires were developed, and answered by a huge number of patients. However, these questionnaires were calibrated not with an independent standard but with "a network of mutually consistent and self-confirming testing devices" (Hacking, 1995, p. 100). That is, instead of the questionnaires being subject to some kind of external control, they were validated by other self-administered questionnaires and by judgements of expert practitioners. They were then responding to opinions present in an existing movement within psychiatry, which also included its patients.

Thus, there were findings about the *continuum* hypothesis, although Hacking argues that the hypothesis was not tested contrary to what the authors claim. According to Hacking, this case demonstrates problems found in the scientific community, both in relation to the self-referencing nature of dissociative scales and in relation to how debates and article publications currently work, since "The peer referees and the journal editor do not look to see if you have tested the hypothesis. They look to see if you have used various prescribed statistical procedures. No one asks about the meaning of those procedures." (Hacking, 1995, p.106)

However, an effort must be made not to generalise the criticisms made by Hacking as the advocacy of a certain normative standard of scientificity that should be followed. The author is categorical in defining himself as a non-normative philosopher of science, always working with the idea that different modes of knowledge production can be deemed scientific, even if they do not share the same epistemological or methodological bases. In the case in question, the Canadian author raises strong objections because he considers that there is an inconsistency between the studies conducted and what they claim to be: they are structured according to a rationality, but their execution fails to respect the established assumptions, which is why they are very fragile. This does not mean that Hacking argues that the correct execution of these experiments should be understood as the only way to validate the theories at stake, but only that they do not validate what they claim to validate.

According to the philosopher, the hypothesis needed not be tested because the *continuum* had already become a fact. This implies that the multiple personality measurements, which legitimise it as a disorder, would result from a misuse of statistics in psychology. We must stress, however, that Hacking has no intention of delegitimising multiplicity as an experience, quite the contrary. If his effort is clearly directed at questioning the patterns used to explain the phenomena studied by doctors and psychiatrists, this is aimed at advocating that, even though the disorder exists, it should be understood in a radically different way: as the fruit of historical, contextual construction.

This does not stop knowledge from producing ontological effects: these effects are not linked to the correctness of the ideas but mainly to their circulation and legitimacy. Discourses and implementations of knowledge cause these ontological truth effects, but they lack epistemological consistency—considering the epistemological bases that the scholars themselves mobilise. This indicates that even if we are not working with an idea of normative epistemology, it is possible not only to sustain that statements are false within specific epistemological systems (as is the case here) but also that the fact that they are false does not stop them from producing ontological effects. The cause is not linked to the correctness of the ideas. The big question is, therefore, how to explain that it has come to this type of experience.

Memory, truth, and causation

Multiple personality disorder is taken up as a particular case produced by something that would have happened a century earlier, which would be the establishment of the sciences of memory as a field of scientific interest and with a great potential for widespread dissemination. The passage between these two moments—between cases of double consciousness (or *dédoublement*) and contemporary cases of multiplicity—depends on a number of factors, especially for multiplicity, in its current form, to have made such an impact. Some of these have been examined earlier, starting with an indication of (1) the role played by situating child abuse as an urgent problem and (2) how scientific discourse reinforces experience and contributes to its dissemination and legitimisation. There is, however, a third element, which is precisely what seems to bridge the two historical moments and which allowed the two former ones to be mobilised the way they were, concerning (3) the centrality of memory and childhood trauma in the etiology of the disorder.

This characteristic of a term that bridges two moments becomes clear when we observe that multiplicity theorists and practitioners regard the early years of Freud's work as an important component of their constructions while at the same time bearing a certain resentment towards the psychoanalyst. This is because the theories of seduction and trauma are rigorously adopted as core elements in the etiology of the disorder, being mobilised as essential keys for understanding its causes. Resentment comes precisely from the advancement of psychoanalytic theory when Freud abandons this centrality. From the point of view of those who work with multiplicity, this was an unforgivable step taken by the Viennese psychoanalyst.

However, as Hacking points out, the interest in this question is not limited to its explanatory capacity since, apart from these hypotheses being pertinent to explain the disorder, their mobilisation reveals something prior: a matrix of thought concerning the subject that would be necessary to produce experiences of this kind. Something that would even predate Freud, although his work provided it with an unparalleled reach.

During the latter half of the 19th century, theories about memory—disseminated by Théodule-Armand Ribot in particular—came to be more present in culture. This even yields the possibility that the term *trauma* could be applied to a hitherto alien field, the psychic field. The idea of a disruptive event, which causes some kind of split, becomes applicable from the moment that memory becomes a scientific object. According to Hacking, there are three practices in the science of memory of the 19th century: neurological studies of location, studies of recall, and the psychodynamics of memory. These practices consisted of a new kind of object, as they were not focused on the contents to be remembered but on *how* they could be remembered. They would all originate from the definition of a previous structure, a conceptual framework that enabled the formation of this type of object. Something that would have been personified in the characters of Ribot and his peers—the first authors ever to address these questions directly.

The evolution of memory studies has defined the boundaries of how we can think of the individual. Ribot, for instance, speaks of two different manners of considering the self from how memory works (Ribot, 1881). In this regard, cases of double personality would be central to the idea that people are constituted by more than one self, connected by memory. Dissociation would be a pathology associated with memory, which would cause the fragmentation of this unity. In delving into these questions, Ribot was allegedly the exponent of this new field, proposing a theory that not only encompassed a specific understanding of memory but also opened the possibility of thinking about its pathologies and the inclusion of the term *trauma* in this field.

This does not mean, says Hacking, that Ribot is the most important theorist or that he is the forerunner of the other authors who came after. He would be, however, the first theorist to have stated, in the field of science, something that was already present in the field of culture, something already established in another level of discursivity. This idea is even compatible with what Jacques Rancière (2001/2009) advocated when he presented how the notion of the unconscious could already be found in artistic manifestations even before Freud's work. Hacking's idea is even more compelling than what is argued by Rancière when he claims that there would be a conceptual matrix that would help delineate memory as a scientific object and that this would bring inevitable consequences for all the fields that stem from it:

> I am not saying that Ribot is a precursor of Freud, the modern multiple movement, or whatever. I am saying that he is an early instance of a man

> whose surface knowledge is worked out within the rules of that underlying depth knowledge which remains the depth knowledge to this very day. One feature of the modern sensibility is dazzling in its implausibility: the idea that what has been forgotten is what forms our character, our personality, our soul. (Hacking, 1995/, p. 209)

Hacking presents a scenario in which the constitution of a scientific object would have defined new possibilities of experience based on the expansion of a mode of rationality into a hitherto unexplored field (unexplored by this mode). A field that will define memory as a possible path to discovering questions linked to truth. Later, Freud would have reinforced this centrality of memory both by locating it as a core etiological element (the absence or repression of memories as the cause of symptoms) and by recognising its therapeutic character (the retrieval of repressed materials as an active part of a healing process). At this point, the philosopher attributes not only to Freud but also to Pierre Janet an essential role in recognising the therapeutic character of working with memories from psychological traumas to treat hysteria, which does not mean that he assigns them the responsibility for establishing the centrality of memory in the public debate.

Depth knowledge and surface knowledge

If Hacking states that the link between memory, truth, and trauma is a legacy from Freud and Janet—because they were the ones who supposedly paved the way for this idea to spread socially—this does not mean that these are the most important authors for thinking about multiplicity, or even the most central influences. According to the author, there is a direct relationship between the etiological hypotheses of multiple personality disorder and the work of these authors (in particular, Freud); however, he states that even Freud and Janet's discussion is an effect of the establishment of another type of discursivity. A discursivity that would give support not only to specific hypotheses but to something broader, which would ground the sciences of memory as a whole. As seen earlier, Hacking points to Ribot and his peers as the leading figures behind the emergence of this new range of scientific thought in the sense that they would have played a central role in the production of enunciations that would give materiality to this endeavour.

This new kind of thinking would bring in novelties, "new kinds of truths-or-falsehoods, new kinds of facts, new objects of knowledge." (Hacking, 1995/2000, p. 198). In this sense, it is about the possibility of new styles of reasoning. It is the moment, alluded to earlier, when scientific thought would expand into a hitherto uncolonised territory, that of the spiritual plane, which could then be actualised through knowledge about memory. This, according to Hacking, consists in the modification of what he defines, based on Foucault, as depth knowledge, something that would have greater depth than specific theories or facts about memory: the very possibility that facts about memory existed, facts that could then be made known and perhaps even lead to future intervention techniques. That would be the foundation of depth knowledge. This is a change in status for certain issues so that "what would previously have been debates on the moral and spiritual plane took place at the level of factual knowledge. These political debates all presuppose and are made possible by this depth knowledge" (Hacking, 1995, p. 198).

Thus, we can see that what Hacking defines as pertaining to depth knowledge—from which specific cases of surface knowledge would be conceivable—denotes a wide-reaching matrix to which various possibilities of theoretical constructions would respond. He proposes this differentiation from what Foucault defines as *connaissance* and *savoir*[20], in the sense that surface knowledge (*connaissances*) would be particular cases of actualisation of depth knowledge (*savoir*), but without exhausting it. In addition, the qualifiers *depth* and *surface* are inspired by Noam Chomsky's proposition, which conjoins these terms to grammar. In this way, in addition to the surface knowledges produced, depth knowledge would also encompass all possibilities of enunciation in that field—including not only 'true' but also false theories, objects, practices, and so on. Depth knowledge is understood as a kind of grammar; something that cannot be known directly but determines what can be considered true or false[21].

From this grammar, surface knowledge is established, shaping some of the foreseen possibilities. Here, a relationship of mutual influence takes place, in which surface knowledge also modifies depth knowledge, although this is a lengthier movement. The reflection on multiplicity implies a movement between these two dimensions: there is the establishment of depth knowledge and how it is actualised, and enunciated through surface knowledge. Surface knowledges are subject to being considered true or false. In contrast, depth knowledge would be precisely what demarcates what can be evaluated according to these terms, as well as the very criteria of truthfulness and falsehood.

We have already indicated the route taken by the author in the movement of practical knowledge that is being established from the latter half of the 19th century in France to the late 20th century in the United States, and now we need to address the question of how this depth knowledge was established. We revisit the central point of this establishment, which Hacking highlights. Regardless of the differences among the routes taken in the development of different theories of memory, there is something that connects them.

According to him, memory became a political issue and can be addressed both in the realm of personal memory and in the realm of collective memory. However, he makes a differentiation in time, stating that it is only after depth knowledge is established that memory can be taken up as a political issue. Personal memory, the case into which he delves, would originate from traumatology and the sciences of memory, something strongly present in the French scene.

If science can follow different paths from the different possible epistemological paths to its development, this can also be said about the different political motivations that reinforce an object's relevance. In the case of memory, there are at least three highly relevant social facts (hysteria, shell shock, and domestic violence) that are directly linked to the sciences of memory of the time, reinforcing the importance of the field. Despite their different forms of actualisation, we must not forget that they share a common ground: "their differences should not conceal what their adherents take for granted. They all suppose that there is knowledge of memory to be had." (Hacking, 1995, p. 213). There is a fundament which manifests itself in particular cases. We can see, therefore, that beyond specific manifestations that can be considered true or false, Hacking indicates another incidence of truth, which responds not to a regimen of truthfulness but to the definition of possible and legitimate objects. And this definition makes it possible to establish political demands.

At this point, Hacking proposes a specific term to name this process: memoropolitics. A term directly inspired by the work of Foucault, based on the proposition of anatomopolitics and biopolitics as two interconnected power practices. Both these conjunctions of power and politics had their own knowledge surfaces (biology and anatomy), hence, specific statistical technologies. Thus, each of these two poles showed specific ways of organising three aspects: power, politics, and science. Therefore, the Canadian philosopher's proposition is the inclusion of a third term that would introduce questions related to the soul and mind into the account of the interweaving of these three poles.

Memoropolitics's central characteristic would then be the expansion of scientific discursivity into territories as yet unoccupied but of great social relevance. It is thus a matter of introducing a mode of thought that shifts the debate from the moral to the scientific field, a movement that consolidated itself in the infamous years between 1874 and 1886:

> Certainly the generation that lived through that time had direct intellectual and practical predecessors. But that is when the depth knowledge, the knowledge that there are facts about memory, came into being. Why did it come into being then? Because the sciences of memory could serve as the public forum for something of which science could not openly speak. There could be no science of the soul. So there came to be a science of memory. (Hacking, 1995, p. 219)

We have arrived, therefore, at the great moment to which the entire historical description responds: the establishment of a depth knowledge that allows questions hitherto linked to the soul and the spirit to follow a scientific path and various discourses, practices, and theories to be established. One of its threads goes through the establishment of psychology as a discipline, the Freudian formulations on trauma and memory, the appearance and disappearance of diagnostic categories, and a particular assimilation in the United States based on local cultural and political influences, leading to what is called multiple personality disorder. The disorder is not, therefore, the only possible resultant. The cases of fugue described in *Mad Travelers* (Hacking, 1998) are also presented by Hacking as something only possible after the establishment of the sciences of memory. In other words, a range of possibilities that only exist because of the establishment of a depth knowledge in the latter half of the 19th century, which allowed questions hitherto linked to the soul to be shifted into the scientific field, producing countless effects. Disorders are thus some possible effects, or better put, possibilities of something produced from the establishment of a knowledge structure.

The big question that arises is in relation to what is actually produced, what constitutes this effect. Hacking claims that this effect can be understood as 'making up people', that is, the creation of specific forms of subjectivity and ontological experiences. The installation of a truth (there are memory facts to be known) not only produces and delimits an epistemological field with specific parameters of truthfulness and falsehood—with particular objects that can then be studied, with validation practices, and possible paths of research development—but also responds to the popular political issues of the moment and, most importantly, enables new modes of subjective experience.

Returning to the question of knowledge production on psychic suffering, we see that, after Hacking, its problematisation leads to the necessity of a kind of ethical questioning. This is because his work allows us to affirm that how we construct knowledge changes the possibilities of experience for the subjects. Its effects must therefore be constantly questioned. Taking the case of biological psychiatry as an example, the possible establishment of a truth such as 'psychic suffering' should be addressed as the result of organic processes that would have an effect on the forms of subjectivation. More than that, if this truth also contains an ideal of normality, the effects could be even more intense.

On the other hand, we see that Hacking effectively presents a way to think about the question of the subject's implication in the production of knowledge. Subjectivity is modified by knowledge, especially by knowledge that attempts to stabilise subjectivity as an object. However, this does not answer the question completely since Hacking's proposition only presents a correlation between established knowledge and recognised symptoms without proposing a causal relationship. Something that leads us back to the question he himself asked, concerning "if there could be a general theory of making up people, or whether each example is so peculiar that it demands its own nongeneralisable story; and I want to know how this idea of "making up people" affects our very idea of what it is to be an individual" (Hacking, 2002a, p. 100). There are, in fact, two questions in this passage. The second is devoted to the retroactive effect of his own work, a pertinent question but one with which we will not deal. The first, on the other hand, points to the possibility of extracting a causal element. After all, what makes this happen? Perhaps psychoanalysis can provide elements for moving forward on this question. To get into this topic, however, we should make a few remarks about the reading that Hacking makes of Freud.

Memory, truth, and psychoanalysis

We briefly pointed out that the philosopher comments on the role of Freud and Janet in establishing the sciences of memory. However, he points out that there is a radical difference between the two physicians, which is delimited based on a connection between memory and truth. Although Janet had acknowledged the therapeutic nature of working with memories, he did not impute to them a status of truth. On the contrary, he reported that he often misled his patients—by asserting the occurrence of events that he knew had not happened—which did not preclude these assertions from having therapeutic effects. On the other hand, Freud would suffer from a "terrible

Will to Truth" (Hacking, 1995, p.195), insisting on the connection between remembrance and truth, especially for its therapeutic effects. Thus, he would force his patients to believe in facts connected to theoretical constructs that showed clear problems regarding their truthfulness. Hacking does not hide a certain disdain for this attitude from Freud, who, according to him, would have gone down in history for being the winner, relegating Janet to a certain oblivion:

> Freud was the exact opposite of Janet. His patients had to face up to the truth—as he saw it. We can have no doubt, in retrospect, that Freud very often deluded himself, thanks to his resolute dedication to theory. Half a century of Freud scholarship has taught that Freud got patients to believe things about themselves that were false, things that were often so bizarre that only the most devout theorizer could propose them in the first place. But there is no evidence that Freud systematically, as a method of therapy, got his patients to believe what he himself knew to be lies. Janet fooled his patients; Freud fooled himself. (Hacking, 1995, p. 196)

Here, however, there is a narrow consideration of Freud's work on the part of Hacking. It is well known, no doubt, that there are several criticisms about a certain conceptual imposition in Freudian interpretations, especially in their reproductions by post-Freudians. There is no shortage of examples, and it is worth recalling the centrality of this question in the work of Heinz Kohut (1979) or even in Jean Hyppolite's intervention in the first session of Lacan's seminar on "Freud's Papers on Technique" (Lacan, 1953-54/1991), where the idea of working through resistances as a possible form of domination is called into question. The Lacanian response is, at first, supported by the thesis that this would be something that concerns the post-Freudians more than Freud himself, pointing to a misguided crystallisation of certain concepts in that which would be named the 'analysis of resistances' (Lacan, 1953-54/1991). As we shall go into more detail below, Lacan's answer is further elaborated afterwards, in such a way that the question of resistance is revisited based on a conceptual reorganisation grounded on the separation between truth and knowledge. While it is not fitting for us to resume the Lacanian debate here, it is interesting to note only that which concerns Freud since it is mobilised directly by Hacking.

If we claim that the author makes a restricted reading of Freud's work at this point, this relates specifically to the fact that Freud problematised, on numerous occasions, the question of truth. It is notorious that this was a central issue for the psychoanalyst, appearing in various texts from the late 19th century to the late 1930s, but imputing to him a naive stance is problematic. Let us take, as an inescapable example of this type of problematisation, the text "Constructions in Analysis" (Freud, 1937), in which Freud begins precisely by alluding to the criticism he had received for his conceptualisation of resistance, which supposedly worked in an infallible way: heads, I win; tails, you lose. The question raised by Freud touches directly on the discussion mentioned by Hacking since it consists of the discussion about the relationship between truth and therapeutic efficacy.

According to Freud, there are three possibilities for the analysand to disagree with the construction proposed by the analyst: it can happen that (1) the analyst is, in fact, wrong, which will not imply any more serious problem, provided it is not something recurrent; (2) the content is too sensitive, so that the negative response would reveal a response of the unconscious to move away from the repressed material, in a more traditional understanding about resistance; and (3) due to the incompleteness of the construction, so that there is an acknowledgement of the accuracy of the enunciation, yet something is missing. Next, and linked to this third point, Freud points to a central issue and one that condenses the whole problem hitherto encountered in the psychoanalytic practice concerning the question of truth: some constructions are admittedly false—that do not fit the patient's background or do not produce any effect of mnemic confirmation—but produce therapeutic effects. Furthermore, Freud is quite clear in this text when he states that the success of a construction is recognisable by whether the analysand's unconscious responds to it. We will go into detail about that in the next chapter; for now, we only indicate that, far from being a naive approach to the question of truth, Freud grants it a privileged status, addressing it in an undeniably complex way.

This point indicates that there is far more nuance and indeterminacy than Hacking seems to acknowledge in this interplay between memory and truth, to which Freud will, in fact, provide more shades in a number of ways—for instance, through distinct forms of truth such as historical truth and material truth (Ambra & Paulon, 2018). More than that, the very adoption of a negative as an element that indicates the accuracy of an interpretation is an example of how the truth will be interpreted within a specific method of reasoning, not being able to be assessed only in stagnant propositions but rather in a process in which denial can have different values depending on its context. That is, a process in which truth can only be inferred from its effects, not requiring any kind of stability or conservation.

We devote special attention to this point not only because it is a misunderstanding on the part of Hacking. But especially because this misunderstanding is the expression of a possibility not seized by the philosopher. As we have been following, he presents a thought that creates tension in the knowledge produced and its ontological effects, which do not respond to the correctness of the ideas in circulation. It is something similar to what he recognises in Janet, opposing him to Freud. As we briefly indicated, this opposition is problematic since Freud will call truth into question mainly based on its effects, connecting it to expressions of the unconscious. If Hacking seems to get carried away by a problematic version embedded within conflicts internal to the psychoanalytic field, its limited approach to Freud's thought prevents something else.

Indeed, he does not give terms like truth or reality the problematising power that Freud grants them. He simply acknowledges that the truthfulness of the content does not interfere with the ontological effects produced, but that does not become an issue. In general, the philosopher adopts a more descriptive position, indicating the elements involved in this dynamic, but without formulating any causal hypothesis on it. This will be, in our view, an absence that limits his understanding of psychopathologies. This limitation is found in a hasty statement about a particular mode of connection between the biological substrate and the statement of a shift in the understanding of the reality of transient mental illnesses. We will look into this in detail below. Broadly speaking, however, we should not let this overshadow the bulk of the philosopher's work, which consists of a critical approach to the relationship between knowledge and experience. As we shall see, something that can also contribute to psychoanalytic understanding.

Chapter 3

A form of truth of its own

The fact that Freud dealt with questions such as truth and reality in complex ways, not backing down in the face of difficulties, is why the question of truth needs to be analysed with care within psychoanalysis. However, we will not limit ourselves to the discussions held by the Viennese psychoanalyst, even because, although he sustained uncomfortable questions without backing down, important progress was made by later authors. Such is the case of Lacan, who strove to draw consequences and advance certain points present in Freud's work, but which cannot be categorically considered as Freudian positionings. This is because, in some cases, Freud did not go beyond preliminary discussions; in others, he kept defending misguided positions, which were in tension with each other resulting in indecisiveness. At any rate, it is not a matter of trying to demonstrate Freud's (or Lacan's) truth but of using his arguments so we can advance the debate. We will therefore pursue a path that moves through Freud, Lacan, and other authors but is based on a conception that is stabilised by Lacanian thought.

We will initially present what could be considered a notion of truth in psychoanalytic thought, and in the next chapter, we will focus on the ontological motifs discussed in chapter 2. Broadly speaking, we will focus on arguing that truth is posited in a twofold sense in psychoanalysis: as a conceptual object and as a specific way of thinking truths-and-falsehoods and constructing objects. Using Hacking's words, it is about taking truth as knowledge and devising a style of reasoning proper to psychoanalysis from psychoanalysis itself.

3.1 The truth and nothing else

At various moments in his work, Lacan places truth as the central axis of psychoanalysis. This occurs based on a diagnosis of the relationship between truth and knowledge, whereby truth emerges as the denial of established knowledge: a clinical phenomenon which brings truth closer to the formations of the unconscious. However, this consideration extends beyond the clinical setting by proposing a historical diagnosis that deals with the conditions of possibility for the emergence of psychoanalysis itself. The hypothesis is that the modern scientific project would refuse to deal with categories such as truth and subject. First, we will present how this question of refusal can be recognised in discussions about the philosophy of science and then analyse how psychoanalysis deals with this question, which would consist in the crystallisation of a new type of object and new modalities of truth or falsehood.

The ideal science of psychoanalysis

The refusal by modern science of categories such as truth and subject is an idea that Lacan derived from Koyré's work, especially from his consideration that mathematisation, as a fundamental feature of modern science, would be a mode of making knowledge independent of subjectivity. This idea, which appears at certain moments in Lacan's work, is stated in "Science and Truth" (1966a/1998), along with an allusion to what could be considered a scientific ideal of Freud. A multifaceted ideal, which leads Paul-Laurent Assoun to call it "epistemological baroque" (Assoun, 1983), but an ideal nonetheless. And according to Lacan, something inseparable from the emergence of psychoanalysis. Lacan thus affirms that Freud was a contributor to the scientism of his time, influenced by authors such as the physiologist Emil Du Bois-Reymond and the physicist, physician, and mathematician Hermann von Helmholtz. The latter, one of the great figures of the scientific scene of that time, served as an ideal of scientism.

In her text "La vérité, toute la vérité, rien que la vérité" [The truth, the whole truth, nothing but the truth] (2007/2012), the physicist and epistemologist Françoise Balibar delves into a famous Lacanian statement that science would care nothing for truth as cause. She does so by using Helmholtz's work as a case study. This choice is not accidental: on the one hand, he is one of Freud's references, as we can see in Lacan's citation; on the other hand, she justifies her particular choice of Helmholtz—rather than other authors who also fit this position—by his closeness to topics that she masters, given that Helmholtz's field of study was physics, among others.

At the outset, the author makes a small clarification regarding the word used by Lacan to describe what the German physicist and physiologist meant to Freud: according to her, the term scientism indicated, still at the time of the publication of "Science and Truth" (1966a/2006), the idea that science would enable a special kind of relationship with truth; this clarification is important since, some years after the rationalist positions in philosophy of science received more direct criticism, this idea of a privileged position began to be frowned upon. The term 'scientism' began to be used in a derogatory way, as this presumed superiority over truth became the main target of the debates.

Balibar states that Helmholtz worked with the idea of integrating all fields of knowledge, which would lead, in turn, to the conception that a single formalisation method would be suitable for all disciplines. Also, this idea of integration implied that one discipline's concepts should be relatable to the others: "The main point is that Helmholtz 'discovered' an invariant quantity. If he discovered it, it was because he was looking for it; and if he was looking for it, it was because he was deeply convinced of the unity of nature and, therefore, of the ultimate unity of all fields of knowledge." (Balibar, 2007/2012, p. 90). In this scope, his great success would be, as part of a study on the variation of body heat in animals, not only to make important contributions to physics but to demonstrate that a physiological concept could have the same status as that of a physical concept. This does not mean elevating physics into a higher discipline, but that, like physics, physiology would be mathematisable. What occupies a privileged position is, therefore, mathematics:

> Scientific physiology thus finds its foundation: the principle of conservation of energy. As with physics, it is based on mathematical principles, which shows how Helmholtz's approach is not reductionist. It is not a matter of making the concepts of physics apply to the field of physiology and so reducing physiology to these concepts, and thus to physics. Helmholtz's ambition is quite different: to establish that physiology can have the same status as physics. Hence the epistemological thesis (later developed by Helmholtz in the 1870s) that finding a relationship that remains unchanged between varying quantities (what we call a 'law') is the supreme form of knowledge. (Balibar, 2007/2012, p. 92).

This very statement has a few subtleties that constitute an important point for us to consider. In fact, when Helmholtz speaks of an unaltered 'relationship', there is a differentiation there between 'relationship' and 'substance'. The German physiologist considered that 'this', which always remains unaltered, concerns a substance; however, it would not be possible to know substances, only the relations which are established between them. A 'law' would then be that which can be gathered from the invariance of a relationship between units that vary. In this way, all relations would be accessible to thought, and thus all would be understandable.

However, we must note that Helmholtz deals with the idea of understanding as something linked to representation, thought, or intuition, something in support of the statement that what is known are relations, not substances. Put another way, the physiologist seems to work with a perspective of the adequacy of the thing to the intellect so that truth ceases to be a question since it is veiled behind the modes of capturing truth (thought, intuition, perception). Commenting on a lecture entitled "Die Tatsachen in der Wahrnehmung", translated into English as "The facts of perception", Balibar says that "we can say, and I think it is no overstatement, that Wahrnehmung is the veneer under which Helmholtz hides the truth" (Balibar, 2007/2012, p. 96). More than that, Helmholtz claims that the science of nature separates what is of the order of definition from what is of the order of reality, of the pure state. In this way, that which appears on the 'other side' of scientific enunciations—that is, that to which the enunciations refer—is reality, not truth.

We have, therefore, the following scheme: the 'empire' of the real is understandable, but not because it is possible to know the truth of its substances; what is possible to be understood are laws that stem from what remains unaltered in the relationship between units, something that can only be accessed from the consideration of reality. Real and reality are not the same thing; however, the laws of reality are adequate to the real. This requires an additional step since the relationship between the laws of reality and the real only makes sense if these laws are stable or, even more so: absolute. Thus, Balibar points out, Helmholtz presents a notion of causality required for this 'collage' between the laws of reality and the real. If the physiologist delimits his knowledge by keeping the truth hidden behind the notion of reality, the notion of reality in itself bears something causal:

> But reality presents itself as *Wirklichkeit* (actual, actualised reality) and appears in the title of the conference as *Tatsachen*, where the word *Sache* cannot fail to resonate; yet Sache in German means, as it does in Latin, both thing and cause—so that the title of this conference finally appears as even more encrypted than it seemed: it exhibits cause and truth side by side, but not in their pure form, as an alliance with other terms, and keeping them carefully at a distance from each other. (Balibar, 2007/2012, p. 98)

What is most surprising, Balibar points out, is not only the complex operation required to make truth conceal itself but also to distance itself from the cause; for Helmholtz continues to present a weakness in his epistemology with regard to the passage from reality to things, even if it is via the causal route: what would cause there to be, in fact, this correlation between the laws of reality that are mathematisable and the things themselves, whose substance and truth are circumvented in the process of knowledge construction? The scientist's answer is stealthy, not resolving the issue, merely stating something like 'trust and do it'.

That is, at this connecting point, what is proposed is a kind of act of faith whereby the question can be left open ('trust'). Furthermore, it also requires that the action is not hampered by this type of questioning ('do'). Such a proposition, so seemingly fragile, is only possible by veiling the question of truth, which, in dealing 'only' with reality, allows the powerlessness present in this act of faith, which gives consistency to the causal law, to go unnoticed. Or, even better, to be actively forgotten:

> In brief, and to put things in simplistic terms, the scientist (identified on this occasion as the one who does science) cannot say "I" in the exercise of his activity as a scientist because it is not this I that is truly speaking, but an Other of which he is the conduit thanks to mathematics, since he has voluntarily "forgotten" the existence of a division within himself and thus left out a whole part of his I: what Lacan designates as the suffering subject which, if I have understood it well, is that part of the subject of science that does not speak in science (but in analysis). Of this shift from the domain of truth to that of reality, we have just analysed at length an example that can be described as paradigmatic. All of Helmholtz's efforts in *Die Tatsachen in der Wahrnehmung* are aimed at constructing an object that is external to him, deliberately forgetting that part of the "I" about which he wants to know nothing – except to be able to remove it from our representations, like a gold digger who, sifting through the gold-bearing sands he has collected, throws away the sand to keep only the pure gold. (Balibar, 2007/2012, p .100)

Thus, the author claims that this avoidance of the question that connects thought and existence is precisely what allows this forgetting of the 'Self' required by the scientific procedure. This is because the produced knowledge can only be sustained by removing this type of question, which would cause great instability to the operations that allow the establishment of the correlation between symbolic laws and real substances that are impossible to be known.

In this sense, mathematics would emerge as a possibility for establishing these operations because it enables establishing this knowledge, respecting the invariance that science requires. If the real (or the substance) is invariable, mathematics will occupy a place of truth because it would enable the construction of effective systems (that touch the real) based on a language that allows the depuration of the researchers' individualities.

However, the author asks, is it possible to do science only in these terms? Her answer is decidedly negative: while mathematisation is an operation that can be present in science, it does not encompass the whole scientific procedure. After all, speaking in purely formal terms, according to Balibar, is the same as not speaking at all. Science only makes sense and is effective when part of it is conducted in vernacular language, not just in formal language, which indicates that this logical and consensual conception of truth is not enough to deal with scientific practice. And, having said that, truth must be approached from another place as well:

> In fact, these passages in ordinary language are not meant to translate what is written in symbolic terms (which is totally unnecessary since, in any case, symbolism is universally understood). They perform a staging role—in the sense that staging is something that succeeds or fails depending on whether the text spoken by the actor-characters addresses (or does not address) the spectator or, as we say, speaks to them (or does not speak to them). Without this 'I' (which is also part of the subject of science) that expresses itself through ordinary language, the subject of science reduced to the diluted 'I' of the principle of relativity speaks to no one. (Balibar, 2007/2012, p. 104).

Based on this presentation, it is possible to pose two questions about the consideration of truth in the production of knowledge: firstly, the question of truth as a guarantor of knowledge, which unfolds in how to sustain the validity of knowledge based on this critique; secondly, the question about the role and the effects that this process has on the subject.

Truth separate from knowledge

In relation to the first question, it is possible, based on Balibar, to find some points of similarity with Hacking's diagnosis of the problem inherent to applying theories of truth (in the sense intended by Kirkham) to the sciences since scientific practice does not seem to be well explained by a theory of truth as adequacy, or by a pragmatic theory, let alone by a semantic theory. We must remember that the philosopher states (Hacking, 2003) that the problem would be in the transition from theory to the world, wherein it does not seem possible to justify, epistemologically, how that which is formalised would actually work with empirical objects. Something quite compatible, therefore, with Balibar's statement about the need for logical statements to be embodied for science to happen. However, what is made of this diagnosis marks a difference concerning the second question.

As indicated in Chapter 1, Hacking will address this issue by claiming that there is no assured fitting but rather a series of practices that would bring some sort of delineation to this gap. This is what he indicates as stabilising techniques, which would be responsible for accommodating knowledge to the empirical problems found and to what is expected of knowledge production. And along with this, the understanding that the very stability of knowledge is self-referential: the result of the combination of several factors that includes everything from constraints imposed by objects to negotiations dictated by the social. It is, therefore, a solution that, by shifting the question from truth to truthfulness, replaces absolute knowledge with historicised knowledge, not guaranteed by any external element and open to some kind of negotiation. That would be the answer to the first question.

Regarding the second question, we saw in chapter 2 Hacking's extensive work on the retroactive effect of scientific practices and discourses on individuals. It is a 'positivised' way of addressing the issue, thinking about the direct influence that established discourses and practices have on defining symptomatic expression and modes of suffering. There is, therefore, the claim for ontological effects based on the establishment of practices and discourses, but this is dealt with through the relationship between the content of the discourses and the possibilities of experiences.

It is thus a matter of inseparability between the ontological effects of knowledge production, combining epistemology and ontology. The general way the subject is placed within the scientific enterprise yields ontological effects: as we shall see below, it concerns, for Lacan, the rejection of truth as a question. According to the psychoanalyst, this rejection would be linked to how fertile modern science is, to the extent that it would allow the transition to formal language and leave aside questions that might place the relevance of this language as a general model for understanding the world.

We must point out, however, that Hacking does not recognise mathematisation as an indispensable feature in the constitution of modern scientific thinking. This was indicated in the previous chapter when we discussed his differences in relation to Koyré's thought. Although Hacking shows great interest in mathematical thinking, he does not consider it necessary to produce scientific knowledge (Hacking, 1982; 2012). This connects with his sympathy for Crombie's work to the extent that there is disagreement over acknowledging a splitting that would mark the emergence of modern science. As we know, the philosopher rejects Koyré's 'rationalism', seeking more detailed explanations and descriptions of scientific thinking (Hacking, 2012).

However, we could mention a problem here: by not supporting this thesis that modern science emerged as something brought about by another mode of organisation of scientific thought, the idea of producing a new type of subjectivity would be called into question. Yet, as we saw in the previous chapter, Hacking's thought allows this kind of dissociation since ontological effects are not dependent on the correctness of the prevailing knowledges. Even if the author disagrees with a rationalist categorisation (in his words) of modern science—which means that he does not fully accept the thesis that the privilege of reason over experiment would have inaugurated and been an indispensable characteristic of modern science—this does not mean that this idea could not have been applied, or that it was not the basis of several scientific practices. Not agreeing with those premises does not mean that those premises were not used (in practices and discourses) and, most importantly, produced ontological effects.

It is possible to disagree with the role of *cogito* in relation to its function within scientific thinking and yet acknowledge the ontological effects of the enunciations produced in this process with which one disagrees. We must remember that Hacking (1995) disagrees with the explanations given about multiple personality, but he still acknowledges the ontological effects of these explanations that he deems wrong. That he rejects a rationalist explanation for science does not mean that he does not acknowledge the existence of a rationalist discourse, including its ontological effects. So there is no inconsistency in the critique of a rationalist approach to explaining modern science and the acknowledgement that this rationalist discourse has produced ontological effects—which reaffirms the relationship between epistemology and ontology, wherein the former produces effects in the latter. However, Hacking makes no effort to explain why this relationship would be established or whether it would respond to something broader. It is possible to acknowledge a relationship between discourses and practices and the production of ontological truths linked to experience, even considering that the effects do not depend on the correctness of the contents mobilised in the discourses. There is no attempt, however, to provide a causal explanation for this that the author acknowledges.

This is the main point of disagreement between Lacan and Hacking. For Lacan, the question of truth must be connected to causation, which has several effects on the debate. We claim this is the main difference, as several points of agreement exist. Concerning the first question, Lacanian criticism of logical positivism (Lacan, 1966a/2006) seems to be quite compatible with Hacking's position: it is not a matter of devaluing knowledge but of refusing an entity that guarantees its truth. However, it is precisely in the way of regarding the question of truth as displaced in relation to knowledge that psychoanalysis will make an innovative proposition when it claims that the fact that knowledge conceals truth produces effects since what is concealed never fails to erupt.

It is a specific way of dealing with the question of truth. A way that answers, in our view, to the specificities of the object and of its reciprocal rationality. Something that brings us back to the quarrel presented by Hacking about Freud and Janet, in which Freud seems to push his uneasiness with the question of truth to the limit.

We will elaborate on this in two moments: first, we will present how the question of truth is dealt with in Lacanian psychoanalysis. In this process, we will use Hacking's work on *styles of reasoning* not only to organise the specificity of psychoanalytic thinking and practice but also to demonstrate that this proposition entails the constitution of a style based on the acknowledgement of strong negativity. This negativity can sustain specific modes of defining objects, mutually with the constitution of methods of thinking that establish specific standards of truth or falsehood and also stabilising techniques. Thus, psychoanalysis establishes a style of reasoning, contemplating the three categories indicated by the Canadian philosopher.

3.2 Truth, psychoanalysis, sciences

If, as stated earlier, Lacan points out that truth would be a kind of centre of gravity of the practice (Lacan, [1951] 1966/2006), we must recognise that his considerations on this matter are spread over a number of years. Given this, we will use the text "Science and Truth" (Lacan, 1966a/1998) as a central reference. This choice is justified as it is a sensitive issue concerning how Lacan addresses not only truth and knowledge but also a precise enquiry about the place of psychoanalysis in relation to these two terms. According to Sidi Askofaré (2013), this is a turning point in Lacanian thought, for it reorganises its pretensions about the question of scientificity.

According to Askofaré (2013), Lacan would have proceeded with the Freudian project of placing psychoanalysis within a scientific worldview (Freud, 1933/2010), but with some adjustments: this effort would rely on the influence of several authors, among them Georges Politzer and the Hegelian philosophy presented by Alexandre Kojève (Simanke, 2002), in addition to a change in the perspective of scientificity marked by the influence of structural anthropology and linguistics.

Besides, Lacan resumed his more direct dialogue with science from 1964 onwards, after he departed from the International Psychoanalytical Association and his seminars were relocated. Askofaré understands that the loss of institutional stability and the expansion of the audience of his seminars brought about by the moving to the École Normale Supérieure—to include a large number of attendants from areas other than psychoanalysis—would be some of the reasons for this resumption[22]. However, this resumption would happen on its own terms. It was not a question of seeking shelter under the umbrella of sciences or even of seeking the scientificity of psychoanalysis at any cost. It was a time when the very ideal of scientificity was already being treated critically, which can be seen in his commentary on his 1964 seminar, when he states that "The question that is my radical project thus abides: the one that goes from: *Is psychoanalysis a science?* to *What is a science that includes psychoanalysis*?" (Lacan, 1965, p.8).

In "Science and Truth", the question of whether there is a science that includes psychoanalysis gets dramatic: if it is correct to say that Lacan is in dialogue with structuralism, he does so to mark a difference. This difference concerns the question of truth and its relationship with causation, so the psychoanalyst mobilises some previous developments about truth to support this differentiation.

This text— originally consisting of the first section of his seminar on *The Object of Psychoanalysis* (Lacan, 1965-66)—summarises earlier developments. It involves the consideration of six points related to the separation between truth and knowledge: the coincidence between the subject of psychoanalysis and the subject of science; the rejection of truth by modern science; the enunciative character of truth (truth speaks); the non-existence of metalanguage; truth as material cause in psychoanalysis and a formal one in science; and the subject's suturing in scientific communication. This brings us, again, to the necessity of choosing how to present these issues. Considering the scope of our work and, especially, the long path we have travelled so far through Hacking's work, we will favour only the necessary points for advancing the debate we propose[23].

In this way, we will have the first point on the perspective guiding our work: it concerns how history makes itself present in this text, indicated by the correlation between the subject of modern science and the subject of psychoanalysis. However, this point will only make sense after more general explanations of how truth is mobilised in psychoanalytic thinking and practice. The question of historicity will then be moved to the next chapter. Thus, before arriving at this guide, we will go through other elements, particularly the *separation between truth and knowledge* and the claim that *truth speaks*. These two ways of presenting the question of truth also work as a more general presentation of the status of truth in psychoanalysis, in its relation to psychoanalytic rationality and to the negativity inherent in its objects—which, as we stated earlier, can be presented as constituting a style of reasoning of its own.

Objects, truths, and falsehoods

Lacan does not hesitate in affirming that truth presents itself as a negation of knowledge. This general construction makes itself present in different, more specific ways in which truth is posed, from how the impaired relationship with truth can be understood as a pathogenic nucleus in Freud's work (Silva Junior, 2017) to the understanding that truth is revealed in the manifestations of the unconscious. According to Lacan, an inalienable characteristic of truth is, in this sense, that it speaks.

This is what he affirms in "The Freudian Thing", with its prosopopoeia of "I, truth, speak" (Lacan, [1955] 1966/2006, p. 340). This formula should not be taken as a primacy of speech over writing, as Porge (2007/2010) rightly points out, but in its enunciative specificity: the truth that speaks or writes. This does not prevent truth from being talked about, but it does indicate that truth would also acquire its own enunciation. Nor does this mean that it speaks the truth; on the contrary:

> I wander about in what you regard as least true by its very nature: in dreams, in the way the most far-fetched witticisms and the most grotesque nonsense* of jokes defy meaning, and in chance—not in its law, but rather in its contingency. And I never more surely proceed to change the face of the world than when I give it the profile of Cleopatra's nose. (Lacan, [1955] 1966/2006, p. 342)

In a context that, on the one hand, involves a strong humanism that was in vogue during the post-war period and, on the other, the beginnings of splitting from certain paths that had been established in the International Psychoanalytical Association (Safouan, 2014; 2017), the Lacanian statement of a 'truth that speaks' is situated at the forefront of his return to Freud, a project that positioned itself critically in the face of these two tendencies. He thus rejected certain passive stances which, whether they advocated a human universal or took too much account of theoretical developments within psychoanalysis itself, ended up heading towards a normative perspective. The reaffirmation of truth as something that has a voice of its own was, therefore, a rejection of this trend: by affirming that whatever may be constructed as a perspective of psychoanalytic cure must bear the indeterminacy that lies in the fact that the truth speaks by itself—it is not a matter of a knowledge that apprehends it[24].

We can also detect an influence of discussions that indicated the reifying power of psychoanalytic theory. Sándor Ferenczi (1930/1992; 1933/1992) often noted this when he expressed his concern that the established order canon might work as a defensive tool for analysts, reducing clinical listening to the sacrosanct facts established by the literature. A concern widely present in Freudian texts but which apparently did not prevent knowledge from assuming this role in clinical practice. By emphasising the connection between truth and the manifestations of the unconscious (dreams, slips, symptoms, etc.) from an eminently clinical position, Lacan creates tension with the established theory. After all, it is a matter of taking what the focal point of any analysis is—the truth—not as the sign of adequacy of an idea or representation but precisely as the thing that eludes what is called knowledge. Truth shows itself, therefore, as *inadequacy*: it is not recognised as an indication or affirmation of positivity but as the effect of a boundary of that which can be captured and stabilised within knowledge. That which creates tension and denies what was established, that which indicates an incompleteness that creates tension in the very idea of adequacy. It thus presents a negative power, always capable of reintroducing a dimension of alterity in what is taken for granted.

Which in turn leads us to the possibilities of recognising truth. In the introduction, we showed how Hegelian dialectics influenced the understanding of truth as one of the terms of a dialectical process, in which it appears precisely as the denial of knowledge. It is a notion that condenses, on the one hand, the traces of the unconscious in its refusal to be objectified; and, on the other, strategies of recognition that are centred on denial. But we must point out that this issue is indisputably clinical.

Resistance between truth and defence

In his seminar, *Freud's Papers on Technique* (Lacan, 1953-54/1991), Lacan dwells quite intently on the impossibility of stabilising truth. We alluded to this in the previous chapter, but we will revisit some points. This is a discussion about the Freudian concept of resistance. In the fourth session of the seminar, Jean Hyppolite asks Lacan about the possibility of understanding the concept of resistance as a power instrument within the clinical practice. This question has the effect of triggering a discussion that encompasses the question of truth in its relation to interpretation, negation, and resistance. It is a moment when Lacan revisits, in addition to the texts on technique, the text "Constructions in Analysis" (1937a) and *Negation* (1925). He even asks Hyppolite to give a presentation on the latter. The problem revolves around the trouble in establishing a criterion for considering the truth in speech, which involves its possibilities of denial.

We must remember that Freud (1914) states that resistance to treatment should not be understood only as an obstacle to be overcome but as something necessary which must be worked through. It is also worth remembering how difficult it is to translate this idea (*durcharbeiten*) since it implies an intention of crossing, which is well expressed, for example, in the English translation *work through*. The working-through would indicate, therefore, that something must be crossed so that it can be transformed, not simply avoided.

The concept of resistance is interesting because it indicates how truth can be found in distinct and apparently contradictory parts of the analytic process. It also indicates the difficulty of keeping a linear and unequivocal thought for explaining an analytic process. One can think, at first, of an opposition: there is an unavailable truth—the one that connects to the cause of symptoms—whose access is hindered by resistance because the latter is initially identified as an obstacle to treatment and to the suspension of the repression (Breuer & Freud, 1895). There is, however, something that also has to do with the truth in resistance, which is why working through resistance is an indispensable part of treatment. Let us remember that Freud uses this argument to differentiate psychoanalysis from suggestion, which would objectify[25] the analysand instead of working through resistance (but rather deviating from it), which is why it is clinically fragile. If we take, for example, the explanation about the traumatic character of an event as the effect of an experience with which the psychic apparatus was incapable of dealing (Freud, 1905), one can think that what makes it impossible to access this experience (resistance) carries the mark of this original incapacity. Something of the truth in the traumatic experience (its excessive character at that moment) is reactivated in the resistance. Besides, based on the need for resistance itself to be worked through, there is an indication that resistance is not completely separate from what it 'defends' the self from, which is compatible with the radial figure Freud uses to explain this mechanism: something that emanates from a nucleus and becomes more intense as it approaches the centre.

Nevertheless, in relation to resistance, Freud points out how insufficient is an interpretation in which the analyst indicates that (and to what) the analysand resists, arguing that it is a process in which the mere intellectual statement does not solve the problem. Instead, it requires an intensification of this mechanism for any transformation to take place:

> One must allow the patient time to become more conversant with this resistance with which he has now become acquainted, to work through it, to overcome it, by continuing, in defiance of it, the analytic work according to the fundamental rule of analysis. Only when the resistance is at its height can the analyst, working in common with his patient, discover the repressed instinctual impulses which are feeding the resistance; and it is this kind of experience which convinces the patient of the existence and power of such impulses. (Freud, 1914, p. 155)

Here we can already recognise a particular form of relationship between knowledge and truth: the simple enunciation of knowledge, even if it is correct, does not necessarily produce therapeutic effects. Instead, it produces unconscious effects, which may even manifest as denial (Freud, 1925). And at that point, the denial would be 'disqualified'; it would be taken as a confirming sign that something important was mobilised, so important that it would still be carrying some kind of censorship. We were referring to this when we talked about the truth contained in resistance. It can be seen from the outset that we have an object that operates according to the dynamics of veiling and that requires reciprocal parameters of truth or falsehood for this object that shows itself through negatives.

On the other hand, the question of resistance is often controversial, blamed for being used as a subterfuge in the face of any possibility of failure on the part of the analyst. Freud does not refrain from confronting this question, using it as a trigger to start the discussion in "Constructions in Analysis" (1937a). In this text, the relationship between resistance, negation, and truth reveals even more interesting features.

Freud begins his discussion with an allegation that the concept of resistance acts as a guarantee of the analyst's infallibility (heads, I win; tails, you lose). And this makes him dwell on what could drive an analysand to refuse the construction offered by the analyst. The first option would be that the analyst is, in fact, wrong. This would not be a serious matter, provided that the mistake was rectified and that it would not be a recurrent situation. In the second place, there is resistance per se: the denial would be an unconscious response mobilised by what the analyst has said. Third, there is a possibility of the construction being incomplete, where there would be partial acceptance, with reservations.

These three points clearly indicate that there are specific parameters of truth or falsehood at work in psychoanalytic practice. After all, a refusal could simply be 'correct' (indicating a mistake made by the analyst) or, conversely, be a sign of a successful intervention. And the possibility of differentiating them, according to Freud, is the acknowledgement of a manifestation of the unconscious, which would happen in the second case. The unconscious speaks and does so independently of any conscious conviction or intention of the analysand. This acquires the name 'truth'. Truth speaks in resistance, which does not mean it tells the truth. But it is the fact that it speaks that matters. And that is only one of the ways in which the unconscious can react. We have, therefore, a truth that is measured by its effects.

It is important to remember, though, that the very way in which the question of truth is mobilised is not always the same. There is, for example, the differentiation between kinds of truth in *Moses and Monotheism* (1939); on several occasions, there is a relationship between truth and desire; and there is also the indication of an incompleteness linked to the question of truth, which can be gleaned from texts such as "Analysis Terminable and Interminable" (1937b) and particularly in the aforementioned "Constructions in Analysis" (1937a). This brings us to the third point listed in the previous paragraph, which, along with the idea of an incomplete construction regarding historical truth, Freud refers to the possibility that constructions have therapeutic effects even if they do not bring back any recollection that what was constructed actually happened:

The path that starts from the analyst's construction ought to end in the patient's recollection; but it does not always lead so far. Quite often we do not succeed in bringing the patient to recollect what has been repressed. Instead of that, if the analysis is carried out correctly, we produce in him an assured conviction of the truth of the construction which achieves the same therapeutic result as a recaptured memory. The problem of what the circumstances are in which this occurs and of how it is possible that what appears to be an incomplete substitute should nevertheless produce a complete result—all of this is matter for a later enquiry. (Freud, 1937a, 266)

Here, we see a facet where the truth in the construction is linked to the transformative capacity of the enunciation, prescinding from a relationship of correspondence with historical truth. The effect of truth, in this sense, bears no direct relation to things themselves or to historical facts, something quite close to what Lacan will deal with under the formula "every truth has the structure of fiction" (Lacan, 1953b/1979). This movement is central to our argument for its assimilation by Lacan. It is not without reason that the French psychoanalyst deals with this text along with *Negation* (1925) for indicating that denial may be a form proper to the work on truth. It is one of the unconscious responses presented by Freud in "Constructions…", but it is of great importance to Lacanian thought because of its connection with dialectics.

Truth and negation: negativity as style

Negation (Freud, 1925) begins with a seemingly simple idea: in certain cases where negation is enunciated, repressed material comes through. The text presents the speech of a patient who says he dreamt of a woman and insists on denying that she is his mother. According to the author, it is clear that an active negation precedes the question with the aim of justifying something about what had just been said. According to Freud, this kind of construction, in reverse, often shows the truth. The idea is intellectually borne by consciousness only because its affection was negated so that repression is still operating, albeit partially. As the author says, "Negation is a way of taking cognizance of what is repressed; indeed it is already a lifting of the repression though not, of course, an acceptance of what is repressed" (Freud, 1925, p. 236).

This statement is based on the assumption that the intellectual functions of judgment are dependent on the functioning of drives (Silva Junior, 2007) since the judgment of existence (if the represented object exists in reality) can only be constituted from the expulsion of an object by the judgment of attribution (attributing qualities to the object; in this case, not wanting the object). In this way, objectivity and subjectivity would present a point of undifferentiation since reality tests only become possible through the denial of the presence of an object in the psychic apparatus, which enables, on the other hand, the dissociation between the denial of the expulsion of the object in the apparatus (it can exist as a representation) and the denial of its attribution (it exists, but I do not accept its meaning).

The central point which interests us is that the enunciation of truth continues to bear something which hinders its acceptance as the truth. At least, it is the reading suggested by Lacan in his commentary on the text:

> What does Freud tell us, in fact? He reveals to us a phenomenon that structures every revelation of truth in the [psychoanalytic] dialogue. There is the fundamental difficulty that the subject encounters in what he has to say; the most common is the one that Freud demonstrated in repression, namely, the sort of discordance between the signified and the signifier that is brought on by all censorship of social origin. The truth can always, in this case, be communicated between the lines. That is, he who wishes to make the truth known can always adopt the technique indicated by the fact that truth is identical to the symbols that reveal it; in other words, he can always arrive at his ends by deliberately introducing into a text discordances that cryptographically correspond to those imposed by the censorship (Lacan, [1953c]1966/2006, p. 310)

This statement, despite indicating only briefly where this difficulty in the enunciation of truth would come from (the discordance between signified and signifier as one of the possible cases), is interesting because it indicates the possible modes of enunciation. It is always an encrypted enunciation that bears the imposed discordances. In this sense, resistance could be seen not as an obstacle to treatment but rather as the possibility of its achievement. This is what Hyppolite ([1953]1966/2006) points to when he locates this movement within Hegelian dialectics. From where it is possible to infer that negation would, therefore, be a moment of truth.

In a commentary about the same text, Vladimir Safatle (2014), already assimilating advances proposed by Lacan regarding the impossibility of achievement without remnants of the subject, indicates that this negation can be understood with a double inscription: on the one hand, it indicates the relevance of the target object of negation, whose repression would have been, in Freud's words, partially lifted; on the other hand, it would bear a statement about the impossibility of adequacy of the object to desire. In this sense, the denial of negation would exhibit a performativity that is only partial, for something in it would persist beyond the interpretation of its specific content. In other words, if the analyst were to interpret it in the sense of indicating that, yes, it is the patient's mother in the dream, that would not solve the issue because the negation would not fully dissipate there—which is compatible with Freud's allusion, in "Constructions in Analysis" (1937a), to the rejection of a construction due to its incompleteness. The negation appears as an effect of truth, a confirmation of relevance that is only accessible by its effects, while at the same time indicating something that remains—a foundational element in the way Lacan works out the presence of denial between knowledge and truth. As Safatle comments:

> the object is merely an occasion to re-present something that is underneath it. It is an occasion for returning, by means of negation, to what has been 'expelled out of oneself.' Something, which is not the mother, returns under the image of the mother. Something that is not the desire for aggression against the analyst returns in the form of the desire for aggression against the analyst. By means of negation, the subject says two things. They say what the immediate object of their desire is; therefore, they affirm something. But they also say that this object appeared as something desirable to them only because they allowed something radically heterogeneous to find a way to manifest itself in their speech; therefore, they deny something. (Safatle, 2014, p. 49)

This persistent character of negation points to a strong trace of negativity present in the reciprocal relation between the object and the mode of reasoning about it. The actual objects are forms of the temporary stabilisation of 'something radically heterogeneous'. This indicates, however, that the very notion of truth in Lacan cannot be reduced to the simple inversion of a statement into its opposite. It is not a matter of stabilising as true that which is made positive through negation since what is accepted as true at a given moment would not remain so. Truth, in this way, involves this tension between the possibility of enunciation, on the one hand, and the impossibility of being enunciated, on the other. Object and rationality share a founding feature, which is negativity. Something close to what Safatle defines as "negative ontology" (Safatle, 2006, 2007), and which we present as constitutive of a style of reasoning. Negativity that proves to structure objects and modes of reasoning since it is not a matter of merely inverting them into oppositions but of something that remains as the potential negation of any form of positivization[26]. It is precisely in relation to this impossibility of stabilising negation in an opposite that Lacan weaves his commentary on the case of Ernst Kris, first in his seminar (1953-54/1991) and then in "The Direction of the Treatment and the Principles of Its Power" ([1958]1966/2006)[27].

Briefly reviewing: Kris (1951) reported on a patient whose symptom was a persistent assurance of being a plagiarist (stealing the ideas of others). He claims that the research he wished to publish had already been published in a treatise that allegedly contained the same basic idea. The analyst confronts him, claiming they were not the same ideas and interprets his narrative by connecting it to the story of the analysand's father and grandfather. After this, the patient reports that he often leaves his sessions and goes to a particular street, where he would look at menus containing his favourite dish: fresh brains. Kris understands his response as a confirmation of the success of his interpretation, taking it as a sublimation of his desire to devour. And that, from then on, the analysand could properly carry out his intellectual activity.

Lacan, in turn, makes a rather fierce criticism, indicating how there might be a process of adequacy to an ideal personified by the analyst, who would have instructed the patient to behave according to a socially accepted standard. Furthermore, he understands the eating of fresh brains as the failure of interpretation, consisting of an *acting out* which would indicate that something was not being heard. As Safatle states,

> That the 'no' of the patient, in saying, "I cannot publish, I am not someone who can publish his own ideas", is reversed by the analyst into a statement of the kind "you can publish, our ideas always come from others", this means a kind of blockage to a more accurate listening of that 'no'. It was not possible to listen to how such a negation was more brutal, as it called for the development of an experience with language in which the confusion of deeply oral relationships could come to the surface and find a form. […] This demonstrates how understanding what is trying to be produced in negation requires more than surface listening. (Safatle, 2014, p. 53)

Which does not mean that any negation can be taken in that sense. There are numerous forms of negation within Freudian thought, and they serve different purposes in his theorisation. The one at stake here would be that which "seems to implicate the analyst's position in the patient's speech or, if we like, of that negation made by a patient whose speech leaves itself open to the oppositions presupposed by the analyst's position" (Safatle, 2014, p.38)—something we have seen earlier on, in "Constructions in Analysis" (Freud,

1937a). This interests us because it indicates some additional aspects about the consideration of how to recognise the truth in clinical practice.

What poses this question is the impossibility of delimiting truth solely as an opposition to knowledge, indicated earlier by the insertion of a temporal character to this process in which the denial of knowledge by truth implies the establishment of something else, of a remnant. If, on the one hand, it is clear that truth is understood as a process, this can now be unfolded in two aspects: firstly, the truth effect of a speech can only be gauged from a point internal to this process, given that its value only exists in the relationship with other speeches and with the analyst (that is, in the transference); furthermore, this other point, in which truth indicates its impossibility of symbolisation, is also something that is marked within a process, which implies the repetition of the negation of something that had already been established as true, indicating the infinitude of this operation.

From these elements, we see that the question of truth exhibits particular traits in psychoanalysis. It is a notion that connects the negativity that is proper to the type of objects from which psychoanalysis is constituted to the rationality that makes it possible to deal with these objects in some way. Thus, it condenses the originality of the objects and the parameters of truth and falsehood introduced by psychoanalysis. Something that reinforces once again the consideration of psychoanalysis as a style of reasoning since it brings together supportive novelties of forms of truth and falsehood and of objects, agreeing with Hacking's (1982) definition. A style marked by the inexorable inadequacy between truths, objects, and knowledges.

From this exposition, it is possible to understand the specificity of truth as a manifestation of denial and the possibilities of dealing with it from a specific way of thinking about methods of reasoning and the delineation of the object. Moreover, it was also possible to indicate the absence of an external referential and a form of strong negativity. However, what has been presented so far will be best sustained from considering the function of language, as proposed by Lacan. This has appeared before under the form of the 'discordance between signified and signifier', and, along with what we have presented about Hegelian dialectics, it is central for sustaining truth as that which escapes knowledge[28].

Language

So let us look at how language is dealt with and its consequences regarding truth. Especially after 1953, language is no longer a resource but a structuring element; that is, what we conceptualise regarding language must always be included in the theoretical and clinical constructions of Lacanian psychoanalysis. In other words, psychoanalysis must, at all times, take into account that it itself is part of language and that this has consequences for what it can, or cannot, say about itself. And in this sense, the way we treat language is radical: it is not a function but a structure. This is precisely the formula of the 'unconscious structured as a language', which will be constructed in the course of those years.

In this way, structural linguistics should be viewed as a line of support for psychoanalysis, more specifically, a possible way of solidifying the very idea of the unconscious. Such an idea is presented in its clearest form in "The Function and Field of Speech and Language in Psychoanalysis" (Lacan, [1953a]1966/2006). As Jean-Claude Milner (1992/2010) points out, the interest resided, at the limit, in the possibility of affirming the materiality of the unconscious, a "corpuscular conception. What structural linguistics provides, from the work of Saussure and Jacobson, is the possibility of a material foundation based on distinctiveness. It may do away with explanations via neurons and quantum of energy, as Freud had done: [...] before Saussure it is the properties that ground the differences (and the similarities); after Saussure, it is the difference that grounds the properties, and there is no possible statute for similarity." (Milner, 1992/2010)

Structural linguistics thus provides the basis for imagining a 'non-physical corpuscle': "a negative, oppositional, and relative entity" (Milner, 1992/2010). This implies that Lacan not only succeeds in sorting out the theory of the unconscious from a whole but also attains, in linguistics, a mechanics "as strict in its order as physical mechanics" (Milner, 1992/2010). Saussure's theory distinguished syntagma from paradigm as forms of relationship. In the first, corpuscles oppose each other over a sequence of positions, whereas in the second, they mutually oppose and exclude each other in a specific position. Jakobson reportedly sorted this from metonymy and metaphor, linking syntagma to the former and paradigm to the latter.

Lacan can thus maintain that the unconscious is structured as a language, based on the realisation that language is "a set in which (i) metaphor and metonymy are possible as internal composition laws, and (ii) in which only metaphor and metonymy are possible" (Milner, 1992/2010). This, however, situates language as one of the particular forms of a more general notion of structure, something that would not be enough for psychoanalysis since the practice would also require some kind of regard for the particular. For, even if it made sense to conceive the unconscious as being structured as a language, it would still be necessary to explain the singularity of the unconscious formations and their productions in each case. This proves to be, according to Milner, the point where psychoanalysis distances itself from structural linguistics:

> We know the structuralists' solution: the general notion is defined as structure. Lacan never accepted this solution, which fails to emphasise totalities (in this sense, Lacan is certainly a staunch anti-structuralist); the name he suggested to designate the specific mode of existence of that which possesses the properties of language (without necessarily depending on language) emphasises not the totality, but the element: it is the signifier. (Milner, 1992/2010)

This distancing strikes at two points that are key to our discussion: the primacy of the signifier and the cause. Regarding the cause, there would be a problem in the conjugation of psychoanalysis and structuralism in terms of a lack of activity on the part of the elements that are part of a structure, so this aforementioned question of totality becomes a problem. This is not a problematic question for psychoanalysis alone, but rather a problem that structuralism seems to have to answer on top of that[29]. Specifically, with regard to psychoanalysis, this is an impossible separation effected by linguistics: "psychoanalysis passes through the exercise of speech; it is also known that linguistics rules out from its object the marks of subjective emergence, that is, that very set which, after Saussure, is summarised under the term speech" (Milner, 1992/2010). We will revisit this later when we deal head-on with the issue of causation. For now, though, we can say that, even though we must take note of this distancing from structuralist linguistics, the role of language remains key. This can even be seen in Lacan's proposition that psychoanalysis is a "science of language inhabited by the subject" (Lacan, 1955-1956/1997).

As for the primacy of the signifier, which was already alluded to earlier through the irreducible difference between signifier and signified, it must be treated in more detail. This is because it situates the understanding that language is structure (with its metaphorical and metonymic operations) while at the same time asserting the lack of meaning as the basis of the organisation of these operations. As much as it is possible to establish temporary meanings, none of them resists the unravelling of the thread since every positivity is always something to be denied. Hence taking the signifier in its radical sense, as Milner (1992/2010) points out: "that which has neither existence nor properties except through opposition, relation, and negation." Something conclusive in relation to what we have been constructing regarding truth: behind its negations of knowledge that can take on some kind of positivity, there always subsists an impossibility that does not allow negativity to lose its central character. In this sense, the inexistence of the truth of the truthful (Lacan, 1966a/2006) is a development linked to the fact that there is no transcendental criterion to set the truth of a signifier—something that refers, specifically, to what Lacan elaborates in relation to metalanguage.

Thus we see how the assimilation of structural linguistics—with the particularity shown by the primacy of the signifier—makes up, along with dialectics, an inescapable feature of what bears the name of 'truth' in Lacanian psychoanalysis. If the psychoanalytic practice suggests that it is impossible to objectify the subject or to make the unconscious conscious, linguistics will provide elements to materialise this negativity. Considering what has been expounded in the previous section on the ways of recognising the effects of the unconscious as 'speeches of truth' and the novelties that this fosters in terms of truth or falsehood, we can see from this work on linguistics a proposition of explanation that includes negativity in a way that is more specific to the object, to the unconscious. A feature that will undoubtedly be present in other concepts and notions that can be taken as objects of psychoanalytic thinking—such as drive, fantasy, transference, etc.

We should also note that it is by following this path towards the unavoidably negative character of the signifier, placed as a central element for thinking about the unconscious, that we shall sustain a critical approach to language: there is, on the one hand, the impossibility of a language being able to guarantee its own truth, and also the nonexistence of a language that tells the truth about another, from where we conclude that metalanguage is non-existent. The non-existence of a primordial meaning—which is why no language tells the truth about itself or about another—is also seen as where Lacan distances himself from Heidegger (Iannini, 2012); for, even if it is possible to recognise certain traces of unveiling in the way the psychoanalyst addresses the question of truth, this feature fades away as a purely negative perspective takes shape[30].

We can see, therefore, how negativity establishes particular modes of considering truths or falsehoods, as well as the type of object that will be delineated. On the one hand, we have seen how truth is seen as something disruptive, something understood within a dialectical process and something that would condense, on one pole, a temporary positivity and, on the other, a radical heterogeneity. On the other hand, we have seen how structuralism (and, more specifically, structural linguistics) provides elements for the substantialisation of this negativity based on its assimilation marked by the primacy of the signifier as something central and irreducible to meaning. So we have the two points Hacking initially presented for constituting a style of reasoning. There is, however, a third one, which concerns the stability of a style. Let us see how this can be thought of in relation to psychoanalysis.

Stabilisation and experimentation

Perhaps the most immediate problem psychoanalysis faces, on account of its objects' particularities and rationality, has to do with sustaining its stability. As we have indicated, stability comes from the congregation of elements of different orders; elements that, in this intertwining, become patterns of objectivity. In relation to psychoanalysis, we can concede that recognising its explanations of stability has been problematic, such that it has been systematically called into question. The questionings encompass productions which are very uneven in quality: at one extreme, there is no shortage of books and articles which accuse Freud of being a charlatan, such as Jacques Van Rillaer's newly released book (2019), which shows an immense capacity to sustain incoherent arguments; on the other hand, points such as the ones made by Adolf Grünbaum (1984), which at least present a more consistent theoretical work. Attacks on psychoanalysis are not recent (Freud, 1917a), and the question of objectivity has always been a preferred target.

This question is already present at the beginning of Freud's work. The clinical reports caused discomfort because of their form, apparently at odds with the scientistic demands of that time (Breuer & Freud, 1895). However, the success of psychoanalysis seems to have trumped this kind of questioning. The publication of cases, along with an intense theoretical production and the employment of psychoanalysis in the reflection on issues not originating in the practice, seems to have been enough, at least for some decades, for the establishment of psychoanalysis as an esteemed praxis.

However, the particularity of psychoanalysis in relation to its modes of producing and communicating knowledge, which seems to have become isolated as nearby fields moved towards more common standards of objectivity, continued to raise serious questions. The most relevant, it seems to us, is of the sort brought by Grünbaum (1984) about conceptual validation. This type of questioning is complex to solve, as it runs up against the challenge of disseminating the process of knowledge production. This derives from the encounter between clinical and research methods (Dunker, 2012), where theoretical research is always subordinate to clinical. And there seems to be no ethically viable way of rendering this method observable or even reproducible (Granger, 1993), thus imposing obstacles to making the process public.

This does not mean that there is no experimentation in psychoanalysis, quite the contrary. As a matter of fact, the way psychoanalysis understands truth as something that can disprove established knowledge at any moment suggests that the practice's supremacy must call theory into question at all times. As Rustin (2019) rightly points out, if we consider an experiment as a controlled environment that entails a certain degree of indeterminacy—so that new facts can erupt and pose problems for established knowledge—there is no reason to rule out the clinical practice as an adequate procedure. In fact, this description is even in line with Hacking's definition (1983) of the production of new facts and the disruptive importance of experimentation. The indeterminacy of the clinical space (Dunker, 2015; Franco, 2018) could be a strong argument for this.

In addition, it is possible to identify elements which deepen this understanding in the texts mobilised up to now. The idea gathered in "Constructions in Analysis" (Freud, 1937a), that it is from the unconscious responses that we can measure the success of an interpretation, introduces an environment that is necessarily experimental in the clinical practice itself. This is recognisable, for example, in the account of the "Rat Man" (Freud, 1909), in which it is possible to follow the psychoanalyst's different attempts at interpretation, which are always assessed based on the analysand's responses. Some years later, in what became known as the case of the "young homosexual" (Freud, 1920), Freud indicated the need to reconsider his theoretical understanding from the analysand's response. What puzzles the psychoanalyst is the fact that the young woman, faced with a very sophisticated construction, responds with indifference. If the psychoanalyst considered that affectively charged denials were signs that an interpretation or construction was appropriate, the lack of affective charge in an acceptance had the opposite effect. And this leads him to question the established theory itself, as Van Haute & Geyskens (2012) point out.

Two elements can be deduced from this consideration. First, that psychoanalytic practice performs an experimental function in the sense of being the space where entities can be mobilised with the aim of producing effects. The production of these effects is central and is guided by the ethical principles of clinical practice. Besides, it is from the produced effects that the theory can be constructed. On the other hand, the theory can also be called into question based on these effects (or the lack of them). We see, therefore, something quite akin to Hacking's considerations about the value of experimental intervention: it is from its effects that we can propose theories and affirm the existence of entities, just as it is from the indeterminacy of experimental activity that new elements can emerge and destabilise a theory.

In the case of psychoanalysis, such an operation is unique. This is because the recognition of the markers that make it possible to decide whether an effect exists and what it is worth depends on the analyst's clinical judgment. Such judgment—elaborated by Wilson Franco (2018) from the idea of phronesis—apart from taking place in a situation in which the analyst's experience and theoretical training are present in an almost immediate way, also demands a specific type of understanding of the reality of the experiment itself (or of the clinical setting).

It is well-known that reality is a field of interest for Freud, which is evident since he proposed the principles of pleasure and reality. The psychoanalyst's considerations about it involve other concepts, such as fantasy, delirium, and repression. But, keeping the focus in our discussion, it is possible to affirm that the point of reference from which the reality of the analytic setting is negotiated is the affective charge mobilised in the words and acts of the analysands. Something which is found in the discussion presented earlier about incomplete or even erroneous constructions being able to produce therapeutic effects: the central point of interest does not lie in the correspondence with the historical truth or with the reality outside the setting but in the effects produced by the speeches. And these effects are recognisable from the affective mobilisation that reveals itself in the responses. However, this recognition, as well as the meaning that can be attributed to these effects, depends on unique elements of each analysand's analysis since the meanings and the way they are experienced are formed in the subject's history. At this point, the analytic process comes close to another concept formulated by Hacking: dynamic nominalism.

Therefore, we can state that psychoanalytic practice as an experimental situation provides possibilities of theoretical construction along the lines of Hacking's dialectical realism, but which are only possible within its own style of reasoning. This style, marked by radical alterity (or negativity), demands the suspension of any attempts at unequivocal connections between speech and its contents so that they must be transposed into a functioning that corresponds to what is known as dynamic nominalism. This does not mean that stable knowledges will not be produced but that these knowledges must be considered within a framework that can also accommodate the flexibility required by nominalist dynamics.

However, this poses a question concerning the tension between truth and knowledge. It is possible to state that this tension is clear in the clinical situation when we take 'knowledge' as knowledges about the analysand themselves. In other words, the emerging unconscious truths destabilise the identifications and narratives we have about ourselves. And when what has emerged as truth is stabilised as new knowledge, it can be destabilised again. However, should we think of an analogous operation for the theory? The answer is yes, although not as quickly. Stabilised knowledge must be able to be criticised based on truths that emerge; that is something widely held in scientific thinking. However, considering the reifying potential that knowledge may exert in clinical practice, this question becomes dramatic since psychoanalytic ethics is guided by an ideal of alterity.

In other words, the main task is to prevent the clinical practice from working as an instrument for reproducing established values. This requires that the relationship with theoretical knowledge be taken in a specific way. It is not a matter of reducing the value of knowledge, but rather of having the possibility of tensioning this knowledge as much as possible so that it can be recognised where it is compromised with established ideals and be transformed. This can be found in several formalisation experiments conducted by Lacan, which aimed at including the impossibility of total knowledge within the very construction of knowledge. An interesting fact since a central feature of the importance of scientific knowledge is the need to be open to criticism and external interpellation. Lacan tries to accomplish this internally, coherently with the style of reasoning specific to psychoanalysis. This does not mean that formalisation experiments are the only way to produce this tension since the very contact with other kinds of experience can have similar effects. It is what we see, just to name one example among the many possible, in the considerations made by Paul B. Preciado (2019) about the replication of traditional values related to gender and sexuality in the psychoanalytic praxis. A critique that is accompanied by a long history of an indisposition on the part of some analysts, as indicated in Beer & Ambra (2022).

We see that the issue of possible external interpellation must be heeded. Historically, this has been addressed in the publication of clinical cases. It would be a way of exposing the experiment, and sustaining the theoretical propositions. If we take the cases published by Freud as an example, we see how they were used, in fact, as crisis presentation (in the Kuhnian sense) since the psychoanalyst usually presented elements that did not work and demanded improvements. In fact, we must add that the publication of cases is not a privilege of psychoanalysis, being a method accepted in several areas.

Something that was pointed out by John Forrester (1996) when he argued that psychoanalysis had a sufficient and particular scientific grounding, subsumed under a style of reasoning grounded in case-based thinking:

> So psychoanalytic discourse combines two unlikely features: it promises a new way of telling a life in the 20th century, a new form for the specific and unique facts that make that person's life their life; and at the same time, it attempts to render that way of telling a life public, of making it scientific. The bridge between these two aims is the case-history, along with the curious and distinctive narratives of transference and countertransference phenomena that increasingly came to dominate 'clinical writing', as it is called. (Forrester, 1996, p. 10)

As we see, Forrester's proposition is quite compatible with what Hacking advocates; there is a specific way of thinking about new objects, which are supportive of the possibility of thinking and talking about them. Besides, this form maintains itself; that is, some kind of self-stabilisation is involved in its existence. Our difference compared to Forrester is that the clinical case would be, in a Lacanian reading of psychoanalysis, subordinated to a particular kind of style rather than the style itself. The style would be marked by negativity; the cases would be a development of this. To give a rather trivial example, when we hear the expression "Freud can explain it", it is not an allusion to the case as rationality, but to a rationality that implies a type of object and explanation marked by the unconscious (generally related to sexuality). The case is part of this universe but not, as we see it, the central element. The determinant therein, as we assert, is negativity.

In any case, it is possible to recognise various stabilising techniques on the part of psychoanalysis. The practice itself would be the main one, but in addition to it are the cases, the theory, and their presence in culture, as well as the associations with other theories. The explanatory power that psychoanalysis exerts on social facts reinforces its applicability. Moreover, its clinical power, which has been increasingly marked as an interesting alternative to biologistic ways of understanding suffering, also accounts for part of the stability of its style of reasoning. As Hacking would say, something here is working.

The cases are nonetheless a controversial tool, which, on the one hand, help to establish the presence of psychoanalysis in the cultural landscape; on the other hand, they have a normative power if they are taken as models to be followed. However, we must bear in mind that there is a lengthy debate on this particular stabilising technique, which encompasses the discussion on whether the case's focus should be on the analyst or the analysand (Porge, 2007/2010), on the role of transference (as pointed out by Forrester), on possibilities of methodological stabilisation of case construction (Dunker & Ravanello, 2019), or even on the relevance of the publication itself (Porge, 2007/2010). More than that, the very fact that there is an ongoing debate about the best form of presentation and alternatives to deal with the problems encountered would already constitute, in itself, an example of stabilising technique, according to Hacking (1992a). This is because stabilisation also responds to the capacity to deal with eventual problems without the need for the style as a whole to be deconstructed. These debates have this twofold purpose: while proposing alternatives for the assimilation of problems found within rationality itself, they also contribute to the permanence of the style in culture, reinforcing its relevance.

Otherwise, psychoanalysis has not abandoned other modes of transmission, whether in the publication of mathemes (Badiou, 2013), or with topological figures (Nasio, 2011), or even betting on Lacan's style as a form of transmission of his 'clinicity' (Porge, 2007/2010). Something we indicated a few paragraphs back by the name of formalisation and transmission experiments. The question of style, which can even be directly linked to the question of truth (Iannini, 2012), finds resonance with Hacking's proposition of a lack of an external criterion that guarantees it: the choice of the term introduces, as the author himself points out (2002), the limitation of sustaining a way of doing science only on epistemological or ontological grounds. According to the philosopher, the act of borrowing a more comfortable term from the field of aesthetics implies that[31].

This appreciation helps to give coherence to Lacan's different experiments in transmission: it would be something broader that would serve as a shared starting point for propositions as diverse as topology, the matheme, the production of misconceptions, etc. If often the psychoanalyst's epistemological discussions are unusual and prove themselves refractory to the composition of a 'Lacanian epistemology' (or at least a normative epistemology), it is possible to affirm, nevertheless, that they share a common style of reasoning. All these efforts show gravitation around negativity. Something we can deduct from analyses of Lacan's writing style, as we see in Nobus (2019) and Vincent (2019): his writing would be intimately indebted to the tension between truth and knowledge, aiming at the production of disruptive effects as effects of the reading.

It is worth remembering that we are largely sticking to what would be a possible strand within the style of thinking. Lacanian psychoanalysis would thus be one possibility inside something broader (which itself would have crystallised). In this sense, the proposition of a particular style of reasoning might help to organise some debates. It allows, for example, to situate something that contemplates the existence of different paradigms (Andrade, 2016) while still maintaining a minimally common rationality. This may give some direction to the ever-recurring question about a break between Freud and Lacan: one can think of a paradigm shift or even the constitution of a new science, but one that retains certain common features that would have been radicalised by Lacan, evidencing the crystallisation of a style of reasoning that was often already found in Freud.

This encompasses the combination of different styles of reasoning within the same paradigm or the same specific science. This does not mean that there is necessarily a compatibility between styles but rather that there is no impossibility, in principle, of accumulation or coordination.

The specificity of this difference between styles and paradigms—or even of specific styles and sciences—is important because Hacking addresses the issue of stability, considering some subtle differences between these levels of classification. If a style is self-referential, this does not mean that a specific science should be: it is constituted within one (or more) style(s) and simply assumes or proposes stabilising techniques (of the specific science itself). These techniques are possibilities afforded by the style. Still, they are not necessarily self-referential since they do not respond only to the internal determinations of the specific science but also to the determinations constituted within the style, which transcends the science. On the other hand, the localisation (and success) of specific sciences within a style of reasoning leads to a reinforcement of the style's stability. That is, by not being self-referential, the specific sciences reinforce the stability of a style.

This implies that the possibility of combination with other styles can also be understood as a stabilising technique. A style does not begin to be defined by another (there is no external criterion), but the fact that it, even if autonomous, can be combined with the other prevailing styles leads to the reinforcement of its relevance.

Validation

That said, we can return to the question of validation. Even if a style is self-referential, the validation of its specific sciences is a stabilising technique. That is, it does not depend on the validation of all its possibilities, but there needs to be some kind of validity in the set of its particular expressions for it to be self-sustaining. And when it comes to psychoanalysis, the question of validation continued to be a question, at least for Grünbaum (1984), who seems to crystallise a growing discomfort with the difference regarding accepted standards of objectivity, specifically in relation to Freudian theory. Even though the critique of the circular nature of psychoanalytic thinking can be objected to (take the many examples of propositions of communication or transmission), its critique of the lack of an external point of validation seems to resonate with social expectations of what consistent knowledge is supposed to be. We must also note that these same expectations change so that what was hitherto accepted may cease to be, according to how society's expectations change in the course of history.

Grünbaum's critique specifically addresses conceptual validation, indicating that the absence of an extra-clinical point of support is a weakness. According to him, there would be no elements to support that the patient's symptoms were anything other than their response to the psychoanalyst's discourse, so the theorisation about these phenomena would be self-confirming. For the philosopher, extra-clinical support would be a way of sidestepping the potential circularity of a type of knowledge production in which experiments are not open to dissemination. This is because the account would already be a way of dealing with the fact by the one producing the knowledge. However, we should bear in mind that the critique is aimed at validation, not at the experiment itself. If it is possible to validate knowledge outside the clinical setting, then the fact that the experimentation (or data collection) is private would not present much of a problem.

Faced with this, the psychoanalyst Howard Shevrin took on the task of responding to Grünbaum's critique. After many years of experiments and correspondence between them[32], the psychoanalyst and his team published the study "Subliminal unconscious conflict alpha power inhibits supraliminal conscious symptom experience" (Shevrin et al., 2013), in which the concepts of unconscious conflict and repression were said to be validated outside the clinical setting. And indeed, the group successfully provided neuroscientific proof that words linked to unconscious conflicts caused specific inhibition responses to the experience of anxiety symptoms, but only when delivered subliminally. Grünbaum himself would have acknowledged it (Brakel, 2015; Bazan, 2017). According to the authors, this is the "first psychophysiological evidence for Freud's unconscious conflict theory of psychopathology" (Shevrin et al., 2013, p. 8).

Two aspects are of particular interest to us in this study. First, the fact that it is constructed in a way that is indissociable from the clinical experience.

This can be seen, as Winograd (2004) points out, as a possible mode of combining psychoanalysis and neuroscience that does not imply a submission of the former to the latter. Neurosciences do not work as a metalanguage of psychoanalysis, explaining phenomena more appropriately. They can simply recognise neurophysiological functioning that can be linked to psychoanalytic theory.

However, and this is the second aspect, this does not imply that the two moments of the study are equivalent. After all, the studied phenomena are only recognisable, in the second moment, based on the clinical moment. Without the interviews, it would not be possible to differentiate what would be linked to an unconscious conflict from what would not since what is possible to be recognised neuroscientifically (alpha wave responses) is far too plastic and broad. There are alpha wave responses in everyday activities such as driving or listening to music. They indicate an inhibitory process, but the possibility of associating this with a specific type of functioning linked to anxiety was only possible in the psychoanalytic practice. That is, if there is no overlap between the fields, there is, however, the fact that the phenomena in question are only recognisable and causally explainable from the perspective of psychoanalysis (in the context of this study).

Psychoanalysis has been doing clinical work based on the concepts of unconscious conflict and repression for over 100 years without needing the help of neuroscience. The neurosciences can help with some issues, just as psychoanalysis can help them (Johnston & Malabou, 2013; Ribeiro, 2019). In this specific case, the only benefit was the confirmation of a theory by other means, from the combination with other sciences and, therefore, with another style of reasoning. This can be considered a stabilising technique: it increases the relevance not only of Freudian psychoanalysis as a specific science but also of its style of reasoning.

We can see from the expounded developments that it is possible to consider psychoanalysis as a style of reasoning in the terms of Ian Hacking (1982). It presents novelties regarding types of objects and truth and falsehood parameters and constitutes diverse stabilising techniques. As we have seen so far, this style is structured around a strong negativity, in which truth can be situated as a term that, while providing a certain temporary substance to forms of enunciation, also gives evidence of the impossibility of total positivisation. In the coordination between the way of dealing with this conception of truth in practice and in theory, we see that despite them not sharing exactly the same elements, the transposition of the tension between truth and knowledge from practice to epistemology produces an effect of constant attention to the reifying potential of theories from their application in the clinical setting. This responds to an ethical dimension in psychoanalysis, which can bring to its epistemological positioning a wariness concerning the possibilities of ideological reproduction. It is thus a matter of negativity being central to the definition of a notion of truth that encompasses both epistemological parameters and the critical observation of its ontological effects. All this is guided by an ethical imperative based on alterity.

Chapter 4

A historical subject

In the previous chapter, we presented some basic features of the way truth is treated in psychoanalysis, coordinating the specificities found in its rationality and the type of object it addresses. We were able to sustain the consideration that psychoanalysis situates itself in a specific style of reasoning marked by negativity, creating novelties in relation to truth and falsehood and also new objects, as well as specific stabilising techniques. Now it is necessary to address how this style includes a historical diagnosis (science would dismiss truth as cause), which indicates the historicity of the possibilities of positive expression of that which pertains to negativity. It is thus a way of understanding categories such as symptoms, subjectivity, and suffering, which places them as expressions of a broader causality linked to how a certain type of question is recognised or denied when circulating in society.

4.1 Science and subject

We begin by indicating the compatibility between Ian Hacking's Historical Ontology proposition and Lacan's claim about the relationship between the subject of modern science—understood as the Cartesian subject—and the subject of psychoanalysis. Lacan deals thoroughly with this question between 1964 and 1968. During this time, one can single out the moment when he claims, in "Science and Truth" (1966a/2006), the existence of "a historically defined moment, the strict repeatability in experience of which perhaps remains to be determined: the moment Descartes inaugurates that goes by the name of *cogito*." (Lacan, 1966a/2006, p. 727). In this sphere, three aspects must be considered: 1) the relationship between the *cogito* and modern science; 2) the relationship between modern science and psychoanalysis; and 3) the relationship between the *cogito* and psychoanalysis.

The first aspect concerns Lacan's reading of Koyré, which leads him to state that what would bring Cartesian thought and modern science together would be "a rejection of all knowledge, but is nevertheless claimed to establish for the subject a certain anchoring in being; I sustain that this anchoring constitutes the definition of the subject of science." (Lacan, 1966a/2006, p. 727). It is important to remember that Koyré, in his studies on the history and philosophy of science, attached special importance to three characters: Galileo (Koyré, 1939/1966), Descartes (Koyré, 1962/1991), and Newton (Koyré, 1968/1985). From these studies, Koyré not only inaugurates a particular way of doing history of science, which would prove to be of special importance for authors such as Thomas Kuhn and Paul Feyerabend (Lacerda Abrahão, 2015) but also argues that the emergence of modern science would be correlated with an overall change in how the universe is understood. This would have an impact on various aspects of people's lives, as is evident in the title of one of his books: *From the Closed World to the Infinite Universe* (1957/1968).

It is worth remembering that the question of the emergence of modern science is anything but settled, being a matter of much—and probably endless—debate. What is most central in Koyré's work is his dispute with Crombie over whether or not there was a rupture from what was regarded as medieval science. According to several authors of whom Crombie appears as a representative, there would be no fundamental aspect to distinguish between modern and medieval science since both share similarities in their methodological and epistemological discussions. This scope should thus be understood as something arbitrary, building up a too rationalist picture of science. Koyré, opposing this idea, does not deny the similarities; on the contrary, he uses them in favour of his argument. According to him, it is a subtlety that would justify this scope, something that is apparently similar but which, at a closer look, would display radical differences. Such a difference can be found in the distinction between the terms *experience* and *experimentation*: "a predominance of reason over simple experience, the substitution of ideal models (mathematics) for an empirically known reality, the primacy of theory over facts." (Koyré, 1961/2011, p. 77).

Even the act of naming it a *simple* experience already indicates the neuralgic point of the author's thought, who understands that two modifications were responsible for the emergence of a new way of doing science. Firstly, the pre-existence of hypotheses (and theories) to experiments so that they are supposed to be built and guided based on expectations and previous conceptual work; along with this, the work of formalising reality via mathematisation or axiomatisation. These two aspects are interrelated since the status granted to mathematics as a language with the potential for explaining the world is important for justifying the precedence of conceptualisation over experimentation. This does not mean that the value of experiments is reduced, but rather that they should be considered on par with theorisation. It is to this interconnection between theory and experiment that Koyré refers by the term 'experimentation'. In relation to Galileo, and this is quite clear, the author states that "it was not experience, but experiment that had nourished [science's] growth and decided the struggle: the empiricism of the modern science is not experiential; it is experimental" (Koyré, 1961/2011, p. 302). It is this change that the author recognises as a distinctive feature in relation to those who advocate continuity with medieval science, the core of his disagreement with Crombie.

It is always worth stressing that this disagreement does not prevent these two authors from reaching common ground, especially in relation to a non-linear conception of science. Koyré's historiographical work, which often delves into issues considered to be lateral or even marginal, is quite competent in showing how the transformations of scientific thinking are not limited to a linear and predictable progress, not even cumulative. The very idea of scope, built into the proposition of the emergence of modern science as opposed to medieval science, is indicative of this view. And this concerns, to some extent, the importance that the author attaches to Descartes's work since it would have laid the foundations for a way of thinking that is firmly based on the study of modes of causality that do not depend on final explanations. These bases would be constituted from the construction of a method which would decisively influence the way of doing science.

This does not mean that Descartes's thought would be the cause of this innovation, but rather that it indicates a change in the possibilities of understanding the subject and its relationship with knowledge—simultaneous and supportive of the change that moves from the closed world to the infinite universe. This must be remembered even when it comes to the connection between the subject of science and that of psychoanalysis. As Biazin and Kessler state in the article "Psychoanalysis and Science: The Equation of the Subjects": "Rather, it is a question of analysing how a zone of compatibility between the subject of science and the Freudian subject is established, inasmuch as the appearance of the *cogito* comes from a broader scope, which is dependent on the constitution of an infinite universe" (Biazin & Kessler, 2017, p. 417). Besides the importance of this scope, as we shall see below, we must also stress that the relationship between the subject of science and the subject of psychoanalysis is not one based on equality, where the subject of psychoanalysis would be made possible out of what remains from the scientific process.

The focus of this construction is Descartes's hyperbolic doubt, which calls into question each and every established knowledge in order to check whether its bases of support are really necessary. Through this method, the primordial enunciation would be established, constituting the *cogito*: I think, therefore, I am. Even if there is some kind of misunderstanding about what is being thought, it is still possible to affirm the act of thinking, and hence the possibility of affirming existence. This is exactly the "rejection of all knowledge" indicated by Lacan (1966a/2006). It is not our intention here to delve too deeply into this theme, which has already been discussed by several authors[33], but only to identify some points of interest. Firstly, to indicate the aforementioned relationship between the *cogito*, the subject of modern science, and the subject of psychoanalysis. As indicated, Lacan's reading of Koyré can be grasped from the understanding that if the advent of modern science is owed to the mathematisation of the world, the *cogito* will provide the philosophical support for such understanding (Biazin & Kessler, 2017, p. 417).

However, the role of Descartes's work in Lacan's teachings is not restricted to a historical coincidence nor to a simple allusion. It transcends a purely epistemological question (Dunker, 2008), preventing the relationship between these two subjects (of psychoanalysis and of modern science) from being reduced to the way of thinking about the subject itself. As Dunker (2008) points out, it is not restricted to the constitution of a theory of the subject but also plays a part in defining the clinical method. Even the very term *method*, so dear to Descartes, is used by Freud in his definition of psychoanalysis as a method of treatment and a method of investigation (as well as a doctrine). Broadly speaking, psychoanalysis would share with the *cogito* a systematic process of challenging established knowledges that would call into question the relationship between thinking and being. However, as we shall see, they arrive at different ends. Our focus in this discussion will lie on the ontological effects (in Hacking's terms) that can be recognised as a result of this operation and the solution offered by Descartes.

We find at this stage a twofold convergence between Lacan and the thought of Ian Hacking. First, in the historical comprehension of the production of a specific subject—what the Canadian philosopher calls *historical ontology* (and which refers, in Lacan, to the acknowledgement that a new type of subject would emerge at a particular historical moment). Second, on the inseparability of epistemology and ontology, indicating that established forms of thinking modify the possibilities of the individuals' experience—given that Lacan recognises this new subject as the result of specific modes of production and social circulation of knowledge. Hacking organises this discussion from the categories of *depth knowledge* and *surface knowledge* (Hacking, 1995) so that the establishment of depth knowledge would define possibilities of subjectivation. It becomes evident how close it is to the idea that the emergence of modern science would be linked to a way of dealing with the truth, producing ontological effects.

However, these approximations do not come without points of difference. The first can be interpreted as a matter of time since Lacan refers to a 17th-century event, while Hacking refers to the latter half of the 19th century. The second difference concerns the specific nature of the change: Lacan refers to an effect caused by an overall modification, by a philosophical statement that indicates a shift in the way of understanding and experiencing life. Hacking indicates similar effects, albeit caused by an event more specific than the *cogito*: the expansion of scientific thinking to issues hitherto related to the soul and spirituality through the constitution of the sciences of memory. This is, in short, a difference in object. Lacan takes the emergence of modern science and the *cogito* as correlates of the production of a new kind of subjectivity. Hacking dwells upon a specific science—subordinate to the modification considered by Lacan—and the effects that its establishment would produce. A first answer, which would encompass these two questions, would be that the points indicated by Hacking are contained in Lacan's statements and provide a more detailed and accurate historical examination. In this way, the very emergence of the sciences of memory would be a possibility opened up by the modifications that happened hundreds of years earlier, which established specific ways of producing knowledge. The sciences of memory would be understood as one of the possibilities opened up by the emergence of modern science, in Koyré's terms.

However, the definition of depth knowledge would require some flexibility to account for this movement. There would be two operations involved in depth knowledge: the first, more general, and the second, more specific. The way Hacking deals with this category does not seem to pose any problem to this stratification, even though it is not possible to affirm—at least from his work—what would be the ontological effects caused by the modifications involved in what is presented as the emergence of modern science and the *cogito*, and which would not depend on the crystallisation of the sciences of memory.

In addition, this greater precision achieved through Hacking indicates that, beyond the general statements about the *cogito*, it is also important to consider the modes of circulation of the theories produced from then on. We can consider that Hacking's work provides examples of how the *cogito* can spread itself in society, assuming it makes itself present in scientific grounding. As the philosopher demonstrates, how theories are connected to issues of daily life, how they are incorporated by institutionalised discourses and treatments, how they are inserted into diagnostic debates, all this is essential for thinking to have an effect on modes of experience. This is obviously not a criticism of the way Lacan mobilises it, but it brings interesting elements, establishing a relationship of complementarity. This even explains the second point mentioned at the beginning of this section, about the *relationship between psychoanalysis and modern science*. To use Hacking's term, the *niche* wherein psychoanalysis first emerged was deeply marked by scientific discourse, something necessary for Freud's invention of psychoanalysis.

However, while these complementarities may be identified and some differences are also understood as supportive of and not contradictory to each other, one possible point of divergence between the directions taken by Hacking and by Lacan must be addressed. This is ultimately a difference in object since, while Hacking dwells on the retroactive effects of scientific discursivity on experience, Lacan focuses on how these discourses (or any discourse) fail to define and stabilise the subject as an object of knowledge. This is something the psychoanalyst alludes to when he states that science's man does not exist, only its subject does (Lacan, 1966a/2006). We should bear in mind, after all, that what Lacan claims to be the definitive feature of the subject, the splitting of the ego (*Spaltung*), is addressed in connection with the splitting between truth and knowledge. In addition, truth is understood as a cause, even causing neurotic suffering (Lacan, 1966a/2006). There we have an evolution that goes beyond what Hacking is dealing with because it calls causality into question. We will construct this idea carefully because it implies a way of dealing with the question that takes as a reference the truth as an expression of the unconscious. In other words, Lacan's interest lies in what remains, what is left over from this operation of knowing, and this is where his and Hacking's approaches differ.

Lacan and Descartes

The way the *cogito* is treated within Lacan's work is not uniform, changing over the course of his teachings. There are texts in which its difference with Cartesian thought (or those influenced by it) is more explicit (Lacan, [1945]1966/2006)[34], while at other times, the reference takes on a broader character that recognises Descartes as the founder of something that would be distinct from psychoanalysis (Lacan, [1949]1966/2006)[35]. However, the most permanent mode of recourse to Cartesian thought is not restricted to univocal agreement or rejection, indicating points of approximation and divergence. This is indicated, for example, by Biazin & Kessler (2017, p. 421), in asserting the compatibility between the subject of psychoanalysis and that of science: "both are devoid of qualities."

Here, we reiterate the importance of considering this relationship beyond an epistemological approximation, thus regarding it as a movement that encompasses not only the ontological effects resulting from it, but also a similarity in terms of method. As Dunker (2008) indicates, hyperbolic doubt can be recognised in certain aspects of the psychoanalytic practice to the extent that it comes close to a sceptical questioning since it continues the search for truth at the same time as it asserts that it is impossible to find it (Dunker, 1998, p.171).

Although we have already shown the main points of convergence, especially the process of rejecting knowledge that would lead to an emptied subject, there is a second step proposed by Descartes that Lacan would not endorse. This is because the *cogito* would also have the effect of establishing this 'anchoring of the self". This anchoring would imply a wager on this subject who has nothing else but his consciousness and, besides, would relegate what remains, what escapes consciousness, to a transcendental dimension. What separates Descartes's thought from what can be referred to as the psychoanalytic thought inherited from the *cogito* relates to the statute granted to the lack of a guaranteeing basis for the pair thought/existence. Speaking very succinctly, Descartes lacks something that guarantees the truth of knowledge, such that he would relegate to God the guarantee of the *cogito*. That is, in the end, the truth of knowledge would be guaranteed by God. In psychoanalysis, lack is the central aspect to be explored.

What Descartes indicated as being of the order of truth, and therefore God's purview, is what Freudian discovery is talking about. Thus the proposition that unconscious truth speaks through thinking "errors" has become more consistent. However, the consequences of this interpretation will be far-reaching since psychoanalysis would then create instability in what should be the cornerstone of the guarantee. More than that, as indicated previously, Lacanian theory would put the established knowledge in tension toward this impossibility of guarantee. By employing the mode of understanding that Hacking presents to talk about other moments, we can recognise that the establishment of a depth knowledge—which defines the possibilities of what may be constituted as surface knowledge—generates a residue, which will be the very material psychoanalysis deals with to constitute its practice and which will be mobilised in its theoretical constructs. Psychoanalysis would, therefore, diverge radically from guarantee, which does not mean, as stated above, a complete rupture with Cartesian thought but the refusal of what is claimed to be a point of stability. Thus, according to Dunker, Lacan would preserve the *cogito* but dismiss the guarantee: "All attributes of the *quaestio* that lead Descartes to the first evidence are conserved in the meaning that Lacan gives to the subject, including its occasional character, its division by doubt, its lack of contents, its immanence to the act, and its positional value related to enunciation." (Dunker, 2008, p. 184)

It is interesting to note that Lacan's work about the *cogito* seems to pinpoint something that can be identified not only as a mode of knowledge production and its ontological effects but also as the recognition of that which would be the cause of subjectivity and the kind of suffering that psychoanalysis would deal with as something refused. The very idea of truth as cause refers to this, to something that would be intrinsic to the establishment of language and that would be denied in this process of establishing a knowledge guaranteed by God. An idea that can be found in other authors, even if through different paths. For example, Cunha & Silveira (2017) point out how it is possible to identify a strong influence of Husserl[36] on Koyré's work.

This means not only that the German philosopher influenced how the French epistemologist thinks of the emergence of modern science but also that Husserl's diagnosis of the "crisis" of modernity is implicit in Lacan's thought. This crisis would arise as an effect of the mathematisation and objectification of Galilean science's expansion to other dimensions of life, where this kind of reasoning would not provide possibilities to produce meaning for a "pre-scientific consciousness". It would thus lie in something quite close to the inversion between theorisation and experience indicated by Koyré: "instead of geometry being applied *based on* the experience of empirical forms, it starts to be applied *a priori*" (Cunha & Silveira, 2017, p. 77). This would lead to this possibility of mathematisation of the world, which would result in the loss of a type of experience. Broadly speaking,

> according to Husserl's diagnosis, the 'crisis' of modern science has very little to do with science's efficacy, with its technical results but is rather connected with the loss of meaning that this science implies. It loses its meaning insofar as its results have no more to say about the everyday, the pre-scientific experience we have in the ‹world of life' and as it, so to speak, institutes a ‹new' subject. (Cunha & Silveira, 2017, p. 78)

In this sense, we can see an undeniable proximity with what part of Lacan's work on the *cogito* will be, as well as a compatibility with what has been presented, based on Hacking, about the effects of the expansion of the scientific field—under the model of the sciences of memory—in relation to the possible modes of experience. We stress, however, that what is indicated by Hacking as the establishment of possible modes of experience of the self is recognised by psychoanalytic practice—and, as we have just seen, also by Husserl—from modes of *loss* of experience (Dunker, 2015). This loss will be associated with how Freud and Lacan will deal with the question of truth.

We can say that the very separation between truth and knowledge would be a way of dealing with this diagnosis of the crisis of modernity, especially if combined with another pair of opposites at the centre of Lacan's thought: the tension between enunciated and enunciation. It is worth remembering that if the idea of dialectical opposition between knowledge and truth can be found in Lacan's thought from a very early stage, indicating a clear influence of the reading of Hegel proposed by Kojève, such an idea remains active in the French psychoanalyst's thought as a whole (Safatle, 2006). From this, it follows that, in his seminar on *Crucial Problems of Psychoanalysis* (Lacan, 1964-65), it is better linked to the understanding of the subject—this subject which is identified as being both the subject of psychoanalysis and that of modern science—as an effect of the *cogito*. Lacan (1966a/2006) dwells on the role of psychoanalytic knowledge in relation to other knowledges that are historically relevant, acknowledging that psychoanalysis was only able to constitute itself as a practice on the basis of what remains from the modern project, of what seems to be left aside for this process to gain traction, but which returns in the form of symptoms and suffering.

It is not possible, at least during this stage of Lacan's thought, to infer the existence of categories correlated to these in other historical moments. However, it is possible to deduce that different types of subjectivity would be produced from distinct modes of dealing with (or refracting from) the question of the cause associated with truth. According to Lacan, denying that the question of truth is a cause would be a shared trait of different types of knowledge (magic and religion, as well as science) and would be linked to what he calls neurotic suffering. However, his focus is on science. In this sense, the path taken by psychoanalysis can be understood as a response to what is often referred to as the crisis of modernity, a place that, besides acknowledging the role played in history by this enterprise, also acknowledges its peers, whether in philosophy or in clinical practice:

> The paradoxical *Freudian* experience, as we know, will clash with the symptom, the dream, the madness; it will confront the instinctual record of what constitutes it. But this does not stop us from noticing the existence of a very obvious parallel between, on the one hand, knowledge and truth in Lacan and, on the other, technique and knowledge in the Husserl of the *Krisis*, or rather, between knowledge and truth as a distinction that establishes the 'subject of modern science' through the opposition between the 'objectivism' of the mathematical science of nature and transcendental subjectivity, insofar as both cases seem to condemn a concealment of subjectivity which is revealed, from its inception, in a kind of constitutive crisis of which empirical psychology seems to be the most obvious symptom (Cunha & Silveira, 2017, p. 81).

This does not mean, of course, that these authors propose similar responses to the crisis of modernity. We can even restate how necessary it is to be careful in this approximation, which seems to indicate with greater certainty what both cases share in terms of the cause of this crisis, but this does not mean that the diagnosis is exactly the same, since they depart from distinct interpretations of several key elements. Nor does it interest us, at this moment, to delve too deeply into this discussion, as it would be an unnecessary diversion from our objective. The mobilisation of this interesting comment on Husserl's presence in Koyré's thought and of his approximation to what Lacan proposes is dear to us because it restates, based on an unusual reference in psychoanalytic thinking, the historicity of the subject. And this historicity establishes key principles on how to think about the question of truth.

The centrality of the recourse to the *cogito*, simultaneously with the refusal to establish something that guarantees existence, carries a particular interpretation, not only of the relationship between subject and metaphysics—in the sense of whether or not it is possible to claim the essence or meaning of existence—but especially of the role played by language in this equation. We can understand what is being discarded as follows: "The scheme is relatively simple: the subject guarantees knowledge and God guarantees the subject. If the *cogito* is the first evidence that constitutes the subject, the proof of the existence of God is the evidence that constitutes the Other as a guarantee of the subject's knowledge" (Dunker, 2008, p.184). This helps us to establish that we must invert the logic underlying the relationship between knowledge and existence: for Lacan, "he [Descartes] brought up a key problem—the implication of the subject in knowledge—but was unaware of its most immediate consequence, namely, that it is the structure of the Other that precedes and constitutes the subject, and not the contrary" (Dunker, 2008, p. 177).

This consideration is twofold: first, it bears the anteriority of language in relation to the subject. Language is understood as a system of differences, marked by the radical separation between signifier and signified, that is, by the denial of any kind of transcendental signification (Lacan, [1953a]1966/2006). A conception that gives autonomy to language in relation to signification since the subject is marked by it and uses language even before giving signification to this use. This is connected to the function of the signifier as cause: "The effect of language is to introduce the cause into the subject. Through this effect, he is not the cause of himself; he bears within himself the worm of the cause that splits him. For his cause is the signifier, without which there would be no subject in the real" (Lacan, [1964]1966/2006). The absence of an *a priori* meaning is a central element, as it paves the way that will be thoroughly explored in relation to the statute of a knowledge that can only be thought of based on a structural absence. This is because the primacy of the signifier, as separate from signification, indicates that the structure of the Other is the cause of the subject itself, but it is an Other emptied of its guaranteeing dimension[37].

In this vein, the recourse to Descartes gains intensity from the seminar on the *Crucial Problems for Psychoanalysis* (Lacan, 1964-65) and climaxes in a painstaking work on the statute of *The Psychoanalytic Act* (Lacan, 1967-68). Thus, Descartes's importance is reinforced not only in laying the foundations of psychoanalytic theory but also in its clinical praxis dimension (Dunker, 2008; Rabinovich, 2000). But it is not confined to recognising the ethical principle of the non-existence of a moral guarantee; it moves forward towards the consequences of this, both in clinical practice and in relation to the knowledge produced by psychoanalysis.

Non-guaranteed knowledge

But what can be said about the effects of this discussion in relation to knowledge production? We restate what was presented at the end of the previous chapter, that it is possible to state that the recognition of the non-existence of an instance that guarantees the truth of knowledge is not a novelty introduced by Lacan, nor is it a feature that destabilises the value of scientific knowledge. Even if we think that there is an effort to constitute modes of formalisation and transmission of knowledge that tries to bring this impossibility of totality or guarantee into the centre at all times. As we have seen, Hacking (1999; 2003) affirms the value of scientific praxis beyond any pretension to establish the ultimate truth. The attempts to constantly recapture these limits work in the sense of re-actualising an ethical principle committed to understanding the reifying effects of knowledge, but they do not take away the value of knowledge per se.

In this direction, we see endeavours such as the one made by Moustapha Safouan (2017), when he points out the compatibility of a nonnormative epistemology with highly relevant scientific productions. The psychoanalyst compares scientific advances, which, despite dealing with completely different interpretations of the truth-value of epistemology, made similarly accepted discoveries. For example, there would be a strong correspondence between theory and world in Einstein's thought, whereas Niels Bohr's ideas were based on a much less normative epistemological understanding.

We should bear in mind that the current crisis in the credibility of science does not seem to stem from its contingency, but it is instead an effect of an excess of authority that asserted itself by denying this very contingency (Beer, 2021). This indicates that the critique of excessive epistemological normativity should not necessarily lead to the denial of knowledges that have already been produced or will still be produced, but they must have a retroactive effect on how the very production of knowledge is organised. This involves considering that it should not be taken only as an epistemological endeavour but also from the perspective of its ontological and political effects.

Hence the reclaiming of truth as a central concept is justified, not only because it has the effect of opposing knowledge (at least in psychoanalytic thinking) but also because it implies a point of inseparability between epistemology and ontology so that the ethical debate becomes unavoidable when dealing with the production of knowledge. The way this problem structures Lacan's thought is why we understand that psychoanalysis has a specific style of reasoning, in which negativity is a gravitational centre, and not merely a remnant or deviation. This is something we maintain from what has been presented so far about how objects in psychoanalysis, specifically, can always be constituted by referring to a lack, as well as the possibilities of considering truth and falsehood.

This does not mean, however, that we have exhausted the questions concerning the specificity of psychoanalytic objects and rationality. Indeed, the work on the *cogito* shows some effects on this. What can be said is that these effects intensify the modification in how the object is thought, which does not deny or invalidate other knowledges, but rather indicates an unavoidable specificity when dealing with the questions psychoanalysis is concerned with. Something briefly mobilised by Lacan when he says that there is something about the object of science that has not yet been clarified (1966a/2006), which can be understood not as the production of a hitherto non-existent entity but through considering that there is a loss caused by the mode of knowledge production in modern science and that this very loss can be taken as the engine of knowledge production. It is, therefore, a statement that touches on the question of causality, considered from the perspective of negativity. We will delve more deeply into this aspect in the next chapter; for now, we will deal more generally with what concerns negativity as a structuring factor of both experience and knowledge, which continues to show points of approximation with what was previously presented about the *cogito* and the diagnosis of the crisis of modernity[38]:

> The subject, as divided by the disparity between enunciated and enunciation, occurs as the negative function of thinking: *I think where I am not, I am where I do not think*. This negative function is demonstrated by the extensive revision of the status of desire in its relation with language and appears in many different ways throughout Lacan's work. He refers, for example, to the negativity of the structural forms of defence (repression, foreclosure, refusal), the negativity of the modes of inscription of the subject in language (trace, letter, signifier), and the negativity of the subject's existential positions (alienation, separation). This does not reduce the unconscious to a figure of irrationality or to pre-reflexive affect, but it situates the problem of the relations between unconscious thinking and this point where the subject that thinks seems not to exist. That is, *the I do not think* is not a synonym for *there is no thinking in my being*, but that there is thinking that is not carried out by the *self* The ego (*moi*, myself, oneself) is the *place* where the subject thinks and where it deposits what is thought. The subject is a *position* that maintains negative

> relationship (*I do not think, I am not*) with its modes of objectification. The subject is a position which subverts the place from where it appears. (Dunker, 2008, p. 184)

If this must be repaired in relation to the subject, we must also be somewhat cautious in relation to the object. We will not go into details about the proposition of object *a*. However, we cannot evade making some general remarks. First of all, when we refer to the objects of psychoanalysis, it must be clarified that we are not referring only to object *a* but to several objects that are targeted by psychoanalytic theory and that carry, as we advocate, a trace of negativity. Among them are notions such as the unconscious, subject, desire, etc. Furthermore, it is important to remember that the proposition of an object is supportive of its rationality.

Thus, it should not be understood as a negative object inserted into a rationality that traditionally deals with positive objects, as if it were merely an object specificity inserted within an established discipline such as psychology or psychiatry. Or even its opposite, a positive object inserted within a rationality marked by negativity. We must not take object a as 'the' object of psychoanalysis, as if this would release the tensions with other fields. Something that can be deduced from the statement that it is not a matter of producing knowledge about the object *a* (Lacan, 1966a/2006)—a caveat that indicates both the peculiarity of not dealing with an object devoid of negativity and that which can be deduced from the very reciprocity between the construction of this object and the structure of psychoanalytic rationality. If the role of solving certain impasses of psychoanalytic thinking, which are usually directly linked to the question of negativity (Silveira, 2005; Garcia, 2015), can be assigned to the object a, this does not mean that the question will be settled by the production of a knowledge about the object, so its importance can be understood in the "possibility of guaranteeing an existential [...] dimension for the theory, a way of thinking of desire through the drive, the body, and the fantasy." (Silveira, 2005, p. 119).

The object *a* responds to a need for dealing with negativity from the perspective of an organiser, which does not unravel this negativity, but rather enables a conceptual coordination. It is, therefore, an operator that makes this loss present, being mobilised in various contexts and often with different meanings. It is worth noting that, even in its most popular definition, it performs a double role that indicates some kind of loss or lack: as the cause of desire and as surplus jouissance. In addition, it is also worth noting that the conceptual proposition of the object *a* comes well after the presence of negativity in psychoanalytic thinking, reasserting the idea that a style of reasoning is something that can be constituted gradually. More than just an object per se, it seems to us that the object is best understood as something that stabilises a general feature shared by possible objects within psychoanalytic thinking. A negativity to which, as we have tried to demonstrate, the question of truth is essential precisely because it can establish points of enunciation without losing its negative character.

As seen previously, the style of reasoning is responsible for determining the possibilities for the construction of its objects, as well as establishing the bases for defining the parameters of truthfulness and falsehood. In the case of psychoanalysis, because it is not merely a theory, we must also bear in mind that its clinical rationality is generally supportive of its style, which, as Iannini (2012) points out, manifests itself in several constitutive features of its thinking. This is compatible with Hacking's redefinition of his "styles of reasoning" as "styles of scientific thinking and doing" (Hacking, 2012) insofar as this expansion aims to account for the inseparability between thought and practices. Adding to the work of Dunker (2015), we may suppose that this style would encompass psychoanalytic etiology, diagnosis, and therapy. After all, negativity would not only be a causal explanation of the symptoms, but it would also affect the very definition of the symptoms, as would therapy, so we must pay attention to the fact that Lacanian psychoanalysis does not aim at an awareness of the unconscious but at the possibility of other ways of dealing with the lack. In this way, a good deal of the particularities of psychoanalytic thinking can be interpreted in this light of a rationality that is built upon the centrality of the notions of loss and lack, of misunderstanding, and the impossible. Upon negativities.

So far, it has been possible to state the compatibility between how psychoanalysis understands the historicity of the subject and the broader idea of historical ontology advocated by Hacking. It concerns the coordination between the idea that the discourses produced about individuals modify the possibilities of experience—as advocated by Hacking—and Lacan's recognition of the emergence of modern science as something related to the production of a specific modality of subjectivity. It is mainly a matter of agreeing that the discourses produced modify the possibilities of experience. This possibility of combination indicates the relevance of the concept of dynamic nominalism within the field of psychoanalysis, a fact that, even if it does not constitute a major conceptual novelty, indicates a well-established path of dialogue between psychoanalysis and the philosophy of science. Of course, the way this coordination is done is not straightforward since psychoanalysis seems to dwell precisely on what remains in Hacking's description. More than that, Hacking develops the question in a much more specific way: suffering is thought of based on the discourses that take individuals as their objects. In psychoanalysis, this dynamic is broader, as it responds not only to moments when individuals are taken as objects but to the effects produced by the subject's own position in relation to language. It is, therefore, a broader and more stable definition, which may even encompass Hacking's proposition.

4.2 Dynamic nominalism in another style of reasoning

Resorting to Hacking's concept of styles of reasoning can be quite productive in making explicit certain points of divergence between his dynamic nominalism and psychoanalytic thinking, particularly in relation to how mental health conditions and their symptoms, or, more broadly, psychological suffering, are understood.

More specifically, retrieving Hacking's concept performs an immediate role: it shows how insufficient dynamic nominalism is for thinking about psychoanalytic developments. Even if dynamic nominalism is suitable for addressing certain aspects that are highly relevant to psychoanalysis, this development is merely a sideline to psychoanalytic thinking, subordinated to a larger construction. Plasticity and the relationship between symptoms and culture are considered an unavoidable question for psychoanalysis, but they do not exhaust the problem expressed by this plasticity.

On the other hand, it seems to us that the lack of what Hacking defines as a "general theory of making up people" (Hacking, 2002) can be indicated as that which would make its presentation weak in causal terms. Something avoided by psychoanalysis. This is because the importance of the forms of expression of suffering and of symptoms is secondary insofar as psychoanalysis does not lose sight of something that would be more general and stable, not only in theoretical but also in clinical terms. For the same reason, clinical intervention cannot be reduced to the suppression of specific symptoms or to an idea of awareness of the unconscious, both because this approach overlooks the cause of suffering and because it fails to understand the most basic aspect of the unconscious, which is the impossibility of total knowledge. This impossibility is mobilised by the question of truth. In this way, the most general problem to which the symptoms would be subordinated (at least in their classical sense) is that which is connected to the dimension of loss.

This differentiation can be named, as does Dunker (2011; 2015), based on the distinction between discontent, suffering, and symptom. This is not a kind of a-historicity; after all, the very recognition of the importance of the emergence of modern science and the *cogito* points to the contextual character of this general dimension that refers to the mode of consideration of this loss; it is, however, a more stable characteristic than the name 'transient' entails—since it refers to symptoms that change over short periods. Besides, the emphasis given to this dimension of loss of experience not only leads to a change in the understanding of what is suffering and what is a symptom but also to a reorganisation of diagnosis and etiology. Revisiting Hacking's work at this point serves a twofold purpose: it indicates that the way the philosopher deals with issues related to psychic suffering is limited by its lack of depth in causal explanations, as well as how another way of thinking about these issues can expand this discussion in a consistent manner.

We must bear in mind the difference between how Hacking thinks about his dynamic nominalism and how this question is mobilised in psychoanalysis. Although they are compatible, Hacking always focuses on the positivised features of pathologies, that which is explicitly expressed through symptoms. What we find is the establishment of a relationship between the bases of possibility of what can be produced as knowledge (depth knowledge), the knowledges effectively produced (surface knowledge), and their ontological effects. Such effects are measured from the recognition of shared features between the two types of knowledge, the discourse (and practices), and the behaviour (and symptoms) of individuals.

The philosopher goes no further than that toward any reflection on what would be the cause of suffering. Perhaps the only moments in which he takes a stand are the ones when he reproduces a biological understanding widely spread in mainstream contemporary psychiatry. In most of his writings on dynamic nominalism and historical ontology, on transient mental illnesses and psychic suffering, he devotes himself almost exclusively to how the proposed categories interact with their objects—hence their characterisation as interactive kinds.

Nor is there any attempt to explain why these elements interact in this way, at least not any explicit effort. Why are certain illnesses transient? Why do symptoms assimilate cultural elements? Ultimately, what is missing is an etiological explanation that addresses the cause of suffering, not simply its modes of expression. This would not be a problem in the works of a philosopher of science; after all, his work focuses on discussing the interactivity or indifference of certain kinds and how these categories help with various discussions. However, as we have stated, this question becomes problematic when a certain biologistic etiology emerges, which even seems to contradict many of the author's own arguments.

As we saw in *Rewriting the Soul* (Hacking, 1995), knowledges that are scientifically fragile can produce modes of experience. Along with this, there is a constant effort to criticise a possible challenging of the *reality* of these illnesses, indicating that reality must always be understood as an agreement and that the historical nature of an experience does not make it any less real. Well, in this effort, something goes beyond mere description. Even if he does not go into detail about how this process would take place on an individual level, there is a general explanation that asserts the retroactive effect of language on experience. However, two elements indicate an inherent and previous hierarchisation that circumscribes the role of this retroactive effect, as it also modifies some of these considerations about reality. This produces a predetermination about the possibilities of explaining these workings and establishes a differentiation between kinds of pathologies. These two elements can be recognised in the claims that (1) there are diseases that are more real than others and (2) this reality is connected to a presumed indifference found in types of classification that include a biological substrate. Such an argument is explicit in *Mad Travellers* (1998) and *The Social Construction of What?* (1999) but can already be identified in earlier passages.

In these moments, the author seems to narrow the scope not only of his dynamic nominalism but also of his propositions about the historicity of ontology. Even if he maintains that interactional kinds connect to indifferent kinds—that is, the way one experiences a non-transient illness is still historical—there is a predefinition of the possibilities of experience that responds to the biological. In these cases, the historical nature of ontology would be diminished. What seems problematic to us is not the consideration that there are organic factors that limit the possibilities of experience but the way and the extent to which this limitation is treated. In this sense, Hacking seems to fall into two misconceptions: first, an overly broad consideration of how the biological substrate restricts the possibilities, downplaying the idea that the organic also responds to the symbolic. Second, there is a problem in considering non-transient illnesses as 'more real'. This point establishes an inevitable tension with the idea of historical ontology since it would rank modalities of experience, narrowing the space of negotiation that the author himself always points out.

The sense of symptoms and the analytic processes

The first issue to be addressed, starting from the idea that lack is structural in psychoanalytic thinking, has to do with understanding symptoms and suffering. We must remember that Freud asserted, on several occasions, the contextual nature of symptoms, which should be understood in terms of their relationship with each patient's personal history and their historical moment. This is what he states in 1917, in "The Sense of Symptoms" (Freud, 1917b). According to the psychoanalyst, there are the 'typical' symptoms, which are those that benefit from a certain stability: "they are approximately the same in all cases, individual distinctions disappear in them or at least shrink up to such an extent that it is difficult to bring them into connection with the patients' individual experience and to relate them to particular situations they have experienced" (Freud, 1917b, p. 270). On the other hand, there are the symptoms that have a specific relationship with the particular experiences of each patient, providing what the author calls a "*historical* interpretation" (Freud, 1917b, p. 271), retracing the history of each individual. According to him, however, there would be no radical difference between the two kinds of symptoms: "If the individual symptoms are so unmistakably dependent on the patient's experience, it remains possible that the typical symptoms may go back to an experience which is in itself typical—common to all human beings." (Freud, 1917b, p. 271)

It is important to note that Freud does not refrain from attaching great importance to typical symptoms on account of their stability by stating that these symptoms "seem to resist any easy historical derivation" (Freud, 1917b, p. 271). We see, however, that it is possible to assert that there is a twofold historicity in a symptom: if, on the one hand, it responds to the social and cultural context where it is inserted, borrowing elements from the symbolic circulation to express itself; on the other hand, there is a more specific historicity, which concerns the history of each individual. This is important since the more 'general' character of typical symptoms does not indicate a denial of their individuality. The fact that these instances are not mutually exclusive but rather coordinated points to the fact that an individual symptom is always expressed through the symbolic elements available, just as a typical symptom is always interwoven with each person's individual history. This interweaving between something more generally recognised and the historicity of individual life gains force precisely from the etiological understanding of the symptom, wherein the word *meaning* is not without consequences.

This kind of connection is found in Lacan's thought at various moments. If we can find, in "The Function and Field of Speech and Language in Psychoanalysis" (Lacan, 1953a/2006), the statement saying the analyst must find within their scope the subjectivity of their time, the mode of understanding symptoms within a symbolic system, in which terms are interrelated based on their differences, is found in various ways, as well illustrated in *The Neurotic's Individual Myth* (Lacan, 1953b/1979). However, that does not answer the question about the cause. The fact that symptoms are understood as inseparable from the culturally available signifiers does not show what the etiological model of understanding would be, nor which role they will play within a psychoanalytic process.

Let us go back to Freud. The psychoanalyst states that the "construction of a symptom is a substitute for something else that did not happen" (Freud, 1917c, p. 280). This brings greater clarity about the need to understand the symptom not as something that should be considered the main target of clinical thinking, but as the effect of a process whose cause should be investigated. In this way, the symbolic constitution of the symptom is made possible through grasping the available elements, but its insertion is made through a kind of intentionality, indicated by the word 'substitute'.

This even implies that the meaning of a word within a symptomatic construction does not necessarily correspond to its meaning in the social context. This is very clearly expounded, for example, in a presentation by Radmila Zygouris, in which a patient talked about a certain fear of being a paedophile in an absolutely particular sense (Zygouris, 2015). The individual nature of the symptom's meaning is always key since the symptom is not self-contained: "We have comprised two things as the 'sense' of a symptom: its 'whence' and its 'whither' or 'what for'—that is, the impressions and experiences from which it arose and the intentions which it serves" (Freud, 1917c, p. 284). If a symptom has its own 'whence' and 'whither', if it is caused by something specific and serves a purpose, then the symptom itself is something that speaks about something else, a displacement. Displacement that is linked to the repressed, to trauma, to that which is not directly bearable by the symbolic. And, as Freud stated in a subsequent lecture called "The Paths to the Formation of Symptoms" (Freud, 1917d/2014), the search for the cause does not fail to land on a point of meaninglessness, in which, like the concept of drive, the symptom is linked to an impossibility of symbolisation.

A few years later, in "Group Psychology and the Analysis of the Ego" (Freud, 1921), Freud presents the relationship between symptom and identification. It indicates not only the famous idea of contagion—in which adolescents identify with a colleague suffering because of a love letter—but also more specific aspects of identification with symptoms of both the object of desire (the daughter's cough matching the father's cough) and with symptoms of the object of rivalry (the daughter identifying with the mother's symptoms out of guilt). Thus, we see how the symptom's meaning cannot be inferred from its phenomenal expression, requiring an etiological approach that considers its inclusion in the discourse for it to be understood. In this way, as Lacan will insist, based on his assimilation of structural linguistics, the value of a symptom must be understood according to the logic of the signifier, in which there is no *a priori* value but rather a value embedded in a system of differences. A system of differences that orbits, in psychoanalysis, around ideas such as lack, repression, and truth:

> The reform of the subject that is inaugural in psychoanalysis must be related to the reform that occurs at the core of science, the latter involving a certain reprieve from ambiguous questions that one might call questions of truth.
>
> It is difficult not to see that, even before the advent of psychoanalysis, a dimension that might be called that of the symptom was introduced, which was articulated on the basis of the fact that it represents the return of truth as such into the gap of a certain knowledge.
>
> I am not referring to the classical problem of error, but rather to a concrete manifestation that must be appreciated "clinically," in which we find not a failure of representation but a truth of another reference than the one, whether representation or not, whose fine order it manages to disturb… (Lacan, 1966b/2006, p.194)

We see, in this sense, how Lacan identifies the symptom as a return of the truth. Thus, the symptom connects an element found in culture to something stemming from the splitting of the subject, something that speaks. It presents itself when knowledge is lacking. It is important to remember that although truth presents itself as a positive symptom, this does not exclude its negativity. As Dany Nobus states,

> Although the truth of a symptom, its emergence and disappearance, lies in the signifier, this truth has to be situated primarily on the level of the unconscious, that is to say within a discourse from which the conscious subject is barred. The absent subject of the unconscious does not prevent the unconscious from expressing itself. On the contrary, as Lacan had

> daringly demonstrated with a lengthy rhetorical figure, the truth (the fact that there is no subject in the unconscious) speaks vigorously and eloquently. (Nobus, 2002, p. 108-109)

Nobus defines truth as "the fact that there is no subject in the unconscious". A formula that mobilises the notion of subject as an organiser so that its absence would refer to the different elements that we have been naming based on the term 'negativity'. But, beyond that, the author is quite clear in his assertion that this truth speaks and, to this end, it uses the available words.

The causality of the symptom, when taken radically within the field of language and referred to an impossibility of signification, consolidates Milner's (1992/2010) statement about the possibility of abandoning a biological or physicalist materiality, which can be done through the incidence of the signifier. Removing the symptom from a rationality that understands it only as an effect of an unequivocal organic causality—albeit loaded with a certain plasticity in relation to its expressions—reinforces the centrality of the question of cause. This means that symptoms that are phenomenologically similar may carry very different meanings for each person; they may come from a variety of origins, destinations, and purposes. Thus, it is not a matter of trying to solve temporary problems faced by a rationality that would be merely finding it difficult to establish organic bases that satisfactorily explain the symptoms; it is rather a matter of recognising that this mode of thinking is unproductive in dealing with this type of object.

Although Freud proposes, on several occasions, the hypothesis of a direct relationship with organic processes, his etiology does not fail to suggest that these processes would not be indifferent but would also respond to the symbolic and the unconscious. This means that the very account of organic processes need not take them as indifferent kinds. Furthermore, this plasticity goes hand in hand with recognising a functioning that does not support stagnant or unequivocal relations of signification. That is to say, the very way the clinical process works is unique since similar moments can have absolutely different meanings depending on what they respond to. As Freud states in "Constructions in Analysis" (1937a), effects are what signals success. If it is possible to state that at times Freud wavers on the matter of organic causality, Lacan is crystal clear about this rupture, which should not be understood as the denial of organic processes, but as the disregard of any advantage that can be gained from biologically-based etiological explanations.

Lacan asserts this rupture in "Presentation on Psychical Causality" ([1946]1966/2006) and revisits it by putting it in a very central position in his seminar on *The Psychoses* (Lacan, 1955-56/1997), among other moments. This is because the way he made his return to Freudian concepts already displayed the central traits of the particular structure of Lacan's negativity-based thinking.

Symptom and truth

These considerations are supportive of the way of understanding the symptom as a manifestation of truth and have a direct impact on how the treatment is carried out. This is what we saw, for example, in the comments on Kris's case (Lacan, 1953-54/2006; [1958] 1966/2006). One of the objectives of the summarised path we have previously followed was to identify the way Lacan searches in Freud for elements to sustain a way of thinking which has, as its organising elements, critical and negative notions (among which are misunderstanding, the impossible, and the like). Among these elements, the notion of *truth* seems to stand out as an operator that moves while playing different roles: it is mobilised in epistemological as well as in clinical and ontological discussions, indicating points of reciprocity between these instances. In relation to symptoms, we have already indicated that they have a direct relationship with truth. This relationship was even a focus for the French psychoanalyst's criticism of the analytic community, especially in relation to how the psychoanalytic technique was used. As Lacan states, also in "Intervention on Transference" ([1951] 1966/2006),

> Whereas Freud assumed responsibility for showing us that there are illnesses that speak (unlike Hesiod, for whom the illnesses sent by Zeus come over men in silence) and for making us hear the truth of what they say, it seems that this truth inspires more fear in the practitioners who perpetuate this technique as its relation to a historical moment and an institutional crisis becomes clearer. (Lacan, [1951] 1966/2006, p. 177)

Thus, the connection between truth and the symptom can be understood in a twofold manner: as the momentary expression of a conflict that exists there in a positive way (the symptom bears the truth of something that is not working), but also as a thing that is pointing to something outside this positivity, indicating that beyond this momentary expression there is something that is not exhausted by the mobilised contents. The first form, linked to a specific content, is also referenced by Lacan as different 'developments of the truth' in an analytic process (which is not the same thing as the truth in the symptom); moments when, based on an interpretation, a dialectical turn inaugurates a discourse in which the truth opposes the previously established narrative (knowledge) (Lacan, [1951] 1966/2006). These developments of the truth, however, are interpreted, producing new dialectical inversions and new developments of the truth.

The inexhaustibility of this dialectics is supportive of this operation so that there could be no truth that is told in its entirety (Lacan, 1973/2001), and also that the positivity present in the 'telling' of a truth will become a knowledge and can be counterposed to a 'new' truth. It is a similar operation to that of denial in its connection with desire: a denial that points to the as yet conflictive character of intellectual representations that remain repressed in relation to affection but which also points, as noted by Safatle (2014), to the impossibility, contained in any representation, of being adequate to satisfaction.

In this way, the truth of the symptom would combine, on the one hand, the disruptive character of something that emerges as an expression of that which does not work and on the other, the impossibility of working without remnants or conflicts. The other end of this combination of the symptom, which points to something more permanent than occasional expressions (or transients, to use Hacking's term), calls for another notion; a notion in which conflicts are not reduced to their positive expressions and which does not believe that isolated resolutions exhaust the problems (which is why we can consider that therapies that work only with symptomatic remission are only producing displacements). Therefore, we need something more comprehensive and originative. As stated earlier, we must bear in mind that Freud says that symptoms have their origins and destinations, which are simultaneously individual and collective. Thus, beyond regarding the symptom as something that transcends the individual meaning, it is also possible to recognise that it connects with collective meanings since it is part of the symbolic universe determined by culture. Hence it is possible to say that this more comprehensive and originative instance concerning symptoms is not only relevant in individual terms but also recognisable as a general trait.

Discontent, suffering, and symptom as effects of negativity

In this respect, perhaps the most popular idea mobilised is that of discontent, introduced by Freud in his famous *Civilisation and Its Discontents* (1930). On this aspect, it is interesting to note that there is a movement of localising the production of a loss which bears some similarities to Lacan's recourse to the *cogito* as the founder of modern subjectivity. Discontent would thus be one of the possible effects of this loss. At the beginning of his text, Freud proposes hypotheses to understand the hostility towards civilisation, which would be one of the effects of this discontent. By suggesting a hypothesis, he reintroduces the idea of renunciation in an extremely trivial way:

> It was discovered that a person becomes neurotic because he cannot tolerate the amount of renunciation that society imposes on him in the service of its cultural ideals, and it was concluded that when these requirements are removed or greatly reduced, he could return to other opportunities for happiness. (Freud, 1930, p. 87)

We can see, therefore, that in Freud, not only is the idea of loss linked to that of civilisation, but it is possible to consider that there is an inevitable loss in the civilising process. A loss linked to renouncing the satisfaction of drives, which is inevitable for socialisation. The psychoanalytic practice focuses on this type of question. It is curious to note that Freud is not all that concerned with defining what exactly he calls discontent, even though he associates it with various terms such as unhappiness, dissatisfaction, indisposition, hostility, etc. The problem, he claims, is that it does not seem correct to affirm that it would be possible to extinguish this indisposition completely. This realisation is similar to other statements about the limits of analytic work, such as the impossibility of fully analysing a dream without there remaining its 'keystone', or even that an analytic therapy exhausts the contents to be analysed (Freud, 1937b). This indicates that, beyond an ontological assumption, discontent is linked to the clinical practice itself and its impossible professions.

What is of special interest is the fact that discontent itself, which already appears as a shapeless and somewhat undefined notion, cannot be regarded as a cause but is instead the effect of something that is part of the constitution of subjectivity in a civilised society. Therefore, there is an original idea of loss linked to something that civilisation seems incapable of supplying, which presents itself as an impossibility produced by this process.

We must bear in mind that Freud does not refrain from diagnosing impossibilities outside the clinical practice as well, following a line of thought that is largely compatible with the idea of a diagnosis of loss in modernity as a project that is unable to fulfil its aspirations of educating, governing, and psychoanalysing (Freud, 1933). The impossibility of fully accomplishing the civilising project appears, therefore, as a limit mark of the clinical practice, which, while it can be understood as its cause, also presents itself as something that can never be resolved—even though the idea of better dealing with it is not discarded. It is, in this sense, a negativity that, while it is a constraint on possible treatment, establishes a specific causality that refers back to the truth of this loss. As Dunker indicates, one way of understanding this diagnosis of modernity "consists of synchronising the singular experience of negativity and of non-identity (which mark the constitution of the subject) with universal experiences that describe the logical inception of the subject, groups, masses and civilisation" (Dunker, 2011, p. 123).

Lacan, in turn, revisits the Freudian impossible professions by adding a fourth impossibility, which deepens this relationship of loss of experience: the impossibility of desire (Lacan, 1969-70/2007). Nevertheless, we can state that the French psychoanalyst unravels the diagnosis of loss, intensifying it, and proposing several other possibilities never examined before. In this sense, the clinical rationality involved in those developments implies regarding symptom and suffering not as expressions of an isolated conflict but rather as elements that must be included in this rationality built around a negativity. Or, if we recall Lacan's words quoted a few paragraphs ago, which orbits around the *truth*.

It is not by chance that Dunker (2011) will propose the triad discontent, suffering, and symptom, starting from the assumption that these categories would share a homology, a common origin connected to the experience of loss. In this way, suffering would be a kind of expression of discontent, a kind that demands social recognition; it can also be associated with the symptom, but not necessarily, since there are symptoms that do not cause suffering to the subject (one should also consider that a symptom can cause suffering to others). In this sense, symptoms would be better defined as that which expresses, through symbolic elements, a more determinate mode of the dysfunctionality inherent in civilisation (Dunker, 2015, p. 34).

The main question that interests us at this point is how symptoms can be understood not as isolated, one-off conflicts but as effects or expressions of something of the order of the loss of experience as a trait of modern subjectivity. The symptom can thus be understood as the result of an operation that selects and defines part of the discontent, which, on the one hand, is far from exhausting it and, on the other hand, runs the risk of standardising it by choosing discursive stability. This kind of consideration already comes, however, from a kind of rationality that imputes to the symptom a circumscribed place of an effect of something larger, even though, as we have seen, the way how this circumscription is done produces effects on experience[39] itself.

The thesis that the symptom is a one-off sign of a functioning that refers to discontent as a wider and shapeless phenomenon is therefore reaffirmed: "It does not indicate anything transitory or chronic and treatable like a symptom, not even a moral deficit of circumstances like the suffering. *Unbehagen* is a condition, an ontological limit, a way of being in the world" (Dunker, 2015, p. 234). But the possibility of recognising it is found in the narratives that deal with suffering. Therefore, the way this notion of discontent is established, as something broad and reactive to attempts at reification, becomes assimilated in processes of social circulation, in which suffering proves to be one step towards the possibility of recognition. As the author puts it,

> We must bear in mind that the terms used by psychoanalysis to speak of the transition from unease to suffering designate, above all, local uses of language: the family romance of the neurotic, infantile sexual theories, the individual myth of the neurotic, and the tragic ethics of psychoanalysis. Romance, theory, myth or tragedy are formal categories, literary or discursive genres that show us how language's social work intersects in the determination of suffering. (Dunker, 2015, p. 25)

Beyond all the possibilities for discussion opened up by Dunker in this proposition, which bears the innovative characteristic of steering the notion of suffering towards something that should be tackled head-on by psychoanalytic thinking, here we are interested in how this construction shows similarities and divergences with Ian Hacking's thought.

As seen, Hacking is precise in indicating how discursivity (which has symptoms as objects) produces effects on the modes of experience of individuals—something compatible with the psychoanalytic understanding of what a symptom is. However, psychoanalysis goes a step further so that the symptom is understood not only as something that modifies the experience but also as something that responds to how one deals with loss, placed as a central element. Not surprisingly, the notion of *truth* assumes a direct relationship with this loss, pointing to both the disruption of the system upon the introduction (or reintroduction) of an element that disrupts its functioning—after all, the truth that opposes knowledge requires a symbolic reorganisation upon its emergence—and the inexhaustibility of this functioning. It thus indicates that the system can never be fully stabilised. This is when the (momentary) equivocation becomes impossible. This, as Dunker states, can be considered the truth of the symptom, 'its discontent' (Dunker, 2015, p. 190). After all, the symptom bears a dimension of loss in relation to its own function; it does not end in itself.

This idea can already be found in Freud, but it will take on more dramatic features when Lacan centralises it. In this way, if the structuring negativity could already be identified in Freudian theory (Safatle, 2007), it will become the engine of several experiments in theorisation, demonstration, and formalisation in Lacan (Badiou, 2013; Porge, 2007/2010), as pointed out in the previous chapter. But how this negativity colonises the questioning of knowledge production posits a distinction between Lacan and Freud that cannot be ignored. This happens because in the way of thinking about the practice, in the sense that it entails or produces ontological considerations about the subject—or even in attempts at surpassing this concept (subject) such as in notions of *parlêtre* (speaking-being) (Boni Junior, 2018)—the centrality of loss and negativity proves to be undeniable, permeating the French psychoanalyst's teaching at various moments.

Although we have not dealt with every single form that lack or loss can assume in Lacan's thought, what we have presented in both the previous chapter and this one is enough to reinforce the constitutive role played by this negativity in establishing a mode of thinking and in delimiting its objects. Something that can even be named as consequences of a *negative ontology* (Dunker, 2007; Safatle, 2006, 2007).

At this point, it is possible to return to the discussion with Hacking to consider the points where his theory and psychoanalytic thinking distance themselves from each other regarding psychic suffering. This distance, as we have tried to demonstrate, comes from the difference in the diagnostics in which they are inserted, which, in turn, are distinguished by the presence of negativity as a central feature in the style of reasoning upon which psychoanalysis is built.

It is worth remembering that diagnostics should not be confused with diagnosis in its traditional sense, of a pathology in a strict sense, but as a "reconstruction of a way of life ", understood as "to reestablish the links between work, language and desire by considering pathology—which is expressed in symptoms, unease and suffering—as a social pathology" (Dunker, 2015, p. 24). It is, therefore, a matter of localising what disturbs, not as a malfunctioning of one part of a system that should function smoothly, but by understanding contradictions and disruptions as effects of the very constitution of forms of living. This psychoanalytic diagnostic is then structured around negativity, which is inseparable from how the symptom is understood, associated with suffering and discontent.

In *Mad Travelers* (1998), Hacking presents some constitutive features of the relationship between niches and forms of suffering: (1) there is a trending diagnostic framework (hysteria or epilepsy) whose discussion intensifies the (2) visibility of the condition; there is a (3) dimension of relief in the subject's identification with the diagnosis; there is a (4) narrative that places the condition between moral poles (tourist and vagabond). Based on psychoanalysis, other elements may be considered: (5) suffering and symptoms bear something of the truth; (6) viewing interactive kinds as indifferent produces a specific retroactive effect of naturalisation (regarding depression as an indifferent kind changes the experience and treatment of depression); and (7) causality must be included in the understanding of interactivity in order to build a more rigorous understanding that prevents interactive kinds from being viewed as indifferent. Even though the latter three points have already been mentioned, they will be explored in greater depth in the next chapter.

By linking this passage with what has already been said about truth, one sees the central role that the term plays in the conceptual economy of psychoanalysis, serving as a kind of intermediate term between the impossible and the stable, appearing as equivocations and disruptions that inscribe this impossible. In this way, we can see how sophisticated is the construction made by psychoanalytic thinking for the establishment of a diagnostic that does not identify the symptom as an issue to be treated in itself but as a displacement of something that not only assumes different, less normative forms but also is understood as an expression of something which is, ultimately, untreatable.

This does not fail to include the historicity of suffering, symptoms, or even subjectivity. As we have seen, psychoanalysis works with historical diagnosis in a double sense. On the one hand, there is the historicity of local forms of expressing and recognising symptoms and suffering, marked by the symbolic elements made available by the prevailing culture. On the other, psychoanalysis focuses on what would be 'outside' these positivised expressions, indicating that the discourses and practices at work would necessarily entail a kind of loss. This consideration also encompasses a historicity since how this loss is dealt with is contextual. For Lacan, the emergence of the subject of science would inaugurate a specific way of dealing with loss, something contextual but somewhat stable. In addition, the possibility of a causal explanation for this operation would reside in considering this dimension of loss, of negativity. This is central for differentiating between ways of dealing with and thinking about psychic suffering, which consists in how, in Lacan's words, truth is treated as a cause.

Chapter 5

Problems and paths

If Ian Hacking claims that the expansion of scientific thinking into areas hitherto occupied by other modes of knowledge—such as mysticism or religion—changed the possibilities of experience for the individuals (the author identified this moment as the emergence of the sciences of memory), psychoanalysis goes one step further: apart from acknowledging the reciprocity between subjectivity and cultural context, it provides a more general diagnosis of how a mode of thinking—exemplified by the Cartesian *cogito*—would set up a broad modality of subjectivity, responsible for the repetition of a common feature of modern experience, to which Dunker (2015) gives the name of experience of loss.

In this sense, there would be a difference with what is considered depth knowledge. If for the Canadian philosopher, the modification that has opened up the possibilities on which he dwells is the acceptance that there are facts about memory yet to be known, the anchor point for psychoanalysis to think about the establishment of a mode of subjectivity is more comprehensive, something that encompasses the sciences of memory, but not exclusively.

This extra step taken by psychoanalysis does not exclude any of Hacking's proposals right from the outset. Both the idea of dynamic nominalism and historical ontology are broadly compatible with this diagnosis of modernity, especially if we consider that Hacking's more specific works would be detailed accounts of phenomena that are not immune to this diagnosis. It is even coherent to consider that psychoanalysis only came into being the way it did because of the expansion of scientific thinking into other areas, both modifying the possibilities for the emergence of new disciplines and influencing the modes of symptomatic expression, recognition of suffering, and consideration of discontent.

This allows both paths (traced by Lacanian psychoanalysis and Hacking's philosophy of science) to arrive at similar positions at various moments. Hacking's constant assertion of the risks of enquiring about the reality of the illness is exemplary in this regard. One of the focal points of *Rewriting the Soul: Multiple Personality and the Sciences of Memory* (1995) is the claim that, although the etiological explanations for the dissociative disorder were extremely feeble—in the sense that the pathology itself could be regarded as the effect of a process that is, first and foremost, discursive—this does not lessen people's suffering. That is, he maintains that suffering coming from pathologies that he considers to be the effects of cultural processes must be acknowledged. This is, to a large extent, his position on what he calls transient illnesses.

This means that the acknowledgement of suffering (or of experience, more generally) does not depend on theoretical correctness. The fact that feeble explanations produce modes of experience—that is, experiences produced from ideas that lack scientific foundation—does not mean that these experiences are false. There is, therefore, a disjunction of the truth in experience and the epistemological truth. And acknowledging suffering is of central importance, even if one does not agree with its etiological explanations or its treatment.

5.1 Non-transient illnesses and stability

However, it does not seem that this issue will be solved so quickly. For, even if suffering is acknowledged, the way Hacking discusses non-transient illnesses seems to leave some loose ends. He speaks, for example, of certain mental illnesses that show a stronger presence in different places and at different times, such as schizophrenia or mental retardation (Hacking, 1999, p.100), both of which he does not regard as transient. This means neither that their diagnoses and treatments are not historical nor that the classification does not exert a retroactive effect on those who are diagnosed, but it does mean that something in them would be more stable than in transient illnesses. In this vein, he also notes that the profiling of the symptoms linked to schizophrenia has changed, which does not prevent him, however, from identifying schizophrenia as a non-transient, more stable pathology.

As a matter of fact, stability is a central element in Hacking's thought. Stability is a measurement of a theory's relevance, its usefulness, and whether it will not become outdated. And in the discussion about the interactivity or indifference of kinds, stability is linked to indifference: an indifferent kind has less variation than a kind modified by its own classification. However, the question of indifference and stability becomes more complex when it comes to mental disorders.

Take the consideration of the supposedly higher stability of schizophrenia compared to neuroses (Hacking, 1998a). According to him, the difference would not lie in symptomatic variation but in that, even if the symptoms are different, schizophrenia can be identified in more places and times. Regarding changes in symptoms, the author states that the way hallucinations (and their contents) are described has changed and that even the role of hallucinations in diagnosis has shifted over time (Hacking, 1999). We can thus recognise a relationship between the effects of the illness and how the person copes with it. At a given moment, the author points out that schizophrenia was a trendy diagnosis, and it was not embarrassing to talk about auditory hallucinations. That has changed, and people have stopped talking about their hallucinations: "The schizophrenic, as a kind of person, is a moving target, and the classification is an interactive kind." (Hacking, 1999, p. 114).

However, the question of the disorder's higher stability—that is, the fact that it appears to be less transient than others—remains open. His answer is that this higher stability would come from the fact that these illnesses have a biological or neurological substrate—a fact that most scientists acknowledged, according to him—so that they could also be considered indifferent, natural kinds. This is something close to what has been said about depression. However, how would it be possible for an illness to be both an indifferent and an interactive kind?

We have already dealt with this issue to some extent earlier when we were concerned with explaining the very idea of interactive and indifferent kinds. The example we mobilised at that moment, childhood autism, is deemed by biological psychiatry, as is schizophrenia, to be an illness with a clear organic etiological substrate, albeit the progress relative to this idea does not seem to match the assurance displayed (Rose, 2018). What interests us here is a topical question: should the use of 'organic' be viewed as an argument for stability?

Hacking claims that the difference between interactive kinds and indifferent kinds is that interactive kinds are concerned with actors who can realise they are a kind—because they are treated or institutionalised that way, experiencing themselves that way. On the other hand, natural kinds are unaware of how they are classified and do not interact with the classification (Hacking, 1999). The classification of natural kinds, since they are indifferent, would be of greater value because of their higher stability.

However, we must recall that, even when considering the higher stability of natural and indifferent types, Hacking claims that mental illnesses can be both interactive and indifferent at the same time. He claims that by indicating categories that present a biological substrate, but they also determine possibilities of experience—as would be the case with autism, according to him. There would be an organic illness called 'autism', and it would be indifferent (it would not change because of the discourse produced about it); and there would be the subjective condition classified as autism, which would undergo modifications. Hence, he states, even, that biological illnesses can and should be treated psychologically since much of the suffering it causes concerns not only the indifferent part but how that indifferent part relates to the interacting part.

Objects, targets, and classifications

In the article "Hacking on the looping effects of psychiatric classifications: what is an interactive and indifferent kind?" (2007), Jonathan Y. Tsou argues that there seems to be a contradiction in defining kinds that would be both indifferent and interactive. Tsou argues that Hacking confuses interactive kinds with indifferent kinds by failing to differentiate between classifications and objects. His criticism falls precisely on Hacking's idea that illnesses such as autism, schizophrenia, and depression can be considered interactive and indifferent kinds. This comes from considering how interactivity would be linked to symptomatic plasticity and possible expressions of something that would be an 'originating' determinant. This originating determinant, in turn, would be notable for its stability, whereat Hacking argues that it should therefore be understood as the biological basis of these illnesses—which would not be modified by the classification produced about them. According to Tsou, the problem would lie in a confusion between kinds of scientific categories and kinds of objects of classification in nature: "As suggested above, what Hacking intends to identify with his notion of interactive and indifferent kinds is a certain type of object of classification in nature, rather than a certain type of scientific classification" (Tsou, 2007, p. 336).

According to Tsou, Hacking's equivocation lies in not differentiating object and classification: the biological object is a natural object, which would be indicative of the 'reality' of the disease (in Tsou's words). However, the classification produced from it would result in looping effects, which would make it possible for an indifferent natural object to be an interactive kind. Briefly put, Tsou argues that natural objects can be interactive kinds and that this would solve Hacking's ambivalence. It seems to us, however, that Tsou misreads Hacking's proposition since ambivalence (acknowledged by the author himself, it is worth emphasising) is connected to a problem that is more complex than the possibility of biological objects being interactive kinds or not. It is linked to the question of stability.

First of all, we must emphasise that Hacking's theory works upon a non-dissociation between object and classification: this does not mean that an object cannot produce effects, but that a 'kind' is a unit in which these two dimensions are indissociable, so that an interactive kind is one whose classification modifies the very object that is being classified, and therefore the classification itself. Hacking works not with the notion of object but of kind, for he understands that objects are indissociable from their classifications—which can be seen in his argument that the possibilities of apprehension of an object are reciprocal to the structuring of a style of reasoning, as we saw in Chapter 1. To take an object rather than a kind, in this sense, would be to assert an ontological realism that is inconsistent with Hacking's thought. Based on classification, an object can only be biological or non-biological, natural, indifferent, or interactive. Therefore, for Hacking, it is about classification and its effects on its targets and upon itself. The word 'target', as used by the author, indicates precisely this non-dissociation of language often forgotten when using the word 'object'.

More specifically, an interactive kind is that whose classification modifies the target of the classification itself rather than that which produces changes in other classifications' targets. Classifying a person as afflicted with Parkinson's may produce effects (e.g. causing depression), but this is not part of Hacking's idea of an interactive kind because the effect does not concern the classification itself: if it does not change the state of the disorder, then it does not concern the classification itself. It seems that when Hacking states that a disease can be both an interactive kind and an indifferent kind, he is talking about two different kinds (or two different targets) brought together under the same name and not under a contradictory effect of the same classification. The problem that seems to be linked to Tsou's equivocation, meanwhile, is quite interesting, as it touches on an aspect of Hacking's thought that deserves to be discussed.

As Tsou declares, "the most convincing arguments for the reality of certain conditions come from research on physiological or biochemical pathways associated with some psychiatric conditions" (Tsou, 2007, p. 336). This passage indicates an idea that can also be found in Hacking, although, as we have already pointed out, there seems to be a point of equivocation in Tsou's reading. For even if Tsou proposes a differentiation between objects and classifications that does not correspond to Hacking's, the idea of a privileged link between organic factors and the reality of illnesses can, indeed, be found in the work of the Canadian philosopher. This does not happen in the same way as in Tsou. Hacking presents an approach that is not only more careful but also much more complex: "But not only am I ambivalent, or worse, about social construction; I am also ambivalent about the use of rigid designation in connection with disease and disorder" (Hacking, 1999, p. 122).

Although he shows his ambivalence, the author still insists that biological arguments are given a certain degree of privilege. Broadly speaking, it seems to us that this is an error induced by an organicist ideal that considers biological indifference as a stable factor, leading to problematic discussions. On the one hand, we can say that the organic would be more stable because it is indifferent to language. This is not entirely true for Hacking, who nonetheless recognises the effects of behavioural therapies in organic markers—in the case of depression, for example. On the other hand, the relationship between the stability of certain illnesses and a presumably neurological or biological relationship leaves this pathway open, as if what is being argued is that the causality of the pathology, even if it can be subject to therapeutic modifications in relation to the suffering it causes, is indifferent. Hence the assertion that there would be two kinds at play: an interactive one (the effects of illness in terms of suffering and sociability) and the cause of the illness itself, biological, which would be indifferent.

The reality of illnesses

Hacking goes even one step further by addressing the question of the reality of the illnesses. Not only does he affirm the real character of transient illnesses, but he also frequently refers to Hilary Putnam to state that the very idea of reality must be taken as something that is the result of constant renegotiation (Hacking, 1999). Thus, Hacking claims that the question of reality is not all that important (for him), even though he always comes back to it because he is aware of its social significance.

Returning to the question about the reality of multiple personality in *Mad Travelers* (1998a), he says that people wonder about this in a way in which 'reality' is a term that is used to define the 'truth' about controversial issues about mental illness:

> People are not going to stop using the word real or its co-workers such as true in connection with controversial mental problems. Reasons for this range from finance to responsibility, from semantic theory to scientific metaphysics. Health insurance should pay only for real mental illnesses,

> right? Responsibility is the crux. We have a profoundly moral attitude to disease. If something is a real disease, you are not responsible for it or are responsible only insofar as you engaged in vice that brought on the disease. Sex, drink, and idleness are typical vices. But if you need costly hip-replacement surgery because you continued playing boyhood games such as basketball into middle age, you are not blamed or held responsible; this is because in our world continued youthful activity is a virtue. In the case of mental illness, responsibility may be diminished or removed altogether if the illness is a real one. And the names for real illnesses have objective, individuated referents; scientific metaphysics and popular science alike demand that the referent is biochemical, neurological, organic, something localized in the body that could in principle be isolated in the laboratory. (Hacking, 1998a, p. 11)

It is interesting to notice how Hacking delineates the moral question connected to illness and suffering. The question of accountability plays a central role in the debate in the sense that the recognition of an 'external' cause would solve the moral problems involved, absolving individuals of any potential charges. Thus, an ethical dimension should be considered since an indifferent cause would allow individuals to be held unaccountable. Furthermore, when it is taken as a non-interactive kind, this also minimises the debate about the course of treatment: after all, if it is something defined and indifferent, there is no possibility for the idea of cure to be morally oriented—it is only a matter of ensuring that what has already been defined works properly. In other words, the question about reality matters both when holding accountable those who suffer and those who treat. We will return to the ethical dimension later. For now, we shall consider that Hacking returns to the question of reality in two different ways. First, he wonders whether the hysterical fugue was real at the beginning of the twentieth century, to which he answers yes; he then claims that it is not real today. For this, he returns to the idea of reality as a negotiation, but always by affirming the reality of pathologies and the suffering caused by them:

> We have the feeling that there is some fixed, super thing about mental illness, a reality that divides the real illnesses from the fakes. I believe that our conceptions of real illnesses are of necessity being, as Putnam puts it, renegotiated at present. This is because of rapid changes in biological and chemical psychiatry… (Hacking, 1998a, p. 95)

According to the author, the advances in psychiatry would be enough to produce a modification in the conception of what would be real or true illnesses. These advances would be largely demonstrated in the therapeutic effects of biologically based treatments. At a certain point, this leads him to state that there are indeed illnesses that are more real than others: those that are physiologically based would be more real. Therein lies a hypothesis of a relationship between biological bases and reality—reality, at that moment, understood not only as something that demands constant renegotiation but also in a pragmatist way, inspired by Charles S. Peirce. The hypothesis is founded on the effects of treatments based on organicist studies and interventions. There would be, therefore, a renegotiation around the reality of mental illnesses in which organicist approaches would gain a certain advantage by delivering compelling results, which leads him to state that "What I hope is that schizophrenia will emerge as one (or several) bodily dysfunctions, neurological, biochemical, or whatever…" (Hacking, 1998a, p. 99).

Picking up on what the author states in his following book, *The social construction of what?* (Hacking, 1999), the main distinguishing feature between schizophrenia (or mental retardation) and other disorders is its recognition in different contexts. This means that 1) although some symptoms change, there is 2) something that remains stable. Thus, it is possible to speak about an indifferent kind whose target remains stable and an interactive kind whose targets (symptoms, behaviours, suffering) are modified. The recourse to organicism is an attempt to explain stability. In this sense, what is constructed is the idea of a presumed stability of biological explanations resulting from an indifference to language, which would bring them closer to reality. The real illnesses are those that persist, while the others will disappear: "My own expectations about the dissociative disorders are different in kind from those for schizophrenia. In the case of dissociation, I hope that history repeats itself, but once only. I hope it goes away, for keeps" (Hacking, 1998a, p. 99).

Later on (Hacking, 1999), there is a greater ambivalence, whose core is the consideration of biolooping. Even if it continues to maintain a certain privilege of organic and neurochemical explanations, it leaves the relationship between the organic question and the indifference of kinds up in the air. Taking behavioural treatments for depression as an example, he claims that it is possible to see a dimension of interactivity in something considered organic since the successful outcome of these treatments indicates that "a certain chemical condition of the brain, thought to be correlated with depression, is alleviated. We have a dynamics working at the level of classification and at the level of biolooping" (Hacking, 1999, p. 123).

That is, surprisingly, the penultimate paragraph of the chapter "Madness: Biological or Constructed?" Hacking presents this idea and makes no further progress, stating in the chapter's conclusion that "If we begin to move among cyborgs, or to become cyborgs, biolooping will become a common fact of everyday life. Classificatory looping will continue alongside it until, perhaps, the two become one in a world that no one can foresee" (Hacking, 1999, p. 124). After this chapter, the theme is never revisited. And even in *Historical Ontology* (2002/2009), the discussion does not go deeper in this direction, being restricted to comments similar to the ones presented already about schizophrenia and autism. The question of cyborgs had already been dealt with in an article entitled "Canguilhem amid the Cyborgs" (1998b), and it harks back to a relationship between body and language in which biolooping would constitute a much broader effect than what had been hitherto assumed.

We must bear in mind, however, that much of the work done in *Historical Ontology* (2002) bypasses reflections on the organic question, and the connection between reality and the presumed stability of the organic is not revisited. That is, it is neither further elaborated nor refuted, although he continues to work with the idea of biolooping in a rather undefined way. However, Hacking is quite clear in asserting the reality of the making up of people, the effects of dynamic nominalism, and the moving targets. This reinforces something pointed out earlier about recognising the importance of experiences that do not necessarily have an established causal and physiological explanation. On the other hand, the question remains the way it had been presented earlier and must therefore be revisited.

The main issue worth addressing is the relationship between organicism and stability. We emphasise that, whether in relation to childhood autism or schizophrenia, Hacking is placing bets on the possibility of explaining things with arguments that allow us to decide in favour of organic causality. And, when dealing with depression, he suggests an interactivity with organic processes, pointing to changes in the classification. He makes no indication of the magnitude of this consideration, so he may simply agree with the idea that, although causality is organic, suffering might be an interactive kind—which justifies the use of, for example, psychodynamic therapies. The word 'relieved' might indicate this limitation on the scope of the idea. In this sense, the relationship between organicism and stability would be maintained.

The question of the reality of mental illnesses being settled based on their biological substratum involves a renegotiation of what is considered real or true so that the agreement on what is real would be rebalanced from the pragmatic consideration of the therapeutic effects produced by lines of research in alignment with this. If he states, in *Rewriting the Soul* (1995), that the sciences of memory have established the truth that there are facts about memory yet to be discovered, it seems that biological psychiatry has established another, that causality must be sought exclusively within the organic: a truth with effects that are epistemological (it defines a way of knowing), ontological (it defines possibilities of experience), ethical (it modifies the accountability of individuals for their suffering) and political (it is part of a power struggle). A truth that needs to be problematised.

5.2 The problem of excessive interactivity

The idea that real (or at least more real) disorders would be those with greater stability—supposedly linked to physiological and neurochemical bases—seems to be changing in recent years. If this kind of thinking were the target of major investments by the pharmaceutical industry in the late 20th century and the first decade of the 21st, this would have changed in the last ten years, according to Nikolas Rose (2018).

According to Rose, this kind of thinking's momentum was mostly coming from pharmacological efficacy, not only through advances in antipsychotic drugs but especially through antidepressants. This efficacy guided much of the etiological explanations so that the causality of the disorders was thought of based on the fact that drugs worked. This organicist thinking gained momentum with the hopes that imaging scans would lead to a better understanding of disorders (Rose & Abi-Rached, 2014). However, something seems to have gone wrong with these two bets (pharmacological and imaging scans), which raises the question about the relevance of organicist rationality per se.

We laid out some related questions in the first chapter, which were revisited occasionally throughout the book. Now we can delve deeper into the question. To do so, let us start with a paradigmatic case.

Depression in Japan

In his book *Crazy Like Us: The Globalization of the American Psyche* (2010), Ethan Watters talks about a case that illustrates a troublesome relationship between problems of pharmacological efficacy, marketing departments, and the creation of markets. He says that, by the beginning of the 1990s, the Japanese market started to be seen as a priority target by certain pharmaceutical companies, which identified there a scenario of high growth potential. This was due both to the high purchasing power of the population and to the fact that, up until that time, depression was a virtually unknown condition in Japanese culture.

Based on interviews with experts on local expressions of depression and with pharmaceutical executives, the author explains in detail that the absence of depression was presented as a barrier in Japanese culture, which did not seem to be receptive to the introduction of a pathological condition of this kind. In view of this, the companies developed a marketing plan to boost their sales in that country.

There were two initial problems: the first was the absence of a condition akin to the disorder. The closest thing to depression was something extremely severe, something that might be described in Western psychiatry as some kind of dementia. A condition that resulted even in long-term hospitalisations. On the other hand, sadness and changes in volition were dealt with in a private context, being culturally inappropriate to share these feelings with others. In addition to these two issues, there was a high suicide rate, which, however, did not seem to be connected to depression-related disorders but rather to an extremely cohesive social organisation, bringing about intense effects of guilt and shame in the face of frustrations and inability to live up to expectations.

The official line from the drug companies, Watters notes, was that depression was underdiagnosed in Japan and that it was due to *scientific backwardness*. In an interview, one company CEO claimed that the cause of the problem would be 'junk science'. The picture that was being painted was that, even though Japanese culture was extremely advanced in several areas, psychiatry and neurology would turn out to be outdated, causing great harm to the population.

This touched on a second and perhaps more complex aspect of the issue: medicines. The Japanese government required that any new drug sold in the country undergo local testing to prove its efficacy. Something that was also understood by the pharmaceutical executives as a hindrance, a sign of Japanese psychiatry's backwardness. Not trusting the studies carried out in other places was not to understand the illness: something biological that similarly affected all individuals. If there were any variability, it would be related to forms of expression and whether or not the pathology itself was acknowledged, but the illness would exist regardless. However, there was one point that made this line of thinking more complicated: local trials by pharmaceutical companies failed to demonstrate positive clinical effects of the drugs: "Drugs such as Pfizer's Zoloft, which were widely prescribed in the United States, had at least one large-scale human trial failure in Japan in the 1990s" (Watters, 2010, p.224).

The way to overcome such a problem was quite creative. First, a number of specialists received invitations to discuss cultural expressions of depression. They were delivered as if they were invitations to speak at academic conferences, but later they turned out to be closed meetings open only to company representatives. According to the accounts, these representatives were highly qualified; however, they did not engage in any kind of discussion about what was being presented. They only took notes and asked questions to get the specialists to develop their ideas further. According to one of the specialists interviewed by Watters, the goal was clear: to think of a way to market depression as a viable product in Japan.

After this first moment, a massive indirect marketing campaign was launched—since direct marketing of pharmaceutical products was forbidden in Japan. Television programmes, celebrities, articles in newspapers and magazines all showed depression as a real problem that should be treated: nothing too serious, but that should be taken care of lest it becomes an uncontrollable disorder. At this point, it was also part of this campaign to channel the question of suicide to the framework of depression, being presented precisely as a possible terrible fate if something initially simple was not treated. In Japanese, the expression used was *kokoro no kaze*, which means something like 'a cold of the soul': a real illness that one need not be ashamed of but should be treated to avoid unnecessary complications. Something easily solved with one or two pills a day.

Apparently, the campaign was very successful. By 2002, after just two years of the launch of Paxil in the Japanese market, it had already made up a significant part of GlaxoSmithKline's $401 million international revenue (worldwide, excluding the US). In 2008, only six years later, in Japan alone, gains from the sale of this same medicine surpassed $1 billion. However, more significant than the enviable success of this campaign, reflected in the increased number of consumers, is that the rise was not only in consumption but also in efficacy, as measured in the tests. After all, if there had been no proof of efficacy, the very sale would not have been allowed. What happened was that, after the marketing campaign, new tests were carried out and produced different results from the previous ones, supporting the efficacy of the drugs. At the outset, this raises the question of whether an advertising campaign could modify the result of a drug's efficacy test.

If this case can be seen as a great achievement for marketing departments, it can also be understood as a prelude to a looming crisis in biological psychiatry.

After all, even if the situation was masterfully manipulated, it shows an incontrovertible instability between diagnosis, etiology, and therapy that is flagged in the difference between the discourse and the very procedure of the companies: that the diagnosis is the result of some kind of social agreement that permeates the acknowledgement of suffering and determines the symptomatic field, that is nothing new (Dunker, 2015, Silva Junior, 2016). Neither is the intimate relationship between diagnosis and therapy since the advances in treatment act as markers—albeit not the only ones—in delimiting a category. This can be said about etiology as well since both diagnostic and therapeutic categories are connected to hypotheses about causality. However, when therapeutic efficacy is called into question, a retroactive effect calls into question the etiology and even the diagnosis itself—especially in this case, where the therapy seemed to overpower the others. All this indicates, at the very least, a presence far greater than expected of contingency and possible social interactions within a field that is intended to be inscribed, as much as possible, on the side of the organic as synonymous with stable, exact.

The discourse that could be gathered about this issue revolves around that. The alleged backwardness of Japanese psychiatry and neurology was understood as the disregard of an illness with a clear neurochemical causality, that is, something that had been there all along but was overlooked. A more advanced science would prove that, and it did except for the detail that the medicines were not working before a process of symbolic intervention. We can see that this was not merely an awareness campaign but an attempt to promote the idea that this disorder could be treated with the available drugs. In this sense, the actions carried out by the drug companies were at odds with their discourse: while they claimed an organic causality, they acted on the culture to produce the expected results. The very possibility of modifying test results for the same drugs calls into question the explanation given about their efficacy. After all, what we have here is an efficacy absolutely permeated by non-organic issues.

Returning to the idea of the efficacy of pharmacological therapy as a sign of the relevance of knowledge based on neurochemical and physiological hypotheses, there are two pressing questions: firstly, what happens if this efficacy is not proven? Second, how to think about the fact that an advertising campaign has resulted in changes in efficacy, i.e. an effect of biolooping linked to what is pointed out as a cause in an indifferent kind?

The Japanese case is paradigmatic because it provides an alternate narrative to underdiagnosis: we must consider the possibility that some illnesses presented as organic—and therefore indifferent—are produced. Something anticipated in Hacking; however, in this case, it poses some problems in relation to his biological wager on mental illnesses. This implies a larger retroactive effect that modifies elements often presented as indifferent. This does not delegitimise the suffering of individuals but rather points to an entirely different direction in their treatment. After all, one possible interpretation is that the marketing campaign produced the suffering for which the industry would like to sell medicines.

The greater amplitude of the retroactive effect would thus indicate a much stronger ethical and political challenging of this type of discursivity, which includes two affirmations that encompass the question of truth: first, the affirmation of the organic cause as a 'truth', since it is something that cannot be called into question; coupled with this is a mode of knowledge production that is self-confirming in relation to this initial truth, but with the twist that those who control it know that things do not work the way they say they do. The circularity between 'good science' (as a guarantee of the truth of organic causality) and the test results (as a guarantee of the truth of good science) makes its failure clear in this case: it is known that, without an active mobilisation of symbolic and cultural elements, experiments do not produce the expected results. It is thus clear that truth as a question, and not as an argument of authority, needs to be reintroduced into the debate. This would allow not only for the interests present in this type of silencing to be called into question but also for a more honest approach to thinking about the best way to produce knowledge about this type of problem.

This is because, at the limit, it is shown that organic causality does not fully explain the phenomena in question, even though this lure is sustained because it is necessary for advocating the value of the knowledge produced; because part of this circularity is the idea that biological targets make up indifferent kinds, being able to produce more reliable knowledge. Besides, because they are indifferent kinds, the affected individuals and the society are held unaccountable for what happens to them, and the relevance or values at stake in the suggested treatment are also not called into question.

This is something that, as we have been saying, is utterly anticipated in Hacking's dynamic nominalism, provided its understanding of the scope of biolooping is expanded. It is not only a matter of modifications in biological markers carried out through behavioural therapies but of the production of symptoms and suffering through the mobilisation of cultural elements.

However, one possible response to this criticism would be to delegitimise Watters's account: to present the Japanese case as an exception, to relate the failures of the initial tests to one-off errors, and to try to sustain the idea of underdiagnosis and scientific backwardness of the Japanese scientific community. Such a defence would be relevant if this were not just a case that raises serious questions about the efficacy of drugs and about the explanatory capacity of organicist etiological proposals for various mental disorders. What seems to happen is that the Japanese case is added to an array of debates that have been gaining momentum and directly affect this way of thinking spread by contemporary biological psychiatry.

The placebo questions

Given the possible argument that would point to a certain singularity of the Japanese case, so it could not be generalised to a wider discussion about depression diagnosis and treatment, some questions should be raised. The first one can be framed as an ethical problem. Thanks to the Freedom of Information Act in the United States, it became possible to request access to previously restricted records. This confirmed the suspicion—which had already been raised long ago—that the industry controls which studies are published and which are not. The procedure was simple: studies that proved too harmful to the company's interests—either because they showed the drugs had low efficacy or because of their side effects, among other issues —were left aside. This includes full unpublished studies as well as those that have been stopped because they yielded partial results that were adverse to the companies' interests. The revealed information suggests problems of varying severity. One of the most striking was the case of pharmaceutical company GlaxoSmithKline, which was investigated by the US Senate for omitting that the use of its antidepressant, known as Paxil, was related to an increase in suicidal ideation among adolescents (Watters, 2010). However, even those cases that at first had little appeal—studies that were left unpublished for no apparent reason or only because of some slight variation in their results—were mobilised to raise important questions for companies, particularly regarding the clinical efficacy of their medicines.

The most paradigmatic example is the discussion led by Irving Kirsch, which we introduced in the first chapter. To briefly recapitulate, these are meta-studies on the efficacy of antidepressant drugs, which lead to the conclusion that the drugs would not prove more effective than active placebos (those that do not contain the therapeutic principle of the drug but which actively produce the expected side effects).

In a early study, conducted in partnership with Guy Sapirstein in 1998, 19 double-blind clinical studies were pooled and analysed. In this first study, the researchers already found disconcerting similarities between antidepressant drugs and placebos. Kirsch (2010) says that the fact that there was a significant placebo effect was no great surprise; after all, not only was it already expected, but it is also something that is always found in drug studies. However, it was the relationship between the placebo effect and the response to the drugs that came as a shock. As expected, this paper (Kirsch & Sapirstein, 1998) made a great impact on the scientific community. Another similar study, submitted to the Food and Drug Administration of the United States, raised untenable questions that attempted to point out problems in the study. But, despite the unsubstantiated comments, the accuracy of the collected data was acknowledged (Kirsch, 2010, p. 37-8).

Recently, a more consistent answer has been presented by a team of researchers led by Andrea Cipriani, a researcher at Oxford University. The team published a study that aimed to answer the question, "do antidepressants work?" (Cipriani et al, 2018). To this end, they conducted a meta-study pooling more than 500 research studies (published and unpublished) examining 21 drugs. Only cases of major depressive disorder in adults were considered, since the authors themselves point out that the efficacy observed cannot be applied to cases of minor depression, nor to adolescents and children. However, based on these criteria, the answer is that, yes, antidepressants work.

But even if the answer was positive, this seems far from conclusive. The sticking point is not whether drugs work in some cases but to what extent they work, how often they work and how often they do not, and, above all, why do they work. These are key questions not only when assessing the applicability of drugs but also since drug efficacy is a kind of proof, a validation of the causal explanations that make up both their development and their sales. In that sense, the data presented by Cipriani and his peers, showing that drugs have an efficacy rate between 55% and 60%, would leave no doubt; after all, who would not take a drug for a severe condition that promises a nearly two-thirds chance of improvement? However, when placebo data is factored into the equation, it changes the picture. According to the meta-study, the placebo effect would have a prevalence of around 35%, which means that the real efficacy of antidepressants should be considered as being between 20% and 25%. And that is without any emphasis on active placebos.

Cipriani and his colleagues understand, however, that this difference is statistically significant in terms of the efficacy of drugs compared to placebos. They, therefore, claim that, yes, drugs work[40]. Kirsch, in turn, comments on this study in association with a colleague, Janus Christian Jakobsen (Kirsch, Jakobsen, 2018), and considers these results clinically insignificant.

The authors state that there is no evidence that the use of antidepressants is clinically beneficial. After all, if it seems reasonable to use a drug with an estimated efficacy of about 65%, using one with a 20-25% chance of working and a high rate of side effects is debatable. Cipriani publishes a rejoinder (Cipriani et al., 2018b) claiming that statistical significance is relevant and that the question of clinical benefits is something to be evaluated on a case-by-case basis for each patient. However, this does not solve the problems identified by Kirsch, who does not discuss the clinical efficacy of treatments as a whole (including the relationship with doctors and other intersections), but rather the question of the indifferentiation between the results of active substances and placebos.

The big question then looms in the explanation of why there was such a high ratio between the response rate to active substances and to placebos. Turning to the 1998 study, we can see that its ideas persist after the advocacy by Cipriani and his colleagues. The initial interpretation, later reinforced by Kirsch's (2009) book, headed in the direction of established studies on placebo. According to the author, this should be understood as the combination of a series of factors involving the placebo effect, mainly including side effects and a certain expectation on the part of patients regarding the treatment. All of this is summarised based on the use of *active placebos*.

Kirsch (2009, p. 21) constructs his hypothesis by stating that the fact that antidepressants cause many side effects poses a problem for the tests. On the one hand, this can be inferred from the fact that the rate of improvement from antidepressants is, statistically, significantly higher than from inactive placebos (which does not mean that it is clinically relevant), and yet it is not significantly different from the rate of improvement from active drugs other than antidepressants. The fact that an active substance, regardless of its chemical action, can cause such similar effects is perceived by the author as a sign of a placebo effect.

Coupled with this, it is very difficult to distinguish efficacy when the test is conducted using active placebos. Furthermore, two statements complete the picture: as the patients experience more side effects, the greater the improvement; and finally, when side effects are controlled, the difference in comparison to placebo is statistically insignificant. That is, if placebos are produced to cause the same side effects, the efficacy is statistically equal to that of the active substance. In this sense, the author corroborates arguments about side effects being necessary for the efficacy of drugs to be greater than that of placebos (Kramer et al., 1998)[41].

Kirsch does not refrain from pointing out other factors involved in the placebo effect, such as the colour of the pills, the price of the medication, etc. This includes the relationship with the person who prescribes and administers the drug and drug substitutions or dosage changes. Kirsch (2009) reports, for example, a study (Bernkert et al., 1997) in which patients who were not improving received an increase in their dosage; 72% of them showed a significant improvement, yet only half of them had actually received an increase in dosage.

From these arguments briefly summarised here, it is possible to conclude that what should be called into question is not only how antidepressants work but also the physiological and neurochemical explanations of depression. Kirsch does not rule out the benefits of using antidepressants but argues that they should be used as 'honest placebos', which are indeed effective but not because of the active ingredient linked to the symptoms. Beyond clinical usability, he reaffirms (2010, 2014) the state of crisis of the biochemical theory of depression since placebo studies undermine its foundation, which was precisely how drugs work.

Going back to Hacking, it seems to us that Kirsch points out intersections that must be taken into account when looking at therapeutic outcomes as a central argument in the advocacy of a theory's relevance. As we see, the symbolic elements that influence the efficacy of drugs are extremely varied, so deriving etiological explanations or considerations about the nature of classifications solely based on this can be problematic when we are dealing with 'psychic' suffering and pathologies. Interactivity proves to be a much broader issue than the biologistic theories seem to realise so that taking the organic as a vindication of indifference proves to be a fragile project.

Crisis in psychiatry

But could this be something limited to depression? Not according to Nikolas Rose (2018): biological psychiatry as a whole would be facing an unprecedented crisis. The impasse would result from diagnostic, explanatory, and therapeutic models having reached their limits. This includes, among other factors, pharmacological innovation coming to a halt, as well as ethical and epistemological problems. The first issue has to do with the fact that, for quite some time now, the pharmaceutical industry has not been able to deliver any major breakthrough or innovation in terms of medications and products, working only with minor new developments while depending excessively on its marketing departments to remain profitable. As Silva Junior (2016) demonstrates, instead of innovations that present new ways for treating disorders or significant improvements in drug efficacy, efforts have been directed towards creating consumer markets—through the suggestion of new disorders—or towards reinforcing the suffering associated with traditionally mundane disorders. This reinforcement is intended to elevate these disorders to the status of urgent concerns, which should, of course, be treated with the drugs sold by these companies.

Previously, Rose and Abi-Rached (2013, 2014) had already suggested that this crisis in psychiatry would be manifold. The stagnation of pharmacology would be one of its facets, but there would be at least three others that would be just as relevant: the disappointment with the localisationist promise of understanding mental disorders by means of brain imaging; the difficulty in making productive progress towards genetic components; and the refractory character of the idea of brain plasticity in turning into marketable treatments.

If pharmacological stagnation has already been further investigated in relation to depression, it is important to state that the authors' diagnosis also includes other disorders, pointing particularly to an unmet expectation of innovation in relation to antipsychotic drugs. In addition, relying on the brain localisation of disorders would have made very little contribution to psychiatry, hence the disappointment it caused (Rose, 2018).

Regarding genetics and plasticity, however, the progress we see is different from what was expected. The author indicates that the most interesting advances concern studies on epigenetics that show how these objects are not as stable as they would like them to be, responding instead to environmental and social issues. It also follows that its applicability to the field of psychiatry has been practically non-existent.

And in relation to plasticity, the main problem is that progress in this field would yield more indetermination than determination in relation to the organic. This is because they suggest that plasticity is strong enough to mean that the causes are not so stable in neurochemical processes, while at the same time, plasticity would not be so easily manipulated that it would be possible to develop treatments that could use it to their advantage.

In this sense, this problem does not only concern clinical practice but also research since it suggests that the methods hitherto employed for knowledge production—or even for technical artefacts, such as medicines—are no longer effective. The problem has not only been the lack of efficacy, but also other developments that suggest that research was being conducted in a problematic way.

The point is that the problems seem to pile up: the combination of "successful marketing cases" (such as the one in Japan), cases involving serious failures (such as the omission of the rise in suicidal ideation in adolescents), the questioning of the efficacy of currently available drugs, and the difficulty in discovering or inventing a new drug that could make a relevant impact on the landscape makes psychiatry an all too risky market (Rose 2018, p. 131).

According to the British social scientist, the clearest indication of the pharmaceutical industry's despondency about psychiatry can be found in the number of new drugs submitted for approval for testing. If in 2008 the number of psychiatric drugs in the pipeline was close to that of cancer drugs (close to 280), in 2013 it was already half of that. The industry has given preference to other types of illness, while a paradigmatic crisis seems to be taking place. In this vein, Thomas Insel announced the National Institute of Mental Health's (NIMH) break with the DSM, arguing that psychiatry needed to seek less speculative grounds (Insel, 2013). The idea is that it should seek clear etiological grounds like those from other medical fields, such as cardiology. That is how the Research Domain Criteria were put forward, a restructuring of research parameters that takes the biological wager a step further.

This movement is also happening elsewhere, becoming consolidated at the turn of the 21st century (Rose & Abi-Rached, 2013; 2014). It has resulted in the centralisation of neuroscience for thinking about mental health research and treatments, which is summarised in the expression "wager on the brain" (Rose, 2016). It is an attempt to unite different conditions under a common field of research and explanation, from neurological diseases, such as Parkinson's, to psychopathological disorders, such as depression and schizophrenia. According to the authors, this new branch of biopolitics would establish the idea that individuals could be explained by neuromolecular studies of the brain. This has attracted billion-dollar investments such as the one made in the European Union's Human Brain Project (which received $1 billion). However, their results do not seem that encouraging:

> These 'big science' projects want to do for the brain what the Human Genome Project (HGP) did for the genome. As with the HGP, the dream of understanding the brain is linked to the pragmatics of finding new explanations and therapies for mental illness—now routinely assumed to lie in or through the brain. This is an interesting comparison, since the unexpected effect of the HGP was to radically transform almost

> everything we thought we knew about genetics, while largely failing to deliver the promised benefits in terms of understanding and treating human diseases. (Rose & Abi-Rached, 2014a, p. 5)

Lately, private companies seem to share this scepticism: they still advocate going ahead with the research, but they claim that it would be basic research and that, therefore, it should be funded by the government. Rose does not spare them from criticism for choosing this path, claiming that there is no reason to doubt that it is a mistake to double down on a strategy that has so far proven to be insufficient. He even quotes a recent interview by Thomas Insel from 2017, in which the now former director of the NIMH issues something of a *mea culpa*, saying that, as the director of research institutes, he was able to allocate a budget of around $20 billion. Still, he cannot tell if he has made progress on any recognised challenges in the field of mental health (Rogers, 2017).

Returning to the Japanese case and the work done by Kirsch and his colleagues, Rose's argument becomes very clear: there seems to be a serious problem in the structure of the argument in support of the supremacy of neurochemical and physiological causality for mental disorders. On the one hand, the dispute over the efficacy of antidepressants—especially selective serotonin reuptake inhibitors—casts doubt upon any association between pharmacological efficacy and causal explanations based on the therapeutic effects of these drugs. In addition, the Japanese case has far broader implications for the influence of symbolic constructions on organic functions, especially given the change in the efficacy of antidepressants in large-scale population-based tests before and after the marketing campaign.

Obviously, this does not mean that no illnesses have neurochemical causes. Nor that the neurochemical part is not of any interest. The problem lies in the inadvertent spread of this sort of understanding, which forces a kind of rationality on cases that bear no relation to it. In this sense, Hacking's idea of an explanatory stability based on the recognition of biological bases might be appropriate for diseases like Alzheimer's or Parkinson's. However, it does not seem to apply to cases such as depression—given the quarrel over drug efficacy—or even schizophrenia if we follow Rose's (2018) line of argumentation, which claims that the lack of progress in pharmacological therapies signals the inadequacy of this explanatory model. The drugs would be effective in treating some symptoms, in inhibiting certain brain activities, among other things. But their performance would fail to provide any evidence for an etiological thesis about the situation. Rose (2015; 2018) points out that the question should not be exclusively focused on the organic but on something that connects it to social and cultural factors. He proposes that psychiatry should turn towards sociology, focusing on the social elements that cannot be ignored when discussing mental health. This means not only a shift in object or method but also a shift in rationality:

> There is conceptual work to be done here. We need to think of gene sequences, not as an inherited programme that merely reveals itself, but as they activate and de-activate, methylate and demethylate over the course of development, and always in relation to their milieu. We need to recognise that neurotransmitter hypotheses of psychopathology are partial at best, and fail to grasp the complex and distributed nature of the brain circuits that subserve cognitive functions by many orders of magnitude. We need to reject a conception of brain functions that is based on the idea of localisations—these may be given support by the technological and methodological routines of functional magnetic resonance imaging (fMRI), but the tools of visualisation should not shape our theories. We have to realise that, when it comes to mental distress, we are dealing with living organisms and that there is a real limit to what we can learn from animal studies in laboratories where a living organism is deprived of the very basic capacities that life requires—the capacity to shape and reshape one's milieu. (Rose, 2016, p. 98-99)

Rose also presents a series of studies showing a correlation between the prevalence of disorders such as alcoholism, depression, and schizophrenia, and situations of social vulnerability, such as unemployment or housing insecurity (Rose, 2015; 2018). The path proposed by the author is undeniably interesting and necessary; however, it is not the only possible route for shifting the way of thinking about causality out of the realm of biological psychiatry. His claim that various disorders will not be clarified solely on the basis of genetic markers or imaging exams can be sustained not only from the intersection of sociology and neuroscience, as it seems to be the author's wager. How psychoanalysis deals with causality seems to agree with this because, as we have seen in the previous chapter, it centralises a conflictual dimension that does not leave room for a splitting between the social and the individual.

5.3 A path: truth as cause

Rose (2018) is quite precise in pointing out how unproductive it is to isolate the organic question for understanding mental disorders and psychic suffering. In fact, the splitting between organic and psychic—as well as their effects on the production of knowledge about their causes—is as ancient as it is far-reaching. Our goal is to engage in this debate from a well-defined point of view, which concerns the sustenance of something along the lines of what Dunker (2015) advocates as a 'non-reductionist monism'. This implies a non-separation of organic and psychic, meant that neither of these terms necessarily overlaps with the other.

Bearing in mind what we have presented so far in relation to knowledge production on psychic suffering, this position is immediately justified by the impasses encountered by an organicist approach. They concern not only the problems met during the course of their research but also the proposition of a mode of treatment which portrays suffering as devoid of a conflictual dimension: something whose explanation benefits from autonomy in relation to the insertion of individuals in culture, the renunciations involved, the effects of power and violence, etc. This involves the rejection of a conflictual dimension that can be acknowledged as an effect of social relations—violence and segregation, just to name a few examples mentioned by Rose (2018)—but also of a constitutive conflict that harks back to the very entrance into language and culture, directly implicating the subjects in their suffering.

This discussion mainly concerns the question of causation. If this debate was initially driven by a diagnostic question concerning the causality of psychic suffering, it is because the problems that are being identified over the last hundred years suggest that something is not working the way certain sectors would like it to—although, as we have seen, they insist on pushing through solutions that have already failed. Whence we can retrieve the question Hacking left unanswered concerning a general theory of making up people: would it not be the very absence of a causal approach to his dynamic nominalism that would make him so vulnerable to a fragile conception such as the one provided by biological psychiatry? In this sense, psychoanalysis can contribute with a very productive shift.

It mainly concerns thinking of causality in terms of 'something that does not work'; nevertheless, something that does not work constitutively—an inescapable impossible, which situates a conflictual dimension as a central etiological element. As we have presented earlier, psychoanalytic thinking and practice will address their problems based on the recognition of a constitutive negativity, which would be found in the different disruptive forms that we can consider as statements of truth. What Lacan focuses on in "Science and Truth" (1966a/2006) is that truth must be regarded as something connected to causation.

The first question that must be answered is the following: to what is Lacan referring when he says "cause"? Two elements define this in the text: first, his statement that it would be "not the cause as logical category, but as causing the whole effect" (Lacan, 1966a/2006, p. 738)—a sentence that becomes clearer when the author retrieves the four Aristotelian causes to formulate the question: the cause is situated as linked to the transformation of something into something different. According to Lacan, it would be possible to think that different knowledges always deal, somehow, with truth as cause, but in different ways. Science, in particular, would see truth as a formal cause. This means that science sets out to think of transformation from the perspective of identifying the formal elements that distinguish objects, establishing theories of how they relate to each other. Mathematics would be, in this sense, an appropriate way of dealing with these formal elements.

It is worth saying, albeit briefly, that Lacan sees in religion a way of dealing with the final cause (the transformation is understood from the perspective of its purpose), and in magic, the consideration of the efficient cause. On the other hand, psychoanalysis would deal with the cause as a material cause, the incidence of the signifier as a correlate to this 'material'. In this splitting, it would be implicit, nevertheless, that there would be, on the part of science, magic, and religion, some kind of refusal to see truth as cause. According to Lacan, while they deal with truth as cause in different ways—the psychoanalyst uses the term 'refraction' to express this (refractions of truth as cause)—something would be left out. This is a refusal that would not be found in psychoanalysis, which would suggest that truth as material cause is presented as a central mode of treatment for truth as cause.

What we have pointed out, at the beginning of Chapter 3, about the rejection of the question of truth based on Françoise Balibar's (2007/2012) remark is directly connected to this question. As Balibar rightly points out, science would be quite effective in producing mathematical axioms, something suitable for dealing with formal causality. However, what the author identifies as the requisite for thinking about the transition from mathematics to the world—what Helmholtz would claim is a matter of belief—concerns the material aspect. This is indeed what Balibar recognises as the truth, which would be avoided in Helmholtz's explanations, but which would inevitably return. The formal cause would not explain why the knowledge produced from the purification of phenomena into formal elements would be effective in its 'return' to objects. In fact, we can think here of two aspects of the material cause: one concerns the incompatibility between signifier and thing, that is, the fact that representation proves to be inevitably inadequate to the world. But still, there is something that, pragmatically, works, which can be found in Helmholtz's statement about "believing and doing" (Balibar, 2007/2012). On the other hand, there is a dimension of the material cause that singularly concerns the field of psychoanalysis since it has to do with the signifying materiality as something that encompasses the very substantialisation of the body. In this sense, the idea of non-reductionist monism shows its power since it is about a non-separation of that which would pertain to language and that which would pertain to the body.

The first aspect can be recognised when Hacking points to the problem of truth as adequacy in the transition from theory to existence (Hacking, 2002b). Hacking differentiates truth from truthfulness, suggesting that truthfulness would consist of the contextual possibilities, which would always be incomplete and mistaken, for enunciating the truth—something in keeping with his rejection of scientific realism. We can see that Lacan identifies an analogous operation in how the sciences work in general. Still, he will say that this cannot simply be circumvented in psychoanalysis since truth—as that which is not included in the enunciation of the truth—erupts, causing problems for what was enunciated. That is, in the case of psychoanalysis, the tension between signifier and signification produces effects that erupt, showing that there is always something conflictual at work.

Furthermore, if both share the lack of guarantee of the knowledge produced as a key element, Lacan's very conception of truth constantly poses this problem. Something which we have previously claimed to be a difference in the way the authors address the question of negativity, so that this centralisation, in psychoanalytic thinking, would constitute a strong negativity. What is revealed, at this point, is how this strong negativity relates to truth as material cause: if there is some kind of refusal in the other ways of dealing with the truth as cause based on its different refractions (final, efficient, and formal), it is because it would be the material cause that would allow us to go a step further in understanding the emergence of conflicts resulting from attempts at signification—something that localises the strong negativity at the heart of how psychoanalysis understands the question of truth.

Truth as formal and material cause

Going back to "Science and Truth" (Lacan, 1966a/2006), we must recall that, unlike Balibar, Lacan's main reference in this text is not the work of Helmholtz. He makes it clear that he is in dialogue with structuralism, a science that has allowed him to logically formulate the separation between truth and knowledge (Lacan, 1966a/2006). He revisits this in the text to indicate that structural anthropology would perform an operation of separating the myth-maker (as the one involved in mythogeny) from the subject that produces the knowledge of mythogeny, the subject of science. This statement by Lacan is relevant because it underlines the fact that a dimension of truth as cause would be refused in this type of operation.

Something similar to what we saw in Milner (1992/2010) when he said that Saussure's structural linguistics discards speech for the purpose of establishing the formal relations between signifiers. This separation would only be possible in part and would even be detrimental to linguistics. After all, one can only be a linguist if one is a speaking subject. Something that is intensified in some cases, such as when one is studying one's own language, which inevitably implies a movement of turning towards oneself. Or when one sets out to study a language one does not speak, which requires learning (even if only the bare minimum) of the language that is its object. Observer and observed meet in moments like this, which creates, according to the linguist, a paradoxical demand: to produce knowledge by removing the subject that provides the necessary support to the knowledge that will be produced. In linguistics, he claims, it is possible to subdue this subject, but not in psychoanalysis: "Linguistics has to cope with this paradox; but psychoanalysis finds a related paradox, since only a being who is affected by the unconscious can be an analyst. However, unlike linguistics, it not merely subdues the subject: it treats the subject empirically and theoretically" (Milner, 1992/2010).

This is a clear way of presenting the problem, given that what is at stake in psychoanalysis is not only knowledge production but also its clinical practice. The subject cannot be silenced. If this is, just like we said, a paradox for structuralism—since the subject that must be eliminated is needed if knowledge is to be produced—there is something that would help to overcome this problem: the subject would be eliminated at the moment when knowledge is communicated, so that, in Lacan's reading, the splitting of the subject would be sutured during the communication of knowledge in its logical form (Lacan, 1966a/2006). In other words, formalisation would help to circumvent the impasses related to the signification present in knowledge production by removing the subject from the equation. Something coherent since it is the subject that emerges as an effect of these impasses.

By making the necessary reductions for communicating the formal cause, truth and knowledge are sutured. In this suturing, truth as the material cause is lost since it would be the truth that would signal the problem in the transition from formalised knowledge to objects. If we consider how Hacking views the validity of theories and the existence of theoretical entities based on the effects that can be produced, we find the subject as an element that produces decidability about the value of what is recognised or not. In other words, we need a subject to declare that something has been transformed, to sanction what has happened. And that, which would be removed in formal communication, would be precisely where we find the conflicts associated with signification—with the material causality associated with the signifying incidence. In psychoanalysis, when the material cause is removed, what remains is the formal cause, but something that is essential to truth is lost.

As we have seen, the signifier hints at the possibility of a corporeal materiality that does not answer to biology (Milner, 1992/2010)—something indispensable to psychoanalysis since its subject cannot be reduced to structure. This shows that language is not limited to communication: language and the signifiers are interwoven with the corporeal matter, becoming an irreversible part of it. Hence thinking of materiality from the perspective of the signifier. In addition, truth as material cause implies a non-univocal relationship between signifier and signified. In this sense, the statement that psychoanalysis sees truth as material cause may be localised as the foundation of what we have been advocating about a specific style of reasoning: the material cause would encompass both the impossibility of any absolute definition of meaning and corporeal materiality, thus instituting the negativity around which this style is constituted. This negativity points to the incompleteness of knowledge at the same time as it gives a destination to the question of materiality and inseparability of the psychic and the organic. In other words, a negativity that requires us to think from the perspective of the opacity of meaning since, at the limit, the objects themselves are produced from the conflicts that stem from the impossibles associated with the subject inhabiting language. It is in this materiality that does not answer to an organic causality but rather to an unavoidable inadequacy that exists within the relationship of the subject with language that truth implicates its nature of impossibility, of radical heterogeneity.

This is not about claiming an incompatibility between psychoanalysis and science—nothing in Lacan's text suggests this. If the suture of the subjective splitting can be seen as a way of refusing truth as material cause, this is due to specific modes of constitution, not to the incompatibility between the different causes. We must also remember that Lacan attributes to the refusal of material causation a question of science's 'fecundity', not a condition of possibility. Recalling what has been said about a diagnosis of modernity found in Koyré via Husserl, this fecundity has to do with a way of dealing with the truth that excludes certain kinds of questions.

By including truth as material cause—even if connected to the formal cause—causality would inevitably be linked to negativity. As we have already seen, desire is tied to lack, but not only desire; so is the symptom. And truth performs this dual function: at the same time as it presents positivised novelties—in opposition to what was already established—it also has the effect of evoking this constitutive lack, producing symptoms. As we have seen, this lack is signalled in the subject's splitting. As we have seen in the previous chapter, the signifier is identified as the cause of the subject[42], for without the signifier, there would be no subject in the Real (Lacan, [1964] 1966/2006). That is, the cause is connected to the lack of meaning (Real). It is the cause in its broadest sense: this lack of meaning that is inseparable from the production of the subject and also of desire, of symptoms, etc. In this way, psychic suffering would be caused by something partly inevitable since it concerns the impossibility of giving meaning to something that simply has none[43].

Taking psychic suffering as an object of knowledge thus establishes the need to consider a causality that addresses negativity in its strongest sense. This must be taken as a constitutive trait that incorporates impossibility as what creates tension in any knowledge that might be produced, in addition to the causality of the very suffering being traced back to this impossibility. Something that, as we have tried to demonstrate, can be accomplished by introducing the question of truth into knowledge production.

Truth, cause, and ethics

Besides being compatible with the way of establishing objects and clinical rationality, this way of thinking of causality also has a dimension of the subject's implication. At this point, we must take into account the accumulation of developments about truth that were presented in the last chapters: the opposition between truth and knowledge, with the particularity that there would be no possible end to this dialectical process; the inexistence of an instance that would guarantee the truth in knowledge; the incompatibility between signified and signifier, placing negativity as a causal engine; and, finally, the material dimension of the signifier, so that the impossibilities described above must be understood as the cause of subjects, of suffering, of symptoms, etc. Retrieving the question of causality in this light—acknowledging Lacan's imperative, according to which psychoanalysts should 'assume' that truth as cause is a central element in psychoanalysis (Lacan, 1966a/2006)—establishes a direct relationship between how causality is understood and the implication of the subject in their suffering.

This positioning becomes clearer if confronted with modes of dealing with the truth that are concerned neither with the ontological effects of knowledge production nor with the effects of the conflicts inherent to the attempts to signify and stabilise knowledge about individuals. As Hacking points out, this positioning centred on establishing 'extraneous' causes—extraneous, here, understood as that which would not concern the individual, either because it responds to external factors or because it responds to internal yet indifferent (biological) factors—creates a possibility of disimplication. On the one hand, the very belief in an absolute truth can be understood as an instance of alienation, which disengages the subject from the knowledge produced by a third party that would guarantee its truth. On the other, the indifference and extraneous nature of the cause of suffering also produces alienation from something that belongs to the subject.

If the development of a notion of truth that is structured around the denial of an instance that guarantees its truthfulness has unique ethical ramifications, resorting to guaranteeing instances can be regarded as alienation. Not least because, as Iannini (2012) argues, to deny the impossibility of telling the absolute truth is associated with the original repression: this impossibility is not only repressed by the subject but also by this Other that supposedly guarantees the truth—a repression that, from the perspective of the assimilation of structural linguistics, concerns the denial of the disjunction of signifier and signified as a constitutive trait. The repressed would be, in this sense, the lack of meaning *a priori*, which would situate any meaning as merely a single moment of an infinite process of signification.

Thus, resorting to metalanguage, or to the truth of truth, would be a way of denying this opacity of the repression, the opacity of the lack of original meaning, of an essence. As stated earlier, psychoanalysis is not concerned with recovering meaning but rather with shifting to signifying materiality as a way of dealing with this impossible. Therefore, says Iannini (2012), the analyst should not occupy this place of Other of the Other because such an attitude would result in silencing the subject, erasing desire, that which is pure lack.

Thus, along with these considerations on the absence of a guaranteeing instance, there is the possibility of establishing a moral guarantee for the subject. Something that directly strikes at the absence of the truth of truth, insofar as it can be connected to the absence of the Other of the Other: since there is no stable point that can guarantee or clarify the truth of a discourse, neither is there an instance that guarantees the correctness of our acts—something that has been addressed by Lacan in his seminar on *The Ethics of Psychoanalysis* (Lacan, 1959-60/1997) and in "Kant with Sade" (Lacan, [1963] 1966/2006).

In this development, there would be an interconnection between the impossibility of establishing a transcendental guarantee and the localisation of the act as a possibility of defining an ethics that does not require any external moral support. It is worth highlighting that the term 'act' refers to a mode of action characterised by a lack of predictability about its effects, in which there would occur some sort of suspension of the possibility of conforming to normative standards. This development is central to the practice since it provides some kind of therapeutic prospect that will constantly create tension with the normative potential that the very word 'therapeutic' calls into question. It would not be, therefore, a case of normative compliance with certain ideals but a process that seeks to transform the way of critically tackling moral concepts.

The act, in this sense, is not shaped in terms of compliance or non-compliance with the Law (as an established code), but rather the possibility of experience beyond this: "the moral act *must be taken* as fallible as if being rational was knowing how to act without guarantees. *As if a moral act only existed where the subject is called upon to act without guarantees*" (Safatle, 2006, p. 169). The act always carries with itself some kind of failure, a failure in its relationship with the Law. It functions neither as compliance nor as oppositional denial but as the possibility of acting beyond compliance, preserving its conflictual dimension.

Therefore, we can recognise a double ethical implication of the question of truth. On the one hand, the opacity of the repression understood from the signifying materiality indicates the impossibility of determining a normative perspective that is not an attempt at subjection. In other words, if suffering and symptoms answer to an impossibility of compliance with established identifications and norms, treatment cannot be an attempt to restore a normative or identifying perspective but rather an opening to another way of coping. The other implication of the question of truth relates to the impossibility of guaranteeing knowledge, something widely shared among sciences in general but especially central to psychoanalysis. It is thus not only a matter of acknowledging the incompleteness of the knowledge produced but also the normative potential of knowledge, which includes the ontological effects produced. This implication proves to be supportive of the former, in the sense that the tension applied to knowledge within the field of psychoanalysis responds to an ethical imperative of not normalising modes of experience—an ethic whose central element is alterity and not adaptation or compliance to ideals.

In this sense, the position of the subject facing this refusal, this lack, appears as an ethical positioning of the subject facing the inconsistency of the Other. The debate on truth, beyond its epistemological and ontological dimensions, entails an ethical implication insofar as the knowledge produced does not speak for itself, nor does it respond to any guaranteeing instance. This does not imply, however, that knowledge should be reduced to ethics, nor a melancholic denial of the value of knowledge due to its lack of transcendental guarantee—something we have been insisting on since the beginning of this text, when we based our discussion on a critique of how the production of scientific knowledge is understood, one that does not produce any kind of radical relativism.

Truth, negativity, and stability

And what does this entail, specifically regarding truth as material cause, in terms of knowledge about psychic suffering? First of all, that there is a stability in what can be recognised as a cause, and that it is connected to the fact that the subject inhabits language. The incidence of the signifier is the cause of the subject as something split; therefore, also of their desire, their symptoms, etc. Thus, the symptoms hark back to a structural lack, something that brings us closer to Freud's concept, which we have presented earlier, about the lack of truth as a pathogenic nucleus (Silva Junior, 2017)—the truth here is no longer restricted to a concept of historical truth, but as something that has been rejected in the mode of structuring the subject of science. According to Lacan's developments, therapy cannot operate based on an idea of restitution of the truth but rather towards opening up other possible ways of dealing with lack. In this way, one cannot alienate oneself in the guarantee of knowledge; after all, this operation is refractory to the consideration of the subject as an object. Nor is there a guarantee of knowledge.

If we take Hacking's work, we see that his justification for the stability of scientific knowledge does not rely on any kind of guarantee: he attributes stability to effectiveness, which results from constant renegotiations based on what is offered by the knowledge produced. The absence of guarantee is evident in the very idea of the self-stabilisation of a style of reasoning; on the other hand, its difference with psychoanalysis becomes explicit in some moments of his work on transient illnesses. Thus, in Hacking, the difference is evident in the lack of any connection between that which would be excluded from truthfulness and the question of cause. If truthfulness is an effect of the impossibility of enunciating the truth about things—something that can be witnessed in the radical separation between signifier and signified—then the effects of dealing with this impossibility have yet to be acknowledged. And this, according to Lacan, is what psychoanalysis cannot do without, something that implies an intensification of this impossibility, which can be recognised through the active nature of its opposition to knowledge.

In this way, we can affirm that Lacan transfers the question of stability to the signifying incidence. The fact that the subject inhabits language would cause an effect, which implies a split: on the one hand, there are the possible knowledges (including about oneself); on the other, there is something that is not reduced to these knowledges, and that manifests itself as a truth that affirms the absence of an original meaning. The relationship between knowledge and truth is historically established, producing distinct modes of subjectivity. Even within our context, marked by what is called the 'subject of science', there are different ways to establish this division, which respond to distinct modes of denial. More specifically, modes of relating to the very language of castration. This is, in general terms, what Lacan tries to stabilise with his resort to clinical structures so that a structure can bear a wide variability of expressions, even though the structure itself shows greater stability. Thus, we see that the centralisation of the material cause enables another way of thinking of stability and variability.

We then see different degrees of stability, something similar to what Hacking argues for differentiating transient and non-transient illnesses: whether they are recognised in different times and places. If we take the clinical structures, it is possible to assert this wider presence so that much of what Hacking calls 'transient illnesses' would be considered as symptoms under a structural reading. Depression would be, above all, a symptom. Like the hysterical fugue, it is a set of possible expressions of some impasses contained within a clinical structure. On the one hand, it is compatible with the philosopher's argument that the symptoms of non-transient illnesses change over time but that something remains constant. Psychoanalysis offers the possibility of thinking of constancy without having to resort to the biological: by treating causality from the perspective of the subject's relationship with language and its effects.

This shift leads to another way of considering the relationship between interactive and indifferent kinds. The subject of science does not cease to be the target of an interactive kind of classification, but this does not mean that no stable knowledge can be produced about it. The interesting thing is that, in psychoanalysis, the most stable fact about the knowledge produced is that this knowledge will always be, in some way, dismissible. It doesn't matter what anyone says about them. It is not a stability that comes from indifference but rather from the acknowledgement of something that would structure the interactivity. That is, if there is any kind of indifference—in the sense of something that is not modified by the discourse produced—then it would be in relation to impossibility. An impossibility that is taken precisely as the central element of causality. The stability is in the cause, but in the cause as something that denies knowledge and interrupts itself in the production of a stagnant knowledge.

However, we must acknowledge that this is not a matter of defining one mode of knowledge production or considering the question of truth as ethical to the detriment of others that might not be ethical. The point we are making is that the kind of ethical debate that is produced also responds to the way in which the question of truth is mobilised. For example, considering the ontological effects of the knowledge produced invites a series of questions that may not be evident in unadvised understandings of these effects. Inviting these questions can motivate a critical stance in relation to the therapies proposed by questioning what the purpose of the therapies should be. We can see, for instance, that mainstream contemporary psychiatry seems to target ideals of adequacy and productivity (Neves et al., 2021), which does not necessarily represent the ethical views of all the professionals involved. This calls for a consideration of the political dimension of knowledge production, which is often relegated to a place less important than it deserves. Which, as we have argued, would take on a more central role when truth is considered as a question worth dealing with.

5.4. One more path: truth and politics

The first challenge is how to think of the political dimension without causing delegitimising effects on the knowledge produced. Using the political dimension has proved to be a recurring subterfuge for denialist positionings (Beer, 2021) and one that can be avoided by factoring in concepts discussed in this very book. For example, when Rose (2018) claims that the centralisation of neuroscience would respond to a new biopolitical branch, does this mean that the knowledge produced is not valid? As we see in Rose's line of argument, it is not about whether knowledge is valid or not but rather about the disputes involved in defining the fields of study and what will be legitimised as a priority.

More generally, the question is formulated in terms of how we can think of decidability in relation to concurring modes of knowledge production. Something that, in the context of psychoanalytic thinking, reintroduces the subject into scientific production. And which was circumvented many times by Hacking's ideas: after all, it is part and parcel of the very definition of techniques for the self-stabilisation of a reasoning style—and of the contingency involved (albeit to a small degree) in explanations of the stability of specific sciences—that knowledge should also be assessed based on its political applicability. Thus, we see that the political dimension is evident not only when choosing specific particulars in specific sciences—such as the appointment of biology as the ultimate arbiter in psychiatry—but also when deciding on how relevant each mode of thinking is—such as in the definition of a style of reasoning. We can claim that this is a matter of reflecting on how knowledge can be produced to create new possibilities (close to the idea of disruptive truth) and not as an instrument for ideological reproduction.

Proposing this move from ethics to politics is not only a matter of recognising that knowledge inevitably becomes an instrument of power. Above all, it is a matter of giving a destination to this ethical imperative without giving way to an apathy towards knowledge production: as Iain Mackenzie (2018) states, this apathy can, on the one hand, lead us to give up on the proposition of new knowledge, since there is always the risk that this knowledge will be assimilated in terms that are absolute and at odds with our ethical positioning. On the other hand, it can lead to an overinflated ethical dimension, as if it could meet demands that have nothing to do with it. Both alternatives culminate reducing other fields, especially epistemology, to ethics (Dunker, 2007). We believe that reclaiming politics as a field of power struggle, where it is possible to implement ethical principles, is a way to confront this risk while also contributing to the non-abandonment of the ongoing struggles in the field of knowledge production—an abandonment that has already caused much damage to psychoanalysis and to the people who could benefit from it through public mental health policies (Beer, 2015, 2017).

We must not overlook the fact that this approach to politics is based on the centralisation of truth as a question. This is because, as we have been arguing, the question of truth brings into play the reciprocity between epistemology, ontology, and ethics, grounded in the effects of the consideration of three elements: 1) the absence of an instance that guarantees the value of knowledge, 2) the ontological effects produced by the discourses and practices of scientific knowledge, and 3) causality as the consideration of a negative dimension that includes the conflictive character of suffering and the implication of the subject. Taking these three dimensions as reciprocal places politics as a fourth inseparable term since how these dimensions interact also involves the power struggles inherent to any kind of knowledge production. In this sense, the political dimension should be viewed from two different angles. On the one hand, this is the critical power of knowledge, in the sense that it can counter and resist established norms and standards; on the other hand, we have the normative potential of knowledge itself—the potential to establish new standards not only of normality but also of legitimacy in relation to what deserves and must be the object of research.

Revisiting Hacking's notion of a style of reasoning, it is his remarks on the self-stabilisation of a style that open up the discussion to the political dimension, even though the author himself does not delve deeply into this aspect. Underlying the minimum required correspondence between the knowledge produced and the world upon which it must exert some kind of effect, there is the necessary negotiation for defining this world: we must not forget that he invariably resorts to the idea that reality is something that is constantly being renegotiated. In this way, if it is possible to acknowledge that the dimension of negotiation does not oppose the idea of objectivity, it does not exhaust what can be thought about political intersections: if the style determines the modalities of experimentation, validation, and communication, standards of objectivity, and so on, we can state that this very definition is part of a political sphere, to the extent that it grants power.

Knowledge and politics

This question is tackled head-on by Isabelle Stengers (1993) when she proposes that politics is unavoidable when it comes to knowledge production. Stengers shares with Hacking a stance that is neither unicist nor normative with regard to epistemology and methodology. She argues that the impossibility of separating knowledge and politics is due to the fact that it is impossible to establish an external point of reference that defines the value of the knowledge produced. To this end, the author claims that modern science emerged exactly when there was a power struggle going on, a struggle whose object would be nothing less than the truth: to be the one able to enunciate the truth was something extremely valuable. This does not mean that science could be reduced to this, nor that it can be detached from this dimension.

In this sense, the separation (and its justification) between scientific knowledge and other modes of knowledge, which would be considered of lesser value, would be key to the constitution of modern science. To this process, named *demarcation*, Stengers associates the projects of epistemological and methodological standardisation of science. However, none of these projects would have succeeded in finding the necessary grounding to justify the separation between scientific and non-scientific knowledge.

The main way of performing such a demarcation would be based on the separation between fictions and non-fictions: a rhetorical strategy already deployed by Galileo when he claimed that mathematics would make things speak for themselves (non-fiction). Scientific knowledge would be non-fictional, as well as capable of silencing concurrent ideas that "are nothing but fiction" (Stengers, 1993, p. 93). Thus, we see a clear power struggle concerning the legitimacy of the enunciation of the truth and the silencing of competitors. To this end, according to the author, the scientific procedure would be a way to build a presentation of facts that would be suitable for a single narrative only. Some choices are made so that mathematics can conform to empirical objects; however, they are not presented as choices but rather as if they were the natural state of things:

> The fictional world created by Galileo is not only the world that Galileo knows how to interrogate: it is a world that no one can interrogate in any way different from his. It is a world whose categories are practical, because they are the categories of the experimental device that he invented. It is, in fact, a concrete world, namely a world that makes it possible to take in the multitude of rival fictions concerning the movements that accompany it and establish the difference between them, to designate the one that legitimately represents it. (Stengers, 1993, p. 99)

In this sense, how one can represent and demonstrate a fact is nevertheless a fiction. This does not mean, however, that all fictions should be treated as if they were of equal value. Such rhetoric would not only be dismissible but even counterproductive, as it would limit the possibilities for discovery. At this point, the political dimension would make its oppressive power explicit, in the sense that the value of scientific knowledge would lie in the power to tell 'the truth' and to silence competitors. Such positioning comes from a dual political intersection: 1) first, to present itself as non-fiction would be a way to establish, from the outset, a higher hierarchical rank, as it would indicate a direct relationship with truth (political, therefore, because it is a power struggle); 2) such hierarchisation relies on the advocacy of a necessary character coming from an epistemological differentiation, which requires the autonomy of science in relation not only to 'external' struggles (politics as a general arena of negotiation and power) but also by removing politics from its 'essential' workings since its advances could be measured against purely epistemological references.

The reintroduction of politics, as proposed by Stengers, repositions politics as a fundamental aspect of practice since it deprives normative epistemology of any real decision-making power, demanding that the choice of winners should also respond to other contentions. This is not an attack on the value of scientific knowledge but an affirmation of its value by including this area of contention. It is not a case of separating fictions from non-fictions but of choosing the most valuable fictions, explaining the reason behind the choices.

Politics is taken, then, as a constituent element of scientific work. Politics is defined here as a space for the production and dispute of interests: something that is always present when an enunciation claims to have enough authority to determine a research programme. If there is no external guarantee of value, the decision about the quality of a theory has, at the limit, a political dimension; besides, the very acceptance of questions and topics as relevant is not fully explainable by epistemology alone either, as Hacking (2000) rightly pointed out. The political dimension is also an integral part of how a problem will be approached, what its criteria of truthfulness will be, the accepted methods, etc. This does not mean that the importance of epistemology or other procedures that try to provide stability to scientific doing has been erased, but rather that these intersections are inevitable. Something that is only possible, as Stengers puts it, by keeping an attentive eye on power (Stengers, 1993, p. 87).

The conclusion is, therefore, that the way to understand the decidability of the value of knowledge necessarily demands taking politics into account. Something that Stengers ascribes to the very workings of science since it would be supportive of the critical openness required for knowledge production: "if it is no longer a matter of eliminating the power of fiction, it is, however, a matter of putting it to the test, of submitting the reasons we invent to a third party capable of putting them at risk" (Stengers, 1993, p. 154). Science would have this potential of being a criticisable knowledge, above all else. This critique must bear the mark of its political inscription since both its constitution, and its effects are inseparable from power struggles.

The question that remains, meanwhile, concerns how to achieve such a permanent critical openness. Acknowledging the political dimension of knowledge production does not necessarily mean solving the problem. Perhaps because, as it is clearly noticeable in psychoanalytic practice, something that emerges as the truth at a given moment may crystallise as knowledge at the next moment. Knowledge thus remains in a position of indecisiveness between critique and reproduction.

Hacking does not fail to acknowledge this dimension. He acknowledges the disruptive power of knowledge, which he links to the question of truth (1999). He does so, however, in a rather apathetic way, commenting on a recurrent splitting between supposedly 'right-wing' and 'left-wing' positions: there would be a tradition of regarding truth as a revolutionary element—embraced by 'leftists'—in the sense that truth would have the potential to critique and resist established power; on the other hand, he recounts his realisation that, over the years, the question of truth has come to be seen as an instrument of oppression used by conservatives ('rightists'), in which the affirmation of what is true would be a form of oppression and domination. Although he shows sympathy towards the most 'leftist' view, his final stance is apathetic, almost melancholic: the author claims to be too old for this discussion (Hacking, 1999, p. 95-96).

Truth and the political

This kind of apathetic attitude does not seem unusual, and, according to Iain Mackenzie (2018), it is a recurring problem concerning the consideration of truth in politics. He thus claims that the debate on truth must transcend this limit of oppression, seeking ways to deal with the question of truth without them resulting in mechanisms of oppression and domination.

Indeed, if the political dimension of truth is taken only as a movement for replacing different forms of knowledge that impose their rules on others, there is always an oppressive perspective that is difficult to overcome. However, limiting the issue to this process of substituting for opposites is an incomplete understanding of what is at stake when dealing with the political dimension of truth. This limitation is what we have previously named as *weak negativity*, which is limited to the fact that a new truth can exist—since the absolute truth would be unattainable—but it fails to account for its effects on the very value assumed by 'truth' in this process.

As we saw in Chapter 3, the consideration of these effects results in the acknowledgement that the process of replacing truths is not limited to the mere transition to its opposite. Rather, it entails the establishment of an original impossibility of adequacy. Within the framework of what we have named as *strong negativity*, truth bears this dual function: on the one hand, it denies the adequacy of a positive enunciation by the opposition of another positive enunciation; on the other, it points to the infinitude of the negative potential by establishing a perspective of radical difference.

As Mackenzie (2018) states, this notion can be quite useful in effecting a politics that assimilates the question of truth. To this end, he resorts to the work of Alain Badiou: for Badiou (1994), truth would be an effect of a disruptive event[44], which would entail not only the establishment of a new form of symbolic organisation but also the possibility of disrupting any established form, instating lack as a structuring point. We must bear in mind that Badiou views the category of event as something rare, which would result in the establishment of an unforeseen and undeniable newness. Establishing this unprecedented newness would require a reorganisation of knowledges since introducing a new element would lead to a restructuring of the symbolic dimension. At the same time, there would also be the acknowledgement that this new (or any) symbolic organisation might be the target of a new disruptive event, suggesting that an element is always left out when the ways of explaining and experiencing the world are constituted. Badiou associates this element with the idea of lack since it refers to the impossibility of a total recapture of the symbolic, suggesting that there always exists a possible difference.

This lack alludes to the fact that a new element can always erupt, explicitly showing that what is taken for granted as necessary and natural can be understood and experienced in a completely different way. This non-necessary nature of the established ways of thinking and experiencing the world will be localised, according to Mackenzie (2018), as the foundation of the *political*: this is an area of dispute and negotiation that arises from the impossibility of a single form of normative determination. The political would be, therefore, the arena inaugurated by negativity in its strong sense since that would be the acknowledgement that the only feature that could be generalised as the hallmark of being would be multiplicity: what can be assured is that it is always possible to be different from what one thinks one is. Thus, we come back to the idea of radical difference or heterogeneity. That is, power struggles exist and are justified precisely because it is not possible to guarantee that one form of existence is more valuable than another.

Which does not mean that what is established should be delegitimised. Mackenzie suggests that the positivised form of this effect of truth produced by the event should not be disregarded. On the contrary, the newly introduced element should be considered as true and thus guide the reconstruction of the symbolic system. On the other hand, the effect of radical difference that also marks it must be present at all times. It is, therefore, a truth that, at the same time, that offers possibilities of construction, also bears the mark of its ever-potential denial. It is something that can be constructed, but without losing the perspective of its possible liquidation, which leads to the radical difference being constantly brought into play.

This brief presentation of the association between truth and the political does not fail to acknowledge the relevance of positivised affirmations, at the same time as it puts them in a permanent state of tension with negativity in its strong sense, pointing to a perspective of radical difference. Regarding the question of truth for the production of knowledge about suffering, what we see is that the definition of the political dimension of truth is capable of establishing an arena for critical debate. A debate capable of connecting positivised propositions to a negative perspective. Thus, we can see that the problems presented in this chapter regarding epistemological, ontological, ethical, and political questions can all be addressed, provided that we do not shy away from the complexity that is required to do so. We must not abandon the truth, but we must instead take it as a question at each and every moment without being afraid of its effects.

Psychoanalysis cannot escape, in this sense, from taking a political stance: on the one hand, in keeping with Hacking's work, it signals the need to consider the contingency of knowledge, which already takes into account the ontological, ethical, and political effects of knowledge production; on the other hand, by pushing to its limits the negativity dictated by the way in which causality can be dealt with in clinical practice, it maintains alterity as the only possible therapeutic perspective. This concerns a political insertion that is an effect of clinical ethics (Frosh, 1999) and which cannot afford to disregard its power effects (Lacan, [1958] 1966/2006; Checchia, 2015).

If we slightly invert the title of the book by Iain Mackenzie (2018), we suggest that truth, as a question, can be understood as a form of resistance. On the one hand, resistance is what must be gone through during the production of knowledge: here we have Hacking's idea that knowledge production is constrained both by its relationship with its objects and by the social agreements of the community in which it is inserted—which implies that knowledge exists because it is at the service of something, suggesting that truth concerns some kind of effectiveness, just as this effectiveness is in itself the product of collective aspirations and negotiations. On the other hand, the questioning of truth acts as a form of resistance in the sense of opposition to power: truth brings to the fore the power of negativity, the radical difference that must be considered as the foundation and perspective of the function of knowledge, the permanent openness to critique. Perhaps this is one of the great contributions that psychoanalysis can make to science, including here other specific sciences but also, of course, itself.

Conclusion

After a long and winding road, perhaps the only possible conclusion is that truth, as a question, tends to produce some sort of critical reflection on the very production of knowledge. This reflection is not meant to lead to the delegitimisation of knowledge but is meant instead to produce opening areas where any effort to stabilise knowledges shows normative or normalising potential. If we bring suffering into the picture, such openness gains drama, for it is a matter of being able not only to think in different ways but to exist and experience the world beyond that which tends towards reproduction.

The first question raised was about the truth value of knowledge. With Hacking, we were able to establish an understanding of the value of scientific knowledge from a non-normative philosophy of science. Along with this, his project of styles lays the foundations for thinking about the relationship between contingency and the need for knowledge by considering a dimension of negotiation that involves what would be indifferent and what interacts with the discourses produced. However, we cannot stress this enough, he does so without falling into some kind of radical relativism.

This general reading on the workings of sciences could be localised within an understanding of truth as something marked by incompleteness and historicity. Something that establishes a movement between notions that attempt to positively stabilise modes of access and communication of the truth, along with the very movement of scientific doing that requires these notions to be revisited. Nevertheless, the definition of truthfulness as possibilities for enunciating the truth organises the field, reaffirming even the lack of guarantee for the truth of truthfulness. In this way, the critique of truth as adequacy and the establishment of the value of knowledge as separate from its consideration as an absolute truth already signalled the need to consider truth (or truthfulness) as the conjunction of questions that are epistemological (the possibilities of truth or falsehood are delineated within the style of reasoning), ontological (the possibilities of consideration of objects are reciprocal to the definition of truth and falsehood; hence, they also fall within the style of reasoning), as well as ethical and political (a style of reasoning self-stabilises, so that there is no external criterion for sustaining it).

From then on, the consideration of the philosopher's work on *historical ontology* has focused on suffering, with the notion of dynamic nominalism as its compass. If a critical appreciation of the question of truth was already in place, Hacking's proposition on interactive kinds dramatically intensified this need: since knowledge produces retroactive effects on certain kinds of classification, the question of truth unfolds. Beyond the abandonment of any illusion to establish an absolute truth, we must consider a specific ontological potential, given the production of possibilities of experience from the production of knowledge. In this sense, not only does the relationship between epistemology and ontology become stronger, but ethics becomes unavoidable.

At this point, the dialogue with psychoanalysis became urgent, but while being aware that there is a difference in what is called truth. Focusing on the Lacanian conception that truth is linked to the unconscious, we have presented a notion grounded in negativity, and that bears a potential for disruption in relation to knowledge. We were able to present how this unfolds from the clinical practice and some theoretical influences, to show both the compatibility with Hacking in relation to acknowledging the historicity of forms of suffering and also some points of divergence. We should notice, then, that psychoanalysis is a specific form of defining truths and falsehoods that are reciprocal to its objects, and it also presents stabilising techniques—pointing to a specific style of reasoning.

Such a consideration leads to a critique and a possible contribution towards Hacking's historical ontology, which concerns the absence of a causal theory that can explain the phenomena involved. An absence that is noticeable in the resort to the effectiveness of biological psychiatry as a differentiation between interactive and indifferent kinds, thus presenting a relationship between biology and indifference. In this regard, we were able to provide reasons that suggest the insufficiency—or even the inadequacy—of a biologicist approach to certain issues. The inadequacy concerns the effects that the discourse of biological psychiatry can produce, which was demonstrated in the discussion on depression. Insufficiency, on the other hand, can be recognised based on Nikolas Rose's notes on the crisis of psychiatry. Far from denying that there is a biological component involved in the issues at hand, it is a matter of affirming the interactivity of the biological and the need to consider the social.

In this vein, we highlight how psychoanalysis deals with the question of causality by indicating its relevance in dealing with suffering. We have presented a clinical rationality that proposes objects and modes of thinking permeated by the connection between causality and the question of truth. This way of (theoretically) dealing with suffering presents the possibility of a permanent questioning of the effects of knowledge. Understanding the cause as something that engages the subject goes hand in hand with a critical approach to knowledge, acknowledging its ontological effects and the absence of a guaranteeing instance. In this sense, ethics and politics have been called into the discussion as something that can be considered as a double inscription: on the one hand, it is a matter of constantly questioning the effects of power and the ethical assumptions that are (or are not) fulfilled in knowledge production, paying particular attention to the fact that the ways in which we treat suffering (both theoretically and in clinical interventions) always bear a potential for a normative form of experience; on the other hand, it is necessary to consider these issues not as effects that should be dealt with after they are produced—as if they were a kind of undesirable by-product of knowledge production—but as something we should care for during the very process of knowledge production. In other words, it is about balancing epistemology, ontology, ethics, and politics in the processes of knowledge production, which must be considered in a way that renews these questions at all times.

Needless to say, the path trodden—and brutally shortened in the paragraphs above—does not leave room for any attempt towards a stagnant or definitive stabilisation of what should be considered as truth. Even if we can say that it is a matter of reclaiming truth as a concept capable of opening up crystallised debates, we do not contend that this is the only way to pursue such an objective. Nor even that the way we mobilise these concepts is the only or the most correct one: by limiting ourselves to the two main references—Ian Hacking and Jacques Lacan—it suffices to remember that the author of this book has no background in philosophy of science, let alone identifies himself as an orthodox Lacanian who would have studied every single word ever spoken (or implied) by the French psychoanalyst. Instead, the reader was able to find a quite unique reading of Hacking, albeit rigorously committed to the debate proposed. On the side of psychoanalysis, it suffices to say that the mobilised material is extremely reduced in relation to discussions that have already taken place, apart from gathering authors who do not necessarily consider themselves part of the same reading tradition of Lacan's work. Again, what matters is not reaching a final verdict but producing movement.

Demanding a critical reflection that scrutinises the ontological, ethical, and political effects of knowledge production is a legacy that can be found both in psychoanalysis and in the philosophy of science. However, it has been historically difficult for these two fields to engage in less contentious exchanges, which have led to intense clashes when they are brought into contact with each other. This can be seen in the contributions psychoanalysis has made to Hacking's thought, but it must also be taken in the opposite sense. A good example is the critical contribution made by Paul B. Preciado concerning the normative and segregating effects of psychoanalytic theory and practice, something that, nonetheless, does not seem to have been entirely welcomed by psychoanalysts (Beer & Ambra, 2021). Even in fields that are actively engaged with such issues, the complexity of the problems often camouflages the pitfalls.

At a time when scientific knowledge is being fiercely attacked, what we can gather is that what fuels the attacks is not too much doubt but too much certainty. Unshakeable certainty is the greatest obstacle to scientific questioning, which suggests that, apart from producing valuable knowledge, it is also necessary to produce befitting modes for engaging with science itself. This involves giving room to doubt, questioning, errors, and the unexpected. After all, if science is done by means of a movement between truth and knowledge, we must care both for what is established and for what may erupt. Who knows, perhaps by being this careful, sufferings and symptoms can be experienced as harbingers of new horizons, new worlds—yet to be invented, of course. So, perhaps, a conclusion is not a good match for this book; after all, this is all about being able to always move on to a new conclusion that resignifies what came before. But, as Foucault would say, it is nevertheless a conclusion. A short one, at least.

Notes

1 Both trends can be found in the technical note on mental health number 11/2019-CGMAD/DAPES/SAS/MS.

2 It is worth briefly recalling there is a certain similarity with the division proposed by Gilles-Gaston Granger in *Pensée formelle et sciences de l'homme* [Formal Thought and the Sciences of Man] (1960/1967) and *A ciência e as ciências* [Science and the Sciences] (1993), which places mathematics as a pole of formalisation in relation to which there would always be some loss when moving on to the empirical sciences. Granger, in turn, takes this issue forward by stressing the importance of other procedures that should be part of scientific practice, especially experimentation and the replicability of experiments.

3 As indicated earlier, we can think about depression this way, and therefore it does not require a confirmation from brain imaging to consider that it exists.

4 In more detail, the author affirms: "The key ideas are as follows: (1) An emphasis upon verification (or some variant such as falsification): Significant propositions are those whose truth or falsehood can be settled in some way. (2) Proobservation: What we can see, feel, touch, and the like, provides the best content or foundation for all the rest of our non-mathematical knowledge. (3) Anti-cause: There is no causality in nature, over and above the constancy with which events of one kind are followed by events of another kind. (4) Downplaying explanations: Explanations may help organize phenomena, but do not provide any deeper answer to Why questions except to say that the phenomena regularly occur in such and such a way. (5) Anti-theoretical entities: Positivists tend to be non-realists, not only because they restrict reality to the observable but also because they are against causes and are dubious about explanations. They won't infer the existence of electrons from their causal effects because they reject causes, holding that there are only constant regularities between phenomena. (6) Positivists sum up items (i) to (5) by being against metaphysics. Untestable propositions, unobservable entities, causes, deep explanation – these, says the positivist, are the stuff of metaphysics and must be put behind us (Hacking, 1983, p. 41-42).

5 There is also a third article in which Hacking addresses this issue directly in relation to mathematics, but we were unable to access it. It is entitled "Immagini radicalmente costruzionaliste del progresso matematico", and it was published in the book *Realismo/Antirealismo* (Pagnini).

6 As Lacan puts it, "the case of psychology which has discovered ways to outlive itself by providing services to the technocracy—sliding, as it were (as a sensational article by Canguilhem concludes, with truly Swiftian humor), like a toboggan from the Pantheon to the Prefecture of Police." (1966/1998, p. 730).

[7] As indicated in the introduction, these strands exhibit a shift from the original use of "evidence-based" practices, whose object would be, for the most part, the resort to epidemiological studies. Nevertheless, the resulting silencing of pertinent discussions seems to be the same.

[8] We must remember that, in this construction, "Self" here is used in a metapsychological sense, indicating that it is not one of the levels of awareness that has control over what goes on.

[9] The author specifically states: "This is why I did not believe I could characterise the unity of science by a true method, but rather indicate its view more generally. Hence, this unity of scientific thought appears more as a project than as a dogma A project whose vigour we have tried to demonstrate, but which could not conceal from us the extraordinary diversity of the forms of scientific knowledge" (Granger, 1993. p. 51).

[10] It is worth remembering that Grünbaum is a tenacious critic of psychoanalytic thought, and that although he disavowed Popper's criticisms, this was part of the construction of his own critiques—which were in turn answered by Shevrin (2013). On this, see Beer (2015; 2017 and 2018).

[11] This is not surprising, since this kind of positioning seems to be recurrent in the history of psychoanalysis, as we can see in Freud (1917a/2010).

[12] We can find criticisms of the Popperian uniqueness in Granger (1960/1967; 1993), Grünbaum (1984), Hacking (1983; 1999), among many others.

[13] See Hacking (1983).

[14] Let us remember what we previously pointed out, based on Hacking (1983), about how early this kind of thinking appeared on the continental intellectual scene, whose traces could already be recognised in authors such as Ludwik Fleck and Bachelard. However, this debate seems to have gained greater power only after the publication of *The Structure of Scientific Revolutions* (Kuhn, 1962/1966), being introduced as a major novelty in the Anglo-Saxon landscape, and kick-starting what would later be known as "*Science Wars*".

[15] It is even worth noting the similarity with the Foucauldian concept of "modes of subjection". According to Foucault, the object of his work was to attempt "to produce a history of the different modes of subjection of the human being in our culture [that is,] of the forms of objectification that transformed human beings into subjects" (Foucault, 1982/2017, p. 1042)

[16] "The concept of psychological trauma has always been presented as emancipatory. We need not disagree to see the effects of power that it produces. Those children and families in a flood-ravaged region of Nicaragua will, for the first time, live in a world in which they experience themselves not just as ravaged by floods, but as having suffered trauma." (Hacking, 2002a, p. 19).

[17] We will return to this question in a critical manner later on.

[18] Based on what we presented in chapter 1, we can see how this discussion can be made more complex. This will be done later on.

[19] The term niche is not limited to Foucault's idea of discourse, because it transcends language. "Of course language has a great deal to do with the formation of an

ecological niche, but so does what people do, how they live, the larger world of the material existence that they inhabit. That world must be described in all its peculiar and idiosyncratic detail. " (Hacking, 1998, p. 86).

[20] In relation to how Hacking presents this division, it is worth noting that different terms seem to occupy similar roles in Foucault's work. Taking, for example, Castro's (2004/2009) vocabulary as a reference, what is named here as *savoir* is often presented as truth [*vérité*]. In any case, it seems that the Canadian philosopher is quite clear about the meaning of his use of the word.

[21] A style of reasoning would be, in this sense, something that can emerge from the possibilities of depth knowledge, and which, at the same time, has the power to modify it. Hacking does not mobilise this concept in this discussion, but it is possible to acknowledge its presence as something that interacts with both depth and surface knowledge.

[22] Further details on this can be found in Beer (2015; 2017).

[23] There are even different ways of approaching how Lacan elaborates the question of truth, not only in relation to the text in question, but also in relation to Lacan's own work. Erik Porge, for example, presents five of them: (1) truth has a structure of fiction; (2) truth speaks; (3) there is no truth of truth; (4) truth and knowledge are incompatible; (5) truth sustains itself in a half-saying. Iannini (2012) states that there are two general sentences: 1) there is truth and 2) there is no truth of truth. He also presents different possibilities for organizing how truth appears in the work of the psychoanalyst: one of them, chronological (between the 1950s and the 1970s, linked to equivocation and contingency, from the 1970s onwards linked to the impossible); another, from the debates in which it is inserted (dialectics, language, style, logic, etc.).

[24] The idea of the clinical practice as a space of indeterminacy is certainly not restricted to the Lacanian tradition (Franco, 2018), which, however, did not prevent it from being a topic of confrontation between Lacan and the IPA.

[25] And it is in relation to this aspect precisely that Hyppolite poses his question, asking whether the confrontation of resistance in psychoanalysis (therefore, a subject's resistance) would not be an even more aggressive act of power than hypnosis, whereby resistance would come from an objectified subject and would not be confronted.

[26] It is worth noting that if it is possible to recognize some kind of negativity in Hacking's work, especially in his presentation on the difference between truth and truthfulness, it is necessary to point out that negativity plays a secondary role there: thought keeps trying to seek positivity, objects are taken based on their positivity, although there is an unavoidable incompleteness. In Lacan, this is not an obstacle, but the structuring element.

[27] There are a few differences in how Lacan describes the case on the two occasions, as well as some emphases put by the French psychoanalyst that are not necessarily the same as those put by Kris. We follow Lacan's line of thought, as we understand that, for our discussion, it is more relevant than the discussion of the case itself. But, for those who are interested, we recommend reading Kris's text (1951).

[28] We should remember that this is actually the path indicated by Lacan in "Science and Truth", after he resumes the prosopopoeia of "I, truth, speak...": "Which quite simply means everything that can be said of truth, of the only truth—namely, that there is no such thing as a metalanguage (an assertion made so as to situate all of logical positivism), no language being able to say the truth about truth, since truth is grounded in the fact that truth speaks, and that it has no other means by which to become grounded. This is precisely why the unconscious, which tells the truth about truth, is structured like a language, and why I, in so teaching, tell the truth about Freud who knew how to let the truth—going by the name of the unconscious—speak" (Lacan, 1966a/2006, p. 736-37).

[29] By way of example, we can cite Michael Löwy's criticism of structuralist Marxism by Althusser, in which Althusser, according to Löwy, advocated a mechanistic view with no room for the subject's intervention.

[30] As Iannini observes: "What Lacan finds in Heidegger is far more a critique of the reduction of language to its propositional structure and the distancing from the notion of truth as adequacy than a proper conception of truth as *aletheia*, even if it were for the sheer fact that what psychoanalytic practice confronts us with is the empirical, or rather material, genesis of subjectivity, totally insensitive to ontological difference as such" (Iannini, 2012, p. 72).

[31] Beyond the mere agreement on the use of the term "style" in Hacking and Iannini (2012), we believe that the way the Brazilian psychoanalyst and philosopher advances the question may open other possibilities for discussion, no less interesting or relevant. While we may have counted on his work as a guide in this field, it was unfortunately not possible to embark on this journey, given the limitations of our project.

[32] More details can be found in Beer (2015, 2017, 2018), Bazan (2017), and Brakel (2015).

[33] For example, Dunker (2008), Biazin & Kessler (2017) and Cunha & Silveira (2017).

[34] In "The Logical Time" (Lacan, [1945] 1966/2006), Lacan's critique of Sartre is highlighted.

[35] This can be seen, for example, in his opening statement of "The Mirror Stage as Formative of the I Function", by defining it as "this experience [that] sets us at odds with any philosophy directly stemming from the cogito" (Lacan, [1949]1966/2006, p. 93).

[36] "Every reader of 'Science and Truth' knows that, in referring psychoanalysis to the separation between knowledge and truth, Lacan is referring it not only to the methodical strategy of doubt which extricates itself from any thetic knowledge and from which something indubitable will result, but, crucially, to Koyré's thesis concerning the nature of the scientific revolution of the 17th century [...]. On the other hand, what is not often made explicit, when it comes to understanding the central issue in 'Science and Truth', is that the origin of Koyré's inspiration lies in Husserl (and, through him, in the Neo-Kantians' readings of Galileo). Therein lies, from the point of view of the discussion now proposed, the importance of the clue." (Cunha & Silveira, 2017, p. 72).

[37] As mentioned at the end of the previous chapter, in "Science and Truth" (1966/2006), Lacan associates the *cogito* to the inexistence of metalanguage—indicated, in turn, in relation to logical positivism. Metalanguage is understood in the wake of developments that affirm the impossibility of total comprehension and the decipherment of the truth of a code based on another, more "appropriate" code: in a first moment, the inexistence of the true meaning of a speech that could be understood by another (Lacan, 1955-56/1997), leading to the impossibility of establishing a language that could enunciate the truth of something enunciated in another language (as, for example, in logical positivism's failed project to define a common language for the sciences). This impossibility would lead, at the limit, to the precariousness of establishing any transcendental guarantee, in relation both to the meaning of a speech and to knowledge.

[38] What is maintained, even in relation to the approximation with Husserl's thought, as Cunha and Silveira indicate, is that: "The other pillar of that which is excluded by modern science is how to look at the object. The mode of its consideration cannot be detached from an experience of loss in the sense of being a loss of something that, for psychoanalysis, is the foundation of any experience. Modern science, says Lacan, produces an object whose statute had not yet been elucidated. This object (which Lacan calls object a) is an object of loss; not of an empirical loss, but of a loss that has always existed. For Lacan, the fantasy of having lost an object needs to be acknowledged in its statute of fantasy and thus as something that has already constituted itself as a defence. It is a defence against a more fundamental condition of lack—not the lack of an object, an object that would have been lost, but lack of being, which would precede any idea related to any object, whether it is deemed lost or not. When we refer to the existence of a body, language is already implied in this existence, and the rupture between signifier and thing must count as prior to what will appear as existence. Therefore, the condition of loss precedes both the notion of object and the place of the object in fantasy" (Cunha & Silveira, 2017, p. 83).

[39] It is also because of this role of making dysfunctionality explicit that the symptom, in its psychoanalytic understanding, is often referred to Marx's propositions on surplus value as an expression of a loss inherent in the economic system (Dunker, 2015).

[40] It is also necessary to point out, out of respect for the researchers, that they clearly state that medication should not be used as the only form of treatment, but always accompanied by psychotherapy.

[41] The author illustrates this with a curious case: "In September 1998 the pharmaceutical company Merck announced the discovery of a novel antidepressant with a completely different mode of action than other medications for depression. This new drug, which they later marketed under the trade name Emend for the prevention of nausea and vomiting due to chemotherapy, seemed to show considerable promise as an antidepressant in early clinical trials. Four months later the company announced its decision to pull the plug on the drug as a treatment for depression. The reason? It could not find a significant benefit for the active drug over placebos

in subsequent clinical trials. This was unfortunate for a number of reasons. One is that the announcement caused a 5 per cent drop in the value of the company's stock. Another is that the drug had an important advantage over current antidepressants–it produced substantially fewer side effects. The relative lack of side effects had been one reason for the enthusiasm about Merck's new antidepressant. However, it may also have been the reason for its subsequent failure in controlled clinical trials. It seems that easily noticeable side effects are needed to show antidepressant benefit for an active drug compared to a placebo" (Kirsch, 2010, p. 14).

[42] On signifying materiality and the role of language in subjective constitution, we recommend Leite, N. V. A. & Silva Jr., P. S. (2021) Corpo e língua materna. In D. Teperman, T. Garrafa, V. Iaconelli (Eds.), *Corpo (pp. 39-52). Autêntica.*

[43] From the 1970s onwards, Lacan will dwell more intently on attempts to deal with this constitutive lack of meaning, often termed "no sexual relationship" (Lacan, 1971-72/1999, 1972/2001). This happens either through an approximation to sophism (Cassin, 2017, Silva Junior, 2019) or through mathematical formalisation (Badiou, 2017). However, as Dolar (2019) rightly points out, neither approach completely solves the question, which revolves around the possibility of communicating this impossible. As stated, this is a highly valuable discussion, although we believe that, for the purposes of this work, the communication of this impossible is secondary. We believe it is more important to dwell on the tension between the positivised knowledge that is produced and the negativity that must be taken into account, rather than delving into the question of the transmissibility of this negativity, as Badiou (2017) argues. On the other hand, an interesting way of conducting this discussion is found in Van Haute's and Geyskens's (2012) reading of the formulas of sexuation, in which they argue for their potential for establishing a clinical anthropology. We strongly recommend reading this book along with our considerations.

[44] "For the process of a truth to begin, something must happen. What there already is, the situation of knowledge as such, only gives us repetition. For a truth to affirm its newness, there must be a supplement. This supplement is committed to chance. It is unpredictable, incalculable. It is beyond what is. I call it an event." (Badiou, 1994, p.178).

References

Ambra, P., & Paulon, C. (2018). O analista é o historiador. *Psicologia USP, 29*(3), 412-417. https://doi.org/10.1590/0103-656420180012

Andrade, L.F.G. (2016). *Lacan. Um Novo Freud? O Paradigma Lacaniano e Seu Alcance Clínico*. São Paulo: Annablume.

Askofaré, S. (2013). *D'un discours l'autre:* la science à l'épreuve de la psychanalyse. Toulouse: Presses Universitaires du Mirail.

Assoun, P. L. (1983). *Introdução à epistemologia freudiana*. Rio de Janeiro: Imago.

Badiou, A. (1994). Verdade e sujeito . *Estudos Avançados, 8*(21), 177-184. Recuperado de http://www.revistas.usp.br/eav/article/view/9668

Badiou, A. (2017). Formulas of "L'Étourdit". In Badiou, A.; Cassin, B. *There's No Such Thing as a Sexual Relationship: Two Lessons on Lacan*. New York: Columbia Univesity Press.

Balibar, F. (2007). La vérité, toute la vérité, rien que la vérité. In: *La vérité: entre psychanalyse et philosophie*. Toulouse: Ed. Érès, 2012.

Bazan, A. (2017). Alpha synchronization as a brain model for unconscious defense: An overview of the work of Howard Shevrin and his team. *Int J Psychoanal*, 98: 1443-1473. doi:10.1111/1745-8315.12629

Beer, P. A. C. (2015). *Questões e tensões entre psicanálise e ciência: considerações sobre validação*. Dissertação de Mestrado, Instituto de Psicologia, Universidade de São Paulo, São Paulo. Recuperado em 2016-05-09, de http://www.teses.usp.br/teses/disponiveis/47/47134/tde-04042016-122531/

Beer, P. (2017). *Psicanálise e ciência: um debate necessário*. São Paulo: Ed. Blucher, 2017.

Beer, P. (2018). Validação em psicanálise e causalidade em psicopatologia: efeitos de um debate. In: *Acta Psicossomática,* São Paulo, n. 1, p. 47-55, Jul/Dez 2018.

Beer, P. (2021). From negation to negationism: the COVID-19 pandemic in Brazil. *Journal of Psychosocial Studies*, 14(3), 187-201. Retrieved Jun 9, 2022, from https://bristoluniversitypressdigital.com/view/journals/jps/14/3/article-p187.xml

Beer, P. & Ambra, P. (2021). Perguntas que importam: o gênero e as fronteiras teóricas da psicanálise. *Recherches en psychanalyse*, 32, 105-125. https://doi.org/10.3917/rep2.032.0105

Benacerraf, P. (1973). Mathematical Truth. *The Journal of Philosophy*, Vol. 70, No. 19, Seventieth Annual Meeting of the American Philosophical Association Eastern Division. (Nov. 8, 1973), pp. 661-679. Available at: http://links.jstor.org/sici?sici=0022-362X%2819731108%2970%3A19%3C661%3AMT%3E2.0.CO%3B2-V

Bhaskar, R. (1975). *A Realist Theory of Science*. London: Verso, 2008.
Biazin, R., & Kessler, C. (2017). Psicanálise e ciência: a equação dos sujeitos. *Psicologia USP*, *28*(3), 414-423. https://doi.org/10.1590/0103-656420160184
Boni Junior, J. O. (2018). As estruturas clínicas na obra de Jacques Lacan: enodamentos do real, simbólico e imaginário?. Tese de Doutorado, Faculdade de Filosofia, Ciências e Letras de Ribeirão Preto, Universidade de São Paulo, Ribeirão Preto. doi:10.11606/T.59.2019.tde-29032019-165701. Recuperado em 2020-01-21, de www.teses.usp.br
Brakel, L. (2015). Critique of Grünbaum's "Critique of psychoanalysis". In S. Boag, L. Brakel & V. Talvitie (eds). *Philosophy, science, and psychoanalysis: a critical meeting* (pp.59-72). London, England: Karnak Books.
Breur, J. & Freud, S. (1895) *Studies on Hysteria*. SE 2. London: Hogarth
Cassin, B. (2017). Ab-sense, or Lacan from A to D. In Badiou, A. & Cassin, B. *There's No Such Thing as a Sexual Relationship: Two Lessons on Lacan*. New York: Columbia Univesity Press.
Castro, E. (2004). *Vocabulário de Foucault — um percurso pelos seus temas, conceitos e autores*. [Trad. Ingrid Xavier]. Belo Horizonte: Autêntica, 2009.
Checchia, M. (2015). *Poder e Política na Clínica Psicanalítica*. São Paulo: Ed. Annablume.
Cipriani, A.; Furukawa, T. A.; Salanti, G.; Chaimani, A.; Atkinson, L. Z.; Ogawa, Y.; Leucht, S.; Ruhe, H. G.; Turner, E. H.; Higgins, J. P. T.; Egger, M.; Takeshima, T.; Hayasaka, Y.; Imai, H.; Shinohara, K.; Tajika, A.; Ioannidis, J. P. A.; Geddes, J. R. (2018). Comparative efficacy and acceptability of 21 antidepressant drugs for the acute treatment of adults with major depressive disorder: a systematic review and network meta-analysis. *The Lancet*, Vol. 391, Issue 10128, pp. 1357-1366, April 07, 2018. Available at https://www.thelancet.com/journals/lancet/article/PIIS0140-6736(17)32802-7/fulltext . DOI:https://doi.org/10.1016/S0140-6736(17)32802-7
Cipriani, A.; Furukawa, T. A.; Salanti, G.; Turner, E. H.; Ioannidis, J. P. A.; Geddes, J. R. (2018b). Network meta-analysis of antidepressants – Authors' reply. The Lancet, Vol. 392, Issue 10152, pp. 1012-1013, September 22, 2018(b). DOI: https://doi.org/10.1016/S0140-6736(18)31780-X
Crombie, A. C. (1994). *Styles of Scientific Thinking in the European Tradition: The History of Argument and Explanation Especially in the Mathematical and Biomedical Sciences and Arts*. London: Duckbacks.
Cunha, J. & Silveira, L. (2017). Revolução científica e condições de possibilidade da psicanálise: sobre a presença de Husserl em "a ciência e a verdade". *Revista Ética e Filosofia Política*. No XX – Vol. I, pp. 69-87.
Dolar, M. (2019). The sophist's choice. *Crisis and critique*. Volume 6, issue 1, 02-04-2019. Available at https://crisiscritique.org/april2019/dolar.pdf
Dunker, C. (2007). Ontologia negativa em psicanálise: entre ética e epistemologia. *Discurso*, (36), pp. 217-242. https://doi.org/10.11606/issn.2318-8863.discurso.2007.38078

Dunker, C. I. (2008). Descartes e o Método Psicanalítico. *Estudos Lacanianos*, v.1, pp.169-191.
Dunker, C. (2011). Mal-estar, sofrimento e sintoma: releitura da diagnóstica lacaniana a partir do perspectivismo animista. *Tempo Social*, 23(1), pp. 115-136. https://dx.doi.org/10.1590/S0103-20702011000100006
Dunker, C. (2012). *Estrutura e constituição da clínica psicanalítica*. São Paulo: Annablume.
Dunker, C. (2015). *Mal-estar, sofrimento e sintoma: uma psicopatologia do Brasil entre muros*. São Paulo: Boitempo Editorial.
Dunker, C. & Ravanello, T. (2019). A garrafa de klein como método para construção de casos clínicos em psicanálise. *Ágora: Estudos em Teoria Psicanalítica*, *22*(1), pp. 99-110. https://dx.doi.org/10.1590/s1516-14982019001010
Erwin, E. (2015). Psychoanalysis and philosophy of science: Basic evidence. In: Boag, S.; Brakel, L.; Talvitie, V. *Philosophy, Science, and Psychoanalysis: A Critical Meeting*. Londres: Karnak Books.
Ferenczi, S. (1992 [1930]) Princípios de relaxamento e neocatarse. [A. Cabral, Trad.]. In *Psicanálise IV*, pp. 53-68. São Paulo: Martins Fontes, 1992 [1930].
Ferenczi, S. (1992 [1933]). Confusão de língua entre os adultos e a criança. [A. Cabral, Trad.]. In *Psicanálise IV*, pp. 97-106. São Paulo: Martins Fontes, 1992 [1933].
Fernandez, B. P. M. (2000). Popper, Hayek e a (im)possibilidade de predições específicas em Ciências Sociais. *Cadernos de Pesquisa Interdisciplinar em Ciências Humanas, Florianópolis*, v. 1, n. 5, p. 1-18, jan. 2000. Available at: <https://periodicos.ufsc.br/index.php/cadernosdepesquisa/article/view/892>. Acesso em: 08 ago. 2019. doi:https://doi.org/10.5007/892.
Feyerabend, P. (1975). Against Method: Outline of an Anarchistic Theory of Knowledge. London: Verso, 1993.
Figueiredo, L.C. & Loureiro, I. (2018) *Os saberes psi em questão: sobre o conhecimento em psicanálise e psicologia*. Petrópolis, RJ: Ed. Vozes.
Forrester, J. (1996). If p, then what? Thinking in cases. *History of the Human Sciences*, 9(3), pp. 1–25. https://doi.org/10.1177/095269519600900301
Foucault, M. (1966). *As Palavras e as Coisas: uma arqueologia das ciências humanas*. São Paulo: Martins Fontes, 2016.
Fox-Keller, E. (1985). *Reflections on Gender and Science*. New Haven and London, Yale Univ. Press.
Franco, W. A. C. (2018). Os lugares da psicanálise: a inscrição clínica e cultural do pensamento psicanalítico. PhD dissertation, Instituto de Psicologia, Universidade de São Paulo, São Paulo. doi:10.11606/T.47.2019.tde-19122018-095103. Recuperado em 2020-01-19, de www.teses.usp.br
Freud, S. (1905). Three Essays on Sexuality. SE 5. London: Hogarth.
Freud, S. (1909). Notes upon a Case of Obsessional Neurosis. SE 10. London: Hogarth.
Freud, S. (1914). Recollection, Repetition, and Working-Through. SE 12. London: Hogarth.

Freud, S. (1917a). A Difficulty in the Path of Psycho-analysis. SE 17. London: Hogarth.
Freud, S. (1917b). The Sense of Symptoms. SE 15. London: Hogarth.
Freud, S. (1917c). Fixation to Traumas—The Unconscious. SE 15. London: Hogarth.
Freud, S. (1917d). The Paths to the Formation of Symptoms. SE 15. London: Hogarth.
Freud, S. (1920). The Psychogenesis of a Case of Homosexuality in a Woman. SE 18. London: Hogarth.
Freud, S. (1921). Group Psychology and the Analysis of the Ego. SE 18. London: Hogarth.
Freud, S. (1925). Negation. SE 19. London: Hogarth.
Freud, S. (1930). Civilization and its Discontents. SE 21. London: Hogarth.
Freud, S. (1933). The Question of a *Weltanschauung*. SE 22. London: Hogarth.
Freud, S. (1937a). Constructions in Analysis. SE 23. London: Hogarth.
Freud, S. (1937b). Analysis Terminable and Interminable. SE 23. London: Hogarth.
Freud, S. (1937). Constructions in Analysis. SE 23. London: Hogarth.
Frosh, S. (1999). *The Politics of Psychoanalysis*. London: Red Globe Press.
Fulford K. W. (2008). Values-based practice: a new partner to evidence-based practice and a first for psychiatry? *Mens sana monographs*, 6(1), 10–21. doi:10.4103/0973-1229.40565
Garcia, L. F. B. (2015). Despertar do real: a invenção do objeto a. Dissertação de Mestrado, Faculdade de Filosofia, Letras e Ciências Humanas, Universidade de São Paulo, São Paulo. doi:10.11606/D.8.2016.tde-22082016-111115. Recuperado em 2020-01-20, de www.teses.usp.br
Goodman, N. (1954). *Fact, fiction and forecast*. London: Athlone.
Granger, G.G. (1967). *Pensée formelle et sciences de l'homme*. Paris: Harmattan.
Granger, G.G. (1993). *A ciência e as ciências*. São Paulo: Editora Unesp.
Grünbaum, A. (1984). *The Foundations of Psychoanalysis: A philosophical critique*. Oakland: University of California Press.
Hacking, I. (1965). *Logic of Statistical Inference*. Cambridge: Cambridge U.P.
Hacking, I. (1975a). *The emergence of probability*. Cambridge University Press, Cambridge.
Hacking, Ian. (1975b). *Why Does Language Matter to Philosophy?* Cambridge: Cambridge University Press.
Hacking, Ian. (1982). Language, truth and reason. In *Rationality and Relativism*, ed. M. Hollis & S. Lukes. Oxford: Blackwell.
Hacking, I. (1983). *Representing and Intervening: Introductory Topics in the Philosophy of Natural Science*. Cambridge: Cambridge University Press.
Hacking, I. (1990). *The Taming of Chance*. Cambridge: Cambridge U.P.
Hacking, I. (1992a). The self-Vindication of the Laboratory Sciences, in Pickering, A., Ed., Science as practice and culture, Chicago: University of Chicago Press, 1992, 29-64.

Hacking, I. (1992b). Statistical language, statistical truth and statistical reason: The self-authentication of a style of reasoning. In *Social Dimensions of Science*, edited by Ernan McMullin. Notre Dame, Ind.: Notre Dame U.P., pp. 130-157.

Hacking, I. (1992c). 'Style' for historians and philosophers. In: *Studies in History and Philosophy of Science Part A*, Volume 23, Issue 1, 1992, Pages 1-20, https://doi.org/10.1016/0039-3681(92)90024-Z

Hacking, I. (1993). On Kripke's and Goodman's use of 'grue'. *Philosophy 68*, pp. 269-295.

Hacking, I. (1995). *Rewriting the Soul – Multiple Personality and the Sciences of Memory*. New Jersey: Princeton University Press.

Hacking, I. (1998a). *Mad Travelers: Reflections on the Reality of Transient Mental Illness.* London: University Press of Virginia.

Hacking, I. (1998b). Canguilhem amid the cyborgs, *Economy and Society*, 27:2-3, pp. 202-216, DOI: 10.1080/03085149800000014

Hacking, I. (1999). *Social Construction of What?* Cambridge: Harvard University Press.

Hacking, I. (2000). How Inevitable Are the Results of Successful Science? *Philosophy of Science*, 67, no. (Sep., 2000b): S58-S71.

Hacking, I. (2002a). *Historical Ontology*. Cambridge: Harper University Press.

Hacking, I. (2002b). « Vrai », les valeurs et les sciences. *Actes de la recherche en sciences sociales*, 141-142(1), 13-20. doi:10.3917/arss.141.0013.

Hacking, Ian (2005). Truthfulness. *Common Knowledge* 11 (1): 160-172.

Hacking, I. (2006a). *Véracité*. Aula dada no Collège de France no dia 31 de janeiro de 2006. Available at https://www.college-de-france.fr/site/ian-hacking/course-2006-01-31.htm

Hacking, I. (2006b). *Objets*. Aula dada no Collège de France no dia 07 de fevereiro de 2006. Available at https://www.college-de-france.fr/site/ian-hacking/course-2006-02-07.htm

Hacking, I. (2006c). *Méthodes de raisonnement*. Aula dada no Collège de France no dia 14 de fevereiro de 2006. Available at https://www.college-de-france.fr/site/ian-hacking/course-2006-02-14.htm

Hacking, I. (2006d). *Démonstration*. Aula dada no Collège de France no dia 21 de feveriro de 2006. Available at https://www.college-de-france.fr/site/ian-hacking/course-2006-02-21.htm

Hacking, I. (2012a). Introdução à edição brasileira. In *Representar e intervir: tópicos introdutórios de filosofia da ciência natural*. Rio de Janeiro: EDUERJ.

Hacking, I. (2012b). Language, truth and reason 30 years later. *Studies in History and Philosophy of Science* 43 (2012) 599–609.

Hacking, I. (2014). *Why is There a Philosophy of Mathematics at All?* Cambridge: Cambridge U. P.

Hanly, C. (1991). *The Problem of Truth in Applied Psychoanalysis*. New York: The Guilford Press

Hayek, F. (1942). Scientism and the Study of Society – Part I. *Economica*, N.S., 267-291.

Hayek, F. (1952). *The Sensory Order: An Inquiry into the Foundations of Theoretical Psychology*. Chicago: The University of Chicago Press.

Hyppolite, J. (1953/1966). A Spoken Commentary on Freud's "Verneinung" by Jean Hyppolite. In Lacan, J. *Écrits*. London, New York: Norton, 2006.

Iannini, G. (2012). *Estilo e verdade em Jacques Lacan*. Rio de Janeiro: Ed. Autêntica.

Insel, T. (2013). Director's blog: Transforming diagnosi. Available at http://www.nimh.nih.gov/about/director/2013/transforming-diagnosis.shtml

Johnston, A. & Malabou, C. (2019). *Self and Emotional Life: Philosophy, Psychoanalysis, and Neuroscience.* New York: Columbia University Press.

Kirkham, R. L. (1992). *Theories of Truth: A Critical Introduction*. Cambridge, MA: MIT Press.

Kirsch, I. (2009). *The Emperor's New Drugs: Exploding the Antidepressant Myth*. Philadelphia: Basic Books.

Kirsch I. (2014). Antidepressants and the Placebo Effect. *Zeitschrift fur Psychologie*, 222(3): 128–134. doi:10.1027/2151-2604/a000176

Kirsch I., Deacon B. J., Huedo-Medina T. B., Scoboria A., Moore T. J., & Johnson B. T. (2008). Initial Severity and Antidepressant Benefits: A Meta-Analysis of Data Submitted to the Food and Drug Administration. *PLoS Medicine*, 5, e45 doi: 10.1371/journal.pmed.0050045

Kirsch, I., Jakobson, J. (2018). Network Meta-Analysis of Antidepressants. *The Lancet Correspondence* 392(10152): 1010, September 22. DOI: https://doi.org/10.1016/S0140-6736(18)31799-9

Kirsch, I., & Sapirstein, G. (1998). Listening to Prozac but Hearing Placebo: A Meta-Analysis of Antidepressant Medication. *Prevention & Treatment*, 1(2). Article 2a. https://doi.org/10.1037/1522-3736.1.1.12a

Kohut, H. (1979). The Two Analyses of Mr Z. *Int. J. Psycho-Anal.* 60:3-27.

Koyré, A. (1939). *Études galiléennes*. Paris: Hermann, 1966.

Koyré, A. (1957). *From the Closed World to the Infinite Universe*. Baltimore: Johns Hopkins University Press, 1968.

Koyré, A. (1961). *Estudos de história do pensamento científico*. Rio de Janeiro: Forense Universitária, 2011.

Koyré, A. (1962). *Introduction à la lecture de Platon suivi d' Entretiens sur Descartes*. Paris: Gallimard, 1991

Koyré, A. (1968). *Études newtoniennes*. Paris: Gallimard, 1985.

Kramer M.S., Cutler N., Feighner J, Shrivastava R, Carman J, Sramek JJ, Reines SA, Liu G, Snavely D, Wyatt-Knowles E, Hale JJ, Mills SG, MacCoss M, Swain CJ, Harrison T, Hill RG, Hefti F, Scolnick EM, Cascieri MA, Chicchi GG, Sadowski S, Williams AR, Hewson L, Smith D, Carlson EJ, Hargreaves RJ, Rupniak NM. Distinct mechanism for antidepressant activity by blockade of central substance P receptors. *Science*. 1998 Sep 11; 281(5383):1640-5. PubMed PMID: 9733503.

Kris, E. (1951). Ego Psychology and Interpretation in Psychoanalytic Therapy. *The Psychoanalytic Quarterly*, 20(1): 15-30.
Kuhn, T. (1962). The Structure of Scientific Revolutions. Chicago: University of Chicago Press, 1966.
Kuhn, T. (1977). The Essential Tension: Selected Studies in Scientific Tradition and Change. Chicago: University of Chicago Press, 2011.
Kupfer, C. (2013). Prefácio. In: Dunker, C. *A psicose na criança: tempo, linguagem e sujeito*. São Paulo: Zagodoni.
Lacan, J. (1945/1966). Logical Time and the Assertion of Anticipated Certainty. In: *Écrits*. London, New York: Norton, 2006.
Lacan, J. (1946/1966). Presentation on Psychical Causality. In: *Écrits*. London, New York: Norton, 2006.
Lacan, J. (1949/1966). The Mirror Stage as Formative of the *I* Function as Revealed in Psychoanalytic Experience. In: *Écrits*. London, New York: Norton, 2006.
Lacan, J. (1951/1966) Presentation on Transference In: *Écrits*. London, New York: Norton, 2006.
Lacan, J. (1953a/1966) The Function and Field of Speech and Language in Psychoanalysis. In: *Écrits*. London, New York: Norton, 2006.
Lacan, J. (1953b) The Neurotic's Individual Myth. *The Psychoanalytic Quarterly*, 48(3): 405-425, DOI: 10.1080/21674086.1979.11926884, 1979.
Lacan, J. (1953c/1966). Introduction to Jean Hyppolite's Commentary on Freud's "Verneinung". In: *Écrits*. London, New York: Norton, 2006.
Lacan, J. (1955/1966). The Freudian Thing. In: *Écrits*. London, New York: Norton, 2006.
Lacan, J. (1953-54). *The Seminar I: Freud's Papers on Technique*. London, New York: Norton, 1991.
Lacan, J. (1955-56). *The Seminar III: The Psychosis*. London, New York: Norton, 1997.
Lacan, J. (1957/1966). On a Question Prior to Any Possible Treatment of Psychosis. In: *Écrits*. London, New York: Norton, 2006.
Lacan, J. (1958/1966). The Direction of the Treatment and the Principles of Its Power. In: Écrits. London, New York: Norton, 2006.
Lacan, J. (1959-60). *The Seminar VII: The Ethics of Psychoanalysis*. London, New York: Norton, 1997.
Lacan, J. (1960-61). *The Seminar VIII: Transference*. London, New York: Norton, 2001.
Lacan, J. (1963/1966). Kant with Sade. In: *Écrits*. London, New York: Norton, 2006.
Lacan, J. (1964/1966). Position of the Unconscious. In: *Écrits*. London, New York: Norton, 2006.
Lacan, J. (1964). *The Seminar XI: The Four Fundamental Concepts of Psychoanalysis*. London, New York: Norton, 1998.
Lacan, (1965). Summary of Seminar XI. Available at: http://www.lacaninireland.com/web/wp-content/uploads/2010/06/S-SUMMARY-OF-SEMINAR-XI-Cormac-Gallagher-1.pdf

Lacan, J. (1964-65). *Séminaire 12: Les problèmes cruciaux de la psychanalyse*. Available at http://staferla.free.fr/S12/S12.htm

Lacan, J. (1965-66). *Séminaire 13: L'Objet*. Available at http://staferla.free.fr/S13/S13.htm

Lacan, J. (1966a). Science and Truth. In: *Écrits*. London, New York: Norton, 2006.

Lacan, J. (1966b). On the Subject Who Is Finally in Question. In: *Écrits*. London, New York: Norton, 2006.

Lacan, J. (1967-68). *Séminaire 15: L'acte psychanalitique*. Available at http://staferla.free.fr/S15/S15.htm

Lacan, J. (1969-70). *The Seminar XVII: The Other Side of Psychoanalysis*. London, New York: Norton, 2007.

Lacan, J. (1971-72). *The Seminar XX: Encore*. London, New York: Norton, 1999.

Lacan, J. (1972). L'étourdit. In: *Autres Écrits*. Paris: Gallimard, 2001.

Lacan, J. (1973). Télévision. In: *Autres Écrits*. Paris: Gallimard, 2001.

Lacerda Abrahão, L. H. (2015). Koyré e a "epistemologia histórica de Kuhn e Feyerabend". In: Leitão Condé, M. L. & Salomon, M. *Alexandre Koyré: história e filosofia das ciências*. Belo Horizonte: Traço Fino.

Lakatos, Imre (1970). Falsification and the Methodology of Scientific Research Programmes. In: I. Lakatos & A. Musgrave (eds.) *Criticism and the Growth of Knowledge*. Cambridge: Cambridge University Press, 91-196.

Latour, B. & Woolgar, S. (1979). *Laboratory Life: The Construction of Scientific Facts*. New Jersey: Princeton University Press, 1986.

Leite, N. V. A. & Silva Jr., P.S. (2021). Corpo e língua materna. In: Teperman, D., Garrafa, T., & Iaconelli, V. *Corpo* (col. Parentalidade e Psicanálise). São Paulo: Ed. Autêntica.

Mendonça, J. (2012). Apresentação. In: Hacking, I. *Representar e intervir: tópicos introdutórios de filosofia da ciência natural*. Rio de Janeiro: EDUERJ.

Milner, J.-C. (1992). Linguística e Psicanálise. *Revista Estudos Lacanianos*, 3(4), 2010. Recuperado em 14 de feveiro de 2020, de http://pepsic.bvsalud.org/scielo.php?script=sci_arttext&pid=S1983-07692010000100002&lng=pt&tlng=pt

Montgomery, K. (2005). *How Doctors Think: Clinical Judgment and the Practice of Medicine*. Oxford: OUP.

Nasio, J.D. (2011). *Introdução à topologia de Lacan*. Rio de Janeiro: Zahar.

Neves, A., Ismerim, A., Donizete da Costa, F., Pedroso dos Santos, L. R., Senhorini, M., Beer, P., Bazzo, R., Coelho, S. P., & Carnizelo, V. C. R. (2021). A psiquiatria sob o neoliberalismo: da clínica dos transtornos ao aprimoramento de si. In: V. Safatle, N. da Silva Junior & C. Dunker (eds.), *Neoliberalismo como gestão do sofrimento psíquico*, pp. 125-175. Belo Horizonte: Autêntica Editora.

Nobus, D. (2002). A Matter of Cause: Reflections on Lacan's "Science and Truth". In: Glynos, J.; Stavrakakis, Y. *Lacan and Science*. London: Karnak Books.

Nobus, D. (2019). O Escritos de Lacan revisitado [Trad. Paulo Beer]. *Lacuna: uma revista de psicanálise*, São Paulo, 7: 6. Available at: <https://revistalacuna.com/2019/08/07/n-7-6/>

Pickering, A. (1984). *Constructing Quarks: A Sociological History of Particle Physics.* Chicago: University of Chicago Press.

Popper, K. (1934). *The Logico f Scientific Discovery.* London: Routledge, 2002.

Popper, K. (1963). *Conjectures and Refutations: The Growth of Scientific Knowledge.* London: Routledge, 2002.

Porge, E. (2007). A ronda dos semi-ditos claros. In: *Literal 13 – A psicanálise e outros saberes.* [Trad. Paulo Sérgio de Souza Junior]. Campinas, 2010.

Preciado, P. B. (2019). Um apartamento em Urano (Conferência) [Trad. C. Q. Kushiner & P. S. Souza Jr.]. *Lacuna: uma revista de psicanálise,* São Paulo, 8: 12, 2019. Available at: <https://revistalacuna.com/2019/12/08/n-8-12/>

Putnam, F. (1989). *Diagnosis and Treatment of Multiple Personality Disorder and Other State-Change Disorders.* Nova York: The Guilford Press.

Putnam, H. (1979). The meaning of meaning. In: *Philosophical Papers, Mind, Language and Reality.* Cambridge: Cambridge University Press.

Putnam, H. (1982). *Reason, Truth and History.* Cambridge: Cambridge University Press.

Rabinovich, D. (2000). *O desejo do psicanalista.* São Paulo: Cia de Freud.

Rancière, J. (2001). *The Aesthetic Unconscious.* Cambridge: Polity, 2010.

Reiner, R., & Pierson, R. (1995). Hacking's Experimental Realism: An Untenable Middle Ground. *Philosophy of Science, 62*(1), 60-69. Retrieved from www.jstor.org/stable/188035

Resnik, D. (1994). Hacking's Experimental Realism. *Canadian Journal of Philosophy,* 24(3): 395-411. Retrieved from www.jstor.org/stable/40231874

Ribot, T.-A. (1881). *Les maladies de la mémoire.* Paris: Baillière.

Ribeiro, S. (2019). *O oráculo da noite: a história e a ciência do sonho.* São Paulo: Cia das Letras.

Rogers, A. (2017). Star Neuroscientist Tom lnsel Leaves the Google-Spawned Verily For ... A Startup? *Wired.* At hnps://www.wired.com/2017105/star-newoscientist-tom-insel-leaves-google-spawned-verily-startup/

Rose, N. (2016). Neuroscience and the Future for mental health? *Epidemiol Psychiatr Sci.* 2016 Apr 25(2): 95-100. doi: 10.1017/S2045796015000621. Epub 2015 Aug 3. PubMed PMID: 26234570.

Rose, N. (2018). *Our Psychiatric Future: The Politics of Mental Health.* Cambridge, UK: Polity Press.

Rose N. & Abi-Rached J.M. (2013). *Neuro: the New Brain Sciences and the Management of the Mind.* Princeton: Princeton University Press.

Rose, N. & Abi-Rached, J.M. (2014) Governing through the Brain: Neuropolitics, Neuroscience and Subjectivity. *Cambridge Anthropology* 32(1), Spring: 3–23 © Cambridge Anthropology. doi:10.3167/ca.2014.320102

Roustang, F. (1978). Sugestão a longo prazo [Trad. P. Beer]. *Lacuna: uma revista de psicanálise,* São Paulo, 4: 1, 2017. Available at: <https://revistalacuna.com/2017/11/20/n4-01/>.

Rustin, M. (2019). *Researching the Unconscious: Principles of Psychoanalytic Method.* London: Routledge.

Safatle, V. (2006) *A paixão do negativo: Lacan e a dialética.* São Paulo: Ed. Unesp.

Safatle, V. (2007). A teoria das pulsões como ontologia negativa. Discurso, (36), 151-192. https://doi.org/10.11606/issn.2318-8863.discurso.2007.38076

Safatle, V. (2014) Aquele que diz "não": sobre um modo peculiar de falar de si. In: Freud, S. *A negação.* São Paulo: Cosac Naif.

Safatle, V.; Dunker, C.; Da Silva Junior, N. (2018) *Patologias do Social: arqueologias do sofrimento psíquico.* Belo Horizonte: Ed. Autêntica.

Safouan, M. (2014) *La psychanalyse: Science, thérapie – et cause.* Paris: Thierry Marchaisse Editions, 2014.

Safouan, M. (2017) *Les puits de la vérité*: la psychanalyse et la science. Paris: Hermann Éditeurs.

Shevrin, H.; Snodgrass, M.; Brakel, L.; Kushwaha, R.; Kalaida, N.; Bazan, A. (2013) Subliminal unconscious conflict alpha power inhibits supraliminal conscious symptom experience. In: *Frontiers in Human Neuroscience.* 7:544, 2013. Available at http://journal.frontiersin.org/Journal/10.3389/fnhum.2013.00544/full.

Silva Junior, N. (2007). *Linguagens e pensamento.* São Paulo: Casa do Psicólogo.

Silva Junior, N. (2017) O sofrimento como hífen na teoria social freudiana e sua atualidade. O exemplo das modificações corporais. In: Silva Junior, N.; Zangari, W. (orgs) (2017) *A psicologia social e a questão do hífen.* São Paulo: Ed. Blucher.

Silva Junior, N. Epistemologia psiquiátrica e marketing farmacêutico: novos modos de subjetivação. Stylus (Rio J.), Rio de Janeiro, n. 33, p. 227-239, nov. 2016. Available at <http://pepsic.bvsalud.org/scielo.php?script=sci_arttext&pid=S1676-157X2016000200018&lng=pt&nrm=iso>. acessos em 06 ago. 2019.

Silva Junior, N. (2019) *Fernando Pessoa e Freud: diálogos inquietantes.* São Paulo: Ed. Blucher.

Silveira Sales, L. (2005) "Ainda o sujeito – Nota sobre o conflito determinação versus subjetividade em Jacques Lacan". Revista de Filosofia, vol. 18, n. 20. Curitiba: PUC-PR, p. 99-124.

Silveira Sales, L. (2007). Passagem da compreensão à verdade: contribuição do estruturalismo à teoria lacaniana da psicose. *Ágora: Estudos em Teoria Psicanalítica,* 10(2), 211-227. https://dx.doi.org/10.1590/S1516-14982007000200005

Simanke, R. (2002) Metapsicologia lacaniana: os anos de formação. São Paulo: Discurso. Editorial; Curitiba: UFPR.

Stengers, I. (1993) *As políticas da razão.* Lisboa: Edições 70.

Suárez, M (2006) *Experimental realism defended: how inference to the most likely cause might be sound.* Technical Report (01/06). Contingency And Dissent in Science Project, CPNSS, London School of Economics and Political Science, London, UK.

Tsou, J. T. (2007) Hacking on the Looping Effects of Psychiatric Classifications: What Is an Interactive and Indifferent Kind?, *International Studies in the Philosophy of Science,* 21:3, 329-344, DOI: 10.1080/02698590701589601

Van Haute, P.; Geyskens, T. (2012) A Non-Oedipal Psychoanalysis?: A Clinical Anthropology of Hysteria in the Works of Freud and Lacan. Leuven: Leuven University Press.

Van Rillaer, J. (2019) *Freud & Lacan Des charlatans ?: Faits et légendes de la psychanalyse.* Bruxelles: Editions Mardaga.

Vincent, B. (2019) *Lacan: style des écris.* Paris: Éditions Le Bord de l'Eau.

Watters, E. (2010) *Crazy Like Us: the globalization of American psyche.* New York: Free Press.

Williams, B. (2002) *Truth and Truthfulness: An Essay in Genealogy.* Princeton, NJ: Princeton University Press.

Winograd, M. (2004) Matéria pensante – a fertilidade do encontro entre psicanálise e neurociência. *Arquivos Brasileiros de Psicologia,* v. 56, n. 1, p. 20-33.

Retirado do World Wide Web http://www.psicologia.ufrj.br/abp/ 27

Young, A. (1997) *The harmony of illusions: inventing the post-traumatic disorder.* New Jersey: Princeton University Press.

Zygouris, R. (2011) *Psicanálise e psicoterapia.* São Paulo: Via Lettera.

Zygouris, R. (2015) A gata de Schrödinger [Trad. P. Beer]. Lacuna: uma revista de psicanálise, São Paulo, n. 0, p. 3, 2015. Available at: <https://revistalacuna.com/2015/09/29/a-gata-de-schrodinger/>.

Acknowledgements

This book is results from an investigation carried out at the Department of Social Psychology of the University of São Paulo, so it is essential to thank everyone who made this possible: workers, teachers, colleagues and friends, who provided the necessary support for this endeavor. Nelson da Silva Junior, from whom I learned valuable and countless lessons, and who showed me the power of boldness, patience, elegance and, above all, partnership. And Stephen Frosh, who helped me to rediscover what made me dive into this work.

Within the many contributions I had the privilege to receive, I particularly thank Ilana Katz, Léa Silveira, Gilson Iannini, Christian Dunker and Marcelo Ferretti, whose contributions were nothing but essential. And Philippe Van Haute (†), who shared great texts and ideas with me.

I have friends who supported me and shared a great part of this path with me. Among them, Diego Penha, Hugo Lana, Paulo Sérgio Sousa Junior, Pedro Ambra and Rafael Lima, who helped me to think better, sometimes within cups of coffee, sometimes within pints. Wilson Franco, with whom I have the pleasure of sharing amazing projects. The colleagues from LATESFIP, for the years of joint research. And friends from the International Society of Psychoanalysis and Philosophy, especially Beatriz Santos, who was decisive in helping me to envision new paths.

I would like to thank my colleagues and friends from NETT, for the common agreement that it is worth fighting for better times, to which the writing of this book subscribes. To my students and colleagues at Instituto Gerar, UNIVAP, USP, and other places where I was able to teach, debate and learn. Thank you for the exchanges, I hope they continue.

Index

Milton Keynes UK
Ingram Content Group UK Ltd.
UKHW022244120424
441043UK00008B/167

9 789462 704060